# FROM
# BERKELEY
## TO
# BERLIN

# FROM
# BERKELEY
## TO
# BERLIN

## HOW THE
## RAD LAB HELPED AVERT
## NUCLEAR WAR

////////////////////////////////

# TOM RAMOS

Naval Institute Press
Annapolis, Maryland

Naval Institute Press
291 Wood Road
Annapolis, MD 21402

Library of Congress Cataloging-in-Publication Data
Names: Ramos, Tom, author.
Title: From Berkeley to Berlin : how the Rad Lab helped avert nuclear war / Tom Ramos.
Other titles: How the Rad Lab helped avert nuclear war
Description: Annapolis, Maryland : Naval Institute Press, [2022] | Includes
bibliographical references and index.
Identifiers: LCCN 2021045929 (print) | LCCN 2021045930 (ebook) | ISBN
9781682477533 (hardcover) | ISBN 9781682477540 (ebook) | ISBN 9781682477540
(epub)
Subjects: LCSH: Deterrence (Strategy)—History—20th century. | Nuclear weapons—
Research—California. | Military research—United States—History—20th century. |
Lawrence Radiation Laboratory—History. | Lawrence Livermore Laboratory—History.
| United States—Foreign relations—Soviet Union. | Soviet Union—Foreign relations—
United States. | Cold War.
Classification: LCC U162.6 .R36 2022 (print) | LCC U162.6 (ebook) | DDC 355.02/17
—dc23
LC record available at https://lccn.loc.gov/2021045929
LC ebook record available at https://lccn.loc.gov/2021045930

∞ Print editions meet the requirements of ANSI/NISO z39.48-1992 (Permanence
of Paper).
Printed in the United States of America.

30 29 28 27 26 25 24 23 22     9 8 7 6 5 4 3 2 1
First printing

/////////////////

# CONTENTS

//////////////

## *ACKNOWLEDGMENTS*

As I write these paragraphs after nine years of research and toil, I recollect how much I owe to some men who mentored me to be an able participant in keeping our country safe from predatory nations who would seek to destroy our way of life. George Maenchen, Ira "Chuck" Gragson, and Bill Grasberger, three outstanding physicists, showed infinite patience while they taught me how to be a professional physicist. I am forever grateful to them.

Some of the first "victims" I cornered to read my work were family members. My son, Mark, was first to inform me that not all readers are as intrigued with "neat physics stuff" as I am, so I should calm down the language a bit to make it intelligible to average people. Daughters Loretta and Ariana dutifully read through pages of early drafts and made some badly needed corrections in my grammar. My wife, Rose, has been my private cheerleader for years, encouraging me to keep to the task. My good friend Gina Bonanno, who is a National Research Council fellow, bravely read through my original manuscript to offer valuable advice about making sense out of the physics. Cherie Turner, my physical therapist who helped me recover from a horrific cycling accident, is a past editor of *San Francisco* magazine and spent hours poring over drafts and performing badly needed editing chores. I am also deeply indebted to my friend Jim Oliver, who helped me with the myriad challenges of digitally preparing this text for publication.

Tremendous encouragement came from my West Point classmates, especially Jim McDonough, Gary Dolan, Bill Taylor, and Skip Bacevich. These Vietnam veterans are awesome professionals who know how to write, and they were not stingy with helpful advice. Collin Agee, one of my former students when I taught at the Academy, introduced me to Steve Pieczenik, an author of best-selling books and a ghost writer for Tom Clancy. John Antal, another successful author and a good friend, read through an early manuscript and gave me encouragement to keep to the task. Steve and John offered valuable suggestions on how to make the book more enjoyable to read. My classmate Jerry Morelock, editor of *Armchair General* magazine, introduced my project to a talented editor at the Naval Institute Press, Pat Carlin. I am indebted to Pat's energy and steadfastness to turn this manuscript into a book.

One of the great pleasures of this project was the opportunity to work with two incredible gentlemen. Ken Ford, the man who did the crucial calculations that designed the world's first hydrogen bomb and is thus part of this history, reviewed my work and gave so much time to help ensure this book's accuracy that I cannot overstate my gratitude. Bruce Goodwin, who directed nuclear-weapons research for several years, also reviewed my work and, importantly, provided me the opportunity to delve into research about those early years of the Cold War—how Ernest Lawrence and his flock of physicists working at a laboratory in Livermore, California, were able to serve our country so well.

The Lawrence Livermore National Laboratory itself has been a good home to me throughout the latter course of my life, and I have grown to appreciate and cherish that institution greatly. The idea that there were "upstarts" at the "Laboratory," significant figures who, early in the Cold War, helped our country face and survive threats from Josef Stalin and Nikita Khrushchev, was a revelation to me. Those upstarts, including Mike May, Johnny Foster, and Harold Brown, offered me hours upon hours of their time to assure me that my interpretation of events in the 1950s was accurate. Former Laboratory director C. Bruce Tarter, who published a history of the institution titled *The American Laboratory* (2018), generously opened up his personal library to me and became an inspiration, encouraging me in my research.

I have interviewed physicists who participated in many of the actions depicted here, gentlemen who are now in their eighties and nineties. They include Bill Grasberger and George Maenchen, two of the aforementioned mentors who helped guide me to be a nuclear-weapons designer in the

1980s. I also had guidance from Dan Patterson, John Nuckolls, and Bill Lokke, three icons from the Laboratory's golden age. My interview with Arne Kirkewoog gave me insight into the world of radiochemistry.

Of course, I treasured reading through the interviews conducted by Laboratory archivist Jim Carothers. Jim sat down with me after I had completed a stint as a designer of X-ray lasers in the 1980s, so I am familiar with how he masterfully conducted his interviews. Those from the 1960s, 1970s, and 1980s of key Laboratory scientists and engineers gave me incomparable insights into what the young and inexperienced professionals were thinking as they made history. Jim's successors on the archives staff, Beverly Bull, Maxine Trost, and Jeff Sahaida, have been extremely helpful in providing the raw materials I used to research events from the mid-twentieth century. I should also thank those hard-working professionals at the Laboratory, especially Cyndi Brandt and Joan Houston, who have provided technical support for the many lectures I have been called on to give.

That all-important task of passing my manuscript through a classification process was accomplished by highly talented experts in the Laboratory's Classification Office, led by David Brown and ably assisted by Edna Didwall. David and Edna spent innumerable hours going over each sentence to ensure that it met classification standards. The three of us once spent two days together during which they gave me sage advice on how to express ideas in a way that fell within an accepted protocol. Without them, this story would never have been told.

# FROM
# BERKELEY
## TO
# BERLIN

//////////////////

# *Introduction*

In a world that has experienced a military conflict practically every year since the end of World War II, how is it that the superpowers have not used a nuclear weapon in anger? Soviet premier Josef Stalin had shown time and again his willingness to use whatever force necessary to achieve his political goals: for example, he ordered the deaths of millions of Ukrainians in the 1930s to achieve his economic plans for the Soviet Union. Nikita Khrushchev, one of Stalin's lieutenants, was just as much a thug. Considering that a highly aggressive Soviet Union, which became a nuclear-armed state in 1949, emerged from a world war intent on spreading communism through revolution, it is indeed a wonder the Soviets did not use nuclear weapons to further their cause. That was not an accident. On a few occasions during the Cold War, the United States and the Soviet Union came terribly close to exchanging nuclear strikes, but something stopped that from happening.

A decade after the Berlin airlift, at the end of President Dwight D. Eisenhower's administration and the beginning of John F. Kennedy's, the United States and the Soviet Union engaged in a full-blown nuclear crisis over the city of Berlin—and almost went to war. Everyone knows about the Cuban Missile Crisis; arguably, the Berlin Crisis was just as critical. It involved the leader of the Soviet Union directly threatening the democratic free world with destruction.

In 1961 Khrushchev, now Soviet premier following Stalin's death, blatantly warned the democratic governments of Europe not to resist his political ambitions for Berlin. He reminded them the Soviet Union possessed rockets capable of delivering superbombs that could reach their capitals—in other words, he would use nuclear weapons, if necessary, to

1

achieve his political aims. The democracies had to take him seriously: in 1956 the Red Army had ruthlessly crushed a revolt of the Hungarian people against Soviet repression. Western leaders realized Hungary fell within the Soviet sphere of influence, yet the violent response to the uprising felt like a warning shot.

In November 1960 Kennedy was elected president on a platform that the United States would stand firm against communism. Regardless, Khrushchev brandished his nuclear diplomacy to also threaten the United States to abandon Berlin or pay the consequences. The stage was set for a major confrontation over the fate of democratic West Berlin.

Unlike two decades earlier, when an unsuspecting America was attacked by the Japanese Empire at Pearl Harbor, the United States did not enter into the Berlin Crisis fully unprepared. Fortunately, a group of distinguished intellectuals had mentored a band of young and vibrant Americans to give America the ability to stop a communist tyrant from using his nuclear arsenal to seek world domination. Six months after the height of that crisis, Kennedy thought about how close the country had come to destruction, and he flew out to Berkeley, California, to meet and thank this small troop of physicists for helping the country avert a nuclear war. What had they done to deserve the president's gratitude? This book tells their story.

*# # #*

One day in 1931, a young South Dakotan, Ernest O. Lawrence, converted a disused wooden building on the Berkeley campus of the University of California into a scientific laboratory—the Rad Lab. Lawrence, who would win the Nobel Prize in Physics in 1939, would give Berkeley respectability in a world dominated by an elite European clique of physicists. He was passionate about the security of American society, so when it was discovered Nazi Germany had the means to build an atomic bomb, he threw all his energy into rousing U.S. government officials to act immediately.

Ten years later, when Stalin's Soviet Union became a nuclear power, Lawrence drove his students to take on the challenge to deter a communist despot's military ambitions. They were upstarts of the 1950s who helped give the United States the means to get through the Cold War without having to engage in a thermonuclear catastrophe, an accomplishment so many

Americans take for granted. Their journey was not easy, having to over-come ridicule over three successive failures, which had led to calls to see them, and their entire laboratory, shut down.

In his 1983 work *The Wizards of Armageddon*, author Fred Kaplan wrote about how the United States developed a nuclear-deterrent strategy that saw the country safely through the Cold War. He traced the careers of researchers at RAND Corporation, a small group of theorists who would devise and help implement a set of ideas that would change the shape of American defense policy. Kaplan argued that their work meant the differ-ence between peace and total war. But their ideas were not fully effective without Lawrence's young professionals, who complemented their strate-gies with the weapons that credibly deterred a militarily powerful Soviet Union from seeking world dominance.

⫽ ⫽ ⫽

History provides the best guide for our expectations of the future. This narrative was written for history buffs and general readers interested in a heroic tale. The subject matter necessarily includes technological events, but I have made an effort to make sure the reader does not have to be a math and science major to enjoy the story. The emphasis here is on the individuals who were participants, not on the gadgets they invented. Of course, it helps to understand what it is that the story's heroes accom-plished and why they are important, so descriptions of those accomplish-ments are made in a language that can be understood by a general reader who is not technically oriented.

After the First Gulf War in 1992, there was a great victory parade held in Washington, D.C. The troops marched across the Washington Mall to the cheers of thousands of grateful Americans. But there was no victory parade for the physicists who orchestrated the victory won in Berlin in 1961. No one knew what they had done. One of them, Mike May, recalled how Kennedy stepped up to him inside the entrance to the Rad Lab on a sunny day in Berkeley in March 1962. The president grasped his hand and warmly thanked him for all he had done for the country. May said that memory is forever etched in his mind—he will never forget the warmth he felt from the young president, who like May, was a veteran of World War II.

Some of the characters in this history, like Mike May and Johnny Foster, are my friends. They are the physicists who worked directly for Lawrence at his Rad Lab in Berkeley. I do not believe American society is aware of how much it owes to those pioneering upstarts. Their contributions deserve to be recognized by the society they have served so well, while they are still living. What follows is the tale of how these Americans made such a difference to our world.

# *1*

////////////////

## *Clouds over Berlin*

Tensions that would grow into a nuclear crisis in 1961 had their roots in events that occurred immediately after World War II. At that time, Premier Stalin was intent on extracting war reparations from Germany. President Franklin D. Roosevelt had agreed in principle at the Yalta Conference (February 1945) that Germany should be made to pay the Soviet Union $10 billion in reparations, but British prime minister Winston Churchill and his government opposed the agreement, realizing Germany, with its economy destroyed by the war, could never afford to make such payments, the onus then shifting to the Allies to prevent surviving Germans from starving. When Harry Truman assumed the presidency after Roosevelt's death in May 1945, he gradually changed the American position on reparations toward the British position, which irritated Stalin.

Following a meeting of the Council of Foreign Ministers in Moscow in March 1947, American secretary of state George C. Marshall worked with his State Department staff to resurrect the economies of the European nations ravaged by war. These efforts emerged as the Marshall Plan, which spent approximately $13 billion to restore the economies of Europe and create an environment in which capitalism and free trade could thrive. Although the Soviet Union was implicitly included as an eligible recipient for this aid, Marshall was certain Stalin would refuse such assistance since he would never allow American engineers and specialists to move freely within the Soviet Union to ensure the funds were being properly utilized.[1]

Marshall's premonitions were correct, for Stalin saw the assistance as a threat, a form of economic warfare that directly threatened Soviet hegemony over Eastern European nations. When the Czechoslovak Republic and Poland quickly agreed to accept aid under the plan, Stalin summoned the Czech leader, Jan Masaryk, the son of the republic's principal founder, and Wladyslaw Gomulka, the Polish Communist Party's general secretary, to the Kremlin and ordered them to withdraw their requests. They quickly acquiesced to Stalin's demands, but the Soviet leader remained unforgiving. Gomulka was later purged from his position of authority in Poland, and in March 1948, Masaryk was found dead in the courtyard of the Foreign Ministry in Prague.

When negotiations over German war reparations among the Allied foreign ministers had run their course without a satisfactory resolution for the Soviet position, the United States, Great Britain, and France united their occupation zones into a single political entity, the Federal Republic of Germany, or as it was more commonly called, West Germany. Konrad Adenaur, the "Alte" as he was called, was elected prime minister of the West German parliament, the Bundesrat. The new country's capital was established in Bonn along the Rhine River. Among Germans, this was accepted as a temporary political solution until the country could be reunited with the Soviet occupation zone in the east, and Berlin, entirely within the Soviet zone, would be reestablished as the nation's capital. Until that political goal could be achieved, Berlin remained a flashpoint of deteriorating relations between the West and the Soviet Union.

In principle, Berlin was a single city jointly occupied and administered by the victorious Allies, with troops of each—Russian, American, British, and French—occupying an assigned sector of the city. But in reality, Berlin had become two cities: East Berlin, the sector under Soviet control, was essentially a part of Communist East Germany, while West Berlin, comprising the other three sectors, was politically part of West Germany. What most troubled communist leaders was that West Berlin quickly became a conduit for those living in East Germany to leave the country. Initiating its own democratic elections, West Berlin soon established its own government. For the time being, the United States, Great Britain, and France ultimately kept order in West Berlin with the few thousand foreign troops stationed there.[2]

Flaunting postwar agreements, in 1948 the Soviets attempted to force the Western Allies out of Berlin by barricading all highway entrances into the city. Rather than force a confrontation between U.S. and Russian troops at a roadside barricade, the American command opted to fly needed supplies into Western sectors in what became called the Berlin Airlift. The need to land aircraft at West Berlin's Tempelhof Airfield, often in inclement weather, brought forward an invention of physicist Luis Alvarez. Eight years before the airlift, Alvarez led a team to develop Ground Controlled Approach Radar. This proved to be a godsend during the crisis, allowing C-47 aircraft to safely navigate and land their precious supplies. Embarrassed that the Americans were able to sidestep the blockade and supply Berlin by air, the Soviets reopened the road routes to Allied military vehicles after nine months, ending the crisis.

Political tension over Berlin significantly rose again in 1958. Following Stalin's death in 1953, the new Soviet leader was Nikita Khrushchev, who asserted there must be a peace treaty between the wartime allies and Germany that redefined the status of West Berlin. He declared if a treaty was not accepted by the West within six months, the Soviet Union would make separate arrangements with East Germany and be free to impose these new arrangements on West Berlin. All previously recognized rights of the British, the French, and the Americans would become void. Khrushchev succumbed to the temptation of using the threat of his newly created nuclear arsenal to further his political ambitions, a tactic political scientists were calling "nuclear diplomacy." He hoped the nuclear strength the Soviet Union had achieved by the mid-1950s would intimidate Western democracies to agree to his terms, exploiting as well a new threat posed by the launch in October 1957 of Sputnik, the Soviet's first satellite.

Khrushchev's ensuing erratic behavior alternated between pressure tactics and relaxation. The sense of urgency created by his six-month deadline was eased in the spring of 1959 when he agreed to a new round of negotiations, first with foreign ministers that would then lead to a summit meeting. The meetings of the foreign ministers took place for nine weeks and extended into the summer months. These were followed by Khrushchev's visit to the United States, which included a trip to Disneyland and ended with discussions with President Eisenhower at the presidential retreat at Camp David, Maryland. The Soviet leader's friendly spirit was temporary, for that winter he made increasingly vociferous speeches demanding a signed treaty to settle the status of West Berlin.

Matters became worse on May 1, 1960, when an American U-2 reconnaissance spy plane was shot down over the Soviet Union. At a summit in Paris, Eisenhower admitted his personal responsibility for the overflight, to which Khrushchev reacted with demands that forced a quick adjournment of the gathering. Several exchanges were held between the American administration and the Kremlin over Soviet demands for U.S. compensation, which the president refused outright.

In his memoirs written years later, Eisenhower confessed to feeling frustrated dealing with Khrushchev. His term of office was coming to an end, and he felt that decisions about dealing with the Soviets over Berlin, as well as nuclear testing, should be more properly handled by the next administration. Khrushchev eventually announced he would await the new American administration before continuing negotiations. The stage was set for a major confrontation over the fate of West Berlin.

*∥ ∥ ∥*

When John F. Kennedy announced his candidacy for president on January 2, 1960, he claimed he was running for the most powerful office in the free world. The Massachusetts senator branded communism as the greatest threat facing the United States, and the country had to confront that despotic ideology head on without reservations. Kennedy won the election that November and, in office, stayed true to his campaign rhetoric. He planned to engage Khrushchev on the status of Berlin, and he would do it by meeting him face to face. A summit meeting was set for June 3, 1961, in Vienna, Austria, for which Kennedy prepared himself to meet the Soviet leader in a spirit of no equivocation and no retreat. Before a large crowd of supporters, the new president proclaimed he would go to Vienna as leader of the greatest revolutionary country on earth. He would not retreat a single inch. He would be heard.[3]

Although the upcoming summit promised to be a dangerously important event, in the weeks preceding it, American newspapers did not focus on it, instead devoting their pages to other events. Reading a newspaper in May 1961, headlines would showcase such things as Alan Shepherd becoming the first American to go to space; Kennedy making a speech before Congress calling for a moon landing before the end of the decade; "Freedom Riders" being pummeled by squads of Alabama State Police;

riots taking place in Montgomery, Alabama; the country of Laos being in total turmoil; and a military coup breaking out in South Korea. The country, and the world, moved ahead, seemingly oblivious to the drama about to take place in Vienna.

Before facing Khrushchev, Kennedy had to make sure he represented a united front among the Western European allies. On Memorial Day, 1961, he visited French president Charles de Gaulle in Paris. The two leaders met quietly for ninety minutes before emerging at a press conference at which they proclaimed their "complete identity of view" to counter any threat to Berlin by the Soviet Union. President de Gaulle told reporters he and Kennedy had agreed to go to war, if necessary, to maintain Western rights in the divided city.[4]

The following day British minister of defence Harold Watkinson warned the Soviets not to assume the West would fight only a limited war to protect Berlin. Referring to the doctrine of "Massive Retaliation" inherited from the Eisenhower administration, Watkinson recognized that in any confrontation there could be a danger of overdependence on nuclear weapons, which could result in all-out war. On the other hand, he did not believe the North Atlantic Treaty Organization (NATO), the formal military alliance of the allied Western nations, should provide such massive conventional forces as could hope to deal with the entire Red Army without recourse to nuclear weapons. He feared that doing so might merely indicate NATO did not have the courage to use nuclear weapons in any circumstances.[5]

Catching up to Kennedy prior to the summit, the veteran diplomat Averell Harriman—who had just arrived from Geneva, where he had been engaged with Soviet negotiators over the status of Laos—held a private meeting with the president. Harriman coached him on how to deal with Khrushchev, telling Kennedy to talk gently, be relaxed, and tell jokes.

One reason for Khrushchev agreeing to the summit meeting was to size up the new American president. First on his mind was a military operation known as the Bay of Pigs. In the first months of his administration, Kennedy had backed an invasion of Fidel Castro's Communist Cuba by a brigade of Cuban expatriates; the action turned into a fiasco, with the president having to bargain to bring back prisoners of war and settle them in

Florida. Much to the disappointment of several CIA operators and Cuban expatriate leaders, in the days leading to the invasion, Kennedy chose not to involve U.S. military forces in direct support of the operation. There was a feeling that his decision may have guaranteed the operation's failure. This was not lost on the Russians; there was a sense among Khrushchev's advisors that Kennedy's national security staff had acted erratically and was not totally in charge of events. Some in the Kremlin thought there was a lack of nerve by Kennedy that could be exploited.[6]

June 3 arrived, and the summit meeting began at a cordial level, with discussions centering on Laos; Berlin was not mentioned. At a mammoth press conference held that afternoon, the atmosphere was so cordial the British journalist Randolph Churchill, son of the former prime minister, abruptly got up and left because he claimed to be bored.[7]

The next morning the two leaders discussed Berlin, and the mood changed. Khrushchev tried to impress Kennedy with his surliness, determined to see the issue resolved the way he wanted and demanding American soldiers depart West Berlin by the end of the year. He was adamant the situation in Berlin had to change: a free West Berlin was out of the question. Khrushchev made it clear he was losing patience, and at some point the Red Army would besiege the city.[8] At a subsequent press conference Kennedy's press secretary, Pierre Salinger, tried to put a positive spin on the meeting that day with a declaration that this was just an opening to continue negotiations; his words sounded hollow.

Kennedy was shaken and showed it. Before he departed Vienna, a photograph in the *New York Times* showed the Soviet leader smiling and sitting upright on the arm of a chair while the U.S. president sat facing him, his hand extended, looking solemn and somber.[9] Nevertheless, after listening to Khrushchev talk endlessly about change through revolution, Kennedy had not lost his sense of humor, nor his nerve. Remembering Harriman's advice, his last words to Khrushchev were, "I see it is going to be a very cold winter."[10]

The political journalist for the *New York Herald Tribune*, Joseph Alsop, described Kennedy's demeanor immediately following the Vienna meeting. The president went to London to confer with British officials. While there, he attended the christening of the daughter of Jackie Kennedy's sister, who was married to a Polish expatriate, Stanislas Radziwill. Alsop met the president at the christening, where Kennedy shoved the journalist into a corner and talked for fifteen minutes in a tense, low bray about what he had just been through. Alsop said he had no idea while in Vienna how serious the situation was and now had the sense that the meeting with Khrushchev had come to Kennedy as a very great shock. He thought it was after the Vienna meeting that Kennedy began to truly understand what it means to be president of the United States.[11]

Reports of the summit soon reached home, and the State Department performed miserably. It took about six weeks to produce a note in response to the Russian ultimatum.[12] The department's director for German affairs, Martin J. Hillenbrand, thought the blunt way Khrushchev presented the Soviet position on Berlin, which led Kennedy to make his remark on the likelihood of a cold winter, had created the prospect of a major crisis. The Soviet leader presented the president, in effect, with a year-end deadline. It seemed clear Kennedy emerged from the Vienna meeting with the feeling a major confrontation with the Soviet Union was about to take place. The energies of the new administration had to be devoted, on an emergency basis, to meeting this challenge.[13]

There were valid reasons to treat Khrushchev's behavior seriously. He had been Stalin's political commissar to the Central Soviet Army in World War II; his area of operations included the absolute devastation of the Battle of Stalingrad. When there were not enough rifles for every Russian soldier in that city, Khrushchev ordered they be given to every third man; if an armed soldier was shot, an unarmed one had to pick up his weapon and continue the fight. Any soldier who retreated during an attack was shot by Soviet machine gunners. Told about the destruction of a nuclear war, one can imagine Khrushchev thinking, after the horror of Stalingrad, he had already seen total destruction and had survived. Kennedy, also a veteran of World War II, knew very well what his adversary was capable of doing.

Dean Acheson, former secretary of state to President Truman, felt if Khrushchev could split the Western alliance over Berlin and force the allies to withdraw ignominiously, abandoning the 2.5 million citizens of West Berlin, all of Germany and the continent would know the Soviets were the masters of Europe. Americans, too, would have shown their acknowledgment of this.[14] The U.S. Army had a brigade of soldiers in West Berlin, so if the Red Army besieged the city, American soldiers would most likely be either killed or taken prisoner. If Kennedy withdrew them before any siege began, he would be acceding to the Soviet ultimatum; that was an action he would not contemplate. Even so, the president was aware a spark of violence ignited in Berlin could quickly lead to an all-out nuclear conflagration. He had a first-class nuclear crisis on his hands.

Pressure continued to build. On June 15 Khrushchev issued a statement flatly reimposing a year-end deadline for resolution of Berlin's status. Kennedy held several meetings with his national security staff and leaders at the Pentagon as they considered responses to the ultimatum.[15] If the Soviets besieged Berlin, could an Army task force make a breakthrough? A relief convoy, escorted by tanks, could try to force its way past Soviet obstacles, but the Red Army vastly outnumbered any conventional forces NATO could put up. If that was the case, could tactical nuclear weapons be used to offset the large Red Army formations? The president asked Acheson to lead a study for a response to the Russians. The former secretary produced a paper calling for highly aggressive action: go on high alert, reinforce NATO forces, and initiate large-scale military maneuvers.[16]

If Khrushchev carried out his threat to occupy all of Berlin, surely he would realize it could provoke a nuclear attack from the United States, so he might plan to forestall such an event by striking America's nuclear weapons first; could the nation's nuclear forces survive a surprise attack? A political "think tank" created by the U.S. Air Force, the RAND Corporation, had conducted studies on whether America's nuclear arsenal was vulnerable to a Soviet surprise attack. These suggested the arsenal was indeed vulnerable. To reduce that vulnerability, Strategic Air Command (SAC) airbases had operated under a program called Reflex, whereby B-47 bombers were ordered into the air within fifteen minutes of a warning. In reality, that response time was often not achieved.[17]

There was a general assumption among Air Force planners that the Soviets would attack across the Arctic. U.S. early warning radar systems pointed that way, and many expected them to provide ample alert of an incoming attack—a questionable assumption. Locations of SAC bases and launch pads of Atlas and Titan intercontinental ballistic missiles (ICBMs), as well as shorter-range Jupiter and Thor missiles, were known. If there was a surprise Soviet air attack, those bombers and liquid-fueled missiles were vulnerable to destruction; they would hardly have the opportunity to take off or be launched in time. This possibility worried planners the most.[18]

With tensions over Berlin mounting, the chief of staff of the Air Force, General Curtis LeMay, urged the president to launch a preemptive all-out nuclear strike against the Soviet Union. If it was inevitable the two nuclear powers were going to war, LeMay reasoned, why wait for the Soviets to execute an annihilation strike the way the Japanese had done at Pearl Harbor in December 1941?[19] The vulnerability of the nation's strategic nuclear forces raised the specter of military operators manning weapon systems in a "hair trigger" state of readiness. It was the stuff of the popular 1964 Hollywood movies *Fail Safe* and *Dr. Strangelove*.

But in the summer of 1961, the situation went from bad to worse. On August 31 Kennedy told the American public Premier Khrushchev had informed him the Soviet Union intended to resume nuclear testing. Soon after, the Soviets conducted an astonishing forty-five nuclear tests in sixty-five days. As though intending to use these as a form of intimidation, fourteen were above one megaton in yield, including a test on October 30 in the Novaya Zemlya Test Range of a fifty-eight-megaton device, the so-called Tsar Bomba. As of 2021, it remains the largest-yield device ever detonated.[20]

Kennedy was furious and wanted to immediately respond to Soviet testing. He called the chairman of the Atomic Energy Commission (AEC), Glenn Seaborg, and asked how soon the United States could respond with a test of its own. Seaborg answered he could have an atmospheric test ready in a few days. Kennedy, however, was not ready to approve anything but underground detonations. Seaborg said that would have to be of a tactical nuclear weapon with a yield in the tens of kilotons. The president was dissatisfied, saying that would not shake the windows of the Oval Office, and pressed for the testing of a large weapon. Seaborg responded that would take several weeks to prepare.[21]

Still uncertain whether to aggressively respond to Soviet nuclear tests, Kennedy met with his national security advisors and asked if another offer to stop testing should be proposed to the Soviets, and if they did not accept, should the United States keep to its testing moratorium. He received varying advice. Secretary of State Dean Rusk, Secretary of Defense Robert McNamara, and Chairman Seaborg all supported this approach.

The military, led by General Lyman Lemnitzer, the chairman of the Joint Chiefs of Staff, voiced his opposition. The military's argument was straightforward. It seemed the country would survive this one excursion by the Soviets to conduct nuclear tests. The question was, could the country live with another one. If the United States was surprised again by the Soviets, how bad would the problem be then? Would the Soviets be tempted to do it again because they thought they had made significant gains from their first excursion? For America to continue a unilateral moratorium would be politically damaging if the Soviets resumed regular testing. Kennedy accepted Lemnitzer's argument.[22] He ordered Seaborg to prepare the AEC to resume nuclear testing.

*// // //*

A half century after these events occurred, several political analysts pointed out the Russians did not have the means to launch a destructive strike against U.S. bomber bases and ICBM sites. They claimed the CIA's intelligence estimate should have told the president and his national security staff Khrushchev's nuclear threats had been bluster. But if these "Monday Morning" analysts had been able to play out that scenario in 1961, they would have been met with skepticism from Kennedy. The president believed his campaign rhetoric that the United States had let its military stature slip into an unsafe condition. As RAND analyst Albert Wohlstetter observed at the time, political pundits greatly overestimated the difficulties of a Soviet surprise attack with thermonuclear weapons and vastly underestimated the complexity of the Western problem of retaliation.[23]

National Security Advisor McGeorge Bundy succinctly described Kennedy's challenge with uncertainty when he observed it was harder to make a decision than it was to see later what the decision should have been.[24] The president's staff had no other recourse but to take Khrushchev at his word. Kennedy himself revealed a foreboding: "Something is bound to happen, the Russians will not sit still. Great cataclysms are coming—I don't believe I'm going to have a quiet term of office."[25]

In a dramatic address to the nation amid the crisis, Kennedy outlined a series of measures the country would take. In what could be imagined as coming directly out of the pages of RAND analyst Bill Kaufmann's 1954 book on deterrence, Kennedy proposed meeting Soviet aggression by increasing the country's conventional strength—to include a one-million-man Army. Just as Kaufmann had argued, the president stated nuclear forces had to be backed up by whatever conventional forces were necessary to meet Soviet threats.

Shying away from the Massive Retaliation strategy inherited from the Eisenhower administration, which heavily relied on nuclear weapons, Kennedy proposed increasing reliance on conventional forces among the three military services. He wanted to double or triple draft calls. He felt the Soviet Union would be less prone to rash action if it was confronted with the necessity of launching a sizable military attack to gain military victories in various trouble spots, such as Berlin.[26] The military buildup proposed by the president won overwhelming bipartisan support in Congress. The administration had ushered in a strategy of "Controlled Response." Still, an invulnerable nuclear force would have to act as the nation's core defense— its ultimate deterrent.

This is where Kennedy showed his ability to lead the nation. Throughout these trying times, from his abrupt meeting with Khrushchev in Vienna to his endless meetings with advisors who differed so much in their approaches to the crisis—from Adlai Stevenson's totally nonprovocative ethic to LeMay and Acheson's calls for highly aggressive responses— Kennedy sought to keep his policies on an even keel. On the one hand, he wanted to make sure Khrushchev understood the U.S. resolve not to abandon Berlin, but on the other hand, he did not want to provoke him into acting irrationally. The way Kennedy accomplished this balancing act was remarkable.

War can be irrational. Despite the best-laid plans going in, its outcome can lead to completely unforeseen consequences, such as Napoleon's ill-considered campaign to lead Europe's largest army into Russia in 1812, or Hitler's disastrous decision to send the Wehrmacht into the Soviet Union in 1941. Regardless of how much plotting went on within the Kremlin, Khrushchev's behavior would not necessarily be rational, so Kennedy could not count on the Soviet premier reacting to an American action sensibly. The best assurance the president had to keep him from acting irrationally was the invulnerability and preponderant strength of an American retaliatory force.

The thought of preemptively striking the Soviet Union before it could launch a surprise strike had crossed Eisenhower's mind, and he had rejected it outright. But he had not faced a crisis of the same magnitude as this one regarding West Berlin. The thought may have crossed Kennedy's mind as well, but he had something Eisenhower had not had until the last year of his administration: a military system that took the country further away from having a hair-trigger mentality.

With its Polaris submarines on station, the United States was in an unequivocal position of knowing its nuclear forces could retaliate against any massive surprise strike. There was at the time no other weapon system like Polaris. Kennedy well knew how valuable submarine-launched missiles were to the country: "Once one has seen a Polaris firing[,] the efficacy of this weapon system as a deterrent is not debatable."[27]

When the Soviets pushed for a comprehensive nuclear-test ban in 1958, they had not realized a thermonuclear warhead could be made small enough to fit on a submarine-launched missile. Thermonuclear warheads of the time were monstrous affairs that required huge bombers or massive land-based missiles to carry them. Kennedy went into the Berlin Crisis knowing, for all Khrushchev's bluster, the Soviets could not destroy the United States without being destroyed themselves. That was not a guarantee a confrontation could avoid an exchange of nuclear weapons, but at least he knew Khrushchev could not preemptively surprise the United States and get away with it. That thought helped the president have confidence to stand up to his convictions.

No one could have predicted that a bunch of twenty- and thirty-year-old scientists operating out of a converted naval air station in a dusty California town would come up with an effective nuclear weapon that could be launched from a submarine. That assembly of heroic Americans in the town of Livermore was not a happy accident. Their presence was a culmination of events that had started thirty years earlier with the arrival in Berkeley of a very young Ernest Lawrence, who created a laboratory that attracted some of the brightest minds in America.

Khrushchev had made the threat in 1961, and Kennedy stood up to it. It was now up to the Soviet leader to make the next move. If the Red Army besieged West Berlin, then war would begin and most likely escalate into an all-out nuclear exchange between the two great powers. It was a scenario Kennedy dreaded, as he had revealed to Alsop in a quiet moment. Yet the president felt he had no choice but to take a stand. Kennedy's instincts were sound; Khrushchev backed down.

# 2

//////////////

# *The Discovery That Started It All*

K ennedy's facing down a thug like Khrushchev was not a given—it did not just happen. Like almost everything in life, it took preparation, and Kennedy needed help to prepare the nation to have the wherewithal to stand up to a war ultimatum. National Security Advisor McGeorge Bundy believed America's preponderant strength was crucial in seeing it through a nuclear crisis. But it had taken time for the country to develop enough preponderant strength, and to learn how to use it, to deter a determined tyrant.

Having the wherewithal to escape a nuclear crisis unscathed in 1961 actually started thirty years earlier with the creation of a scientific laboratory devoted to the study of nuclear physics. In 1930 Robert G. Sproul became president of the University of California. He was intent on developing the university from a scientific backwater into a world-class center of scientific innovation. To accomplish this, he promoted an associate professor of physics, Ernest O. Lawrence, a South Dakota native and grandson of Norwegian immigrants, to be a full professor. Lawrence was an up-and-coming physicist recently recruited to the Berkeley campus, and Sproul thought Lawrence's passion and zeal to accomplish things would do the trick. He would not be disappointed.[1]

True to expectations, Lawrence sought to do something new and exciting. He invented a machine that accelerated subatomic particles to penetrate the atomic nucleus. He called his invention a magnetic resonance accelerator, but it became known as a cyclotron. Newspaper journalists called his creation the "atom smasher."

In August 1931 Sproul gave Lawrence a disused civil-engineering building to house a new twenty-seven-inch cyclotron. Lawrence called his new home the Penetrating Radiation Laboratory, but within a year it became the University of California Radiation Laboratory (UCRL); most called it the Rad Lab. (As will become evident, UCRL is the hub around which the principal characters and events of this history will revolve.) Lawrence's cyclotron attracted the top experimental-physics students in the country, who flocked to join the Rad Lab and become "cyclotroneers."[2]

Two early recruits to the Rad Lab played significant roles in developing America's preponderant strength and, like Lawrence himself, would become Nobel laureates. One was Edwin McMillan. Slight of build, freckled, and sandy-haired, McMillan was reared in Pasadena, California, and had earned bachelor and master of science degrees from the California Institute of Technology (Caltech) by the age of twenty-two. In 1932 he received a doctorate in physics while at Princeton University; within two years, he joined the Rad Lab. McMillan made his mark almost immediately, inventing schemes to improve the performance of the cyclotron.

The other recruit was Luis Alvarez, a tall and ruddy man with a crop of blond hair. His Celtic looks belied his Hispanic surname, which came from a Cuban émigré grandfather and a father who was a renowned researcher at the Mayo Clinic; his fair complexion came from his mother, Harriet Smyth, the daughter of Irish missionaries to China. In 1936 he held a doctorate in physics when Lawrence offered him a position at the Rad Lab. Within a year, Alvarez had won the right to conduct experiments of his own design with one of the world's most powerful tools for nuclear research.

At about the time Lawrence moved to Berkeley, the university hired a theoretical physicist named J. Robert Oppenheimer. Tall and gangly, Oppenheimer had a narrow face and piercing blue eyes. He and Lawrence complemented each other well. Oppenheimer became the theorist for the Rad Lab, assembling a group of theoretical physicists who provided frameworks that explained what the cyclotroneers were discovering. By 1933, Oppenheimer's genius attracted the top fellows of the National Research Foundation to Berkeley and the Rad Lab.

These two friends, Lawrence, the rural Lutheran South Dakotan, and Oppenheimer, the urban Jewish New Yorker, had so many different characteristics. Unfortunately, with the advent of the atomic bomb in the

1940s, a rift would form between them and lead to passionate battles over thermonuclear research.

///

Young professionals who choose to make physics their lifelong careers have two general paths they can follow, becoming either experimental or theoretical physicists. In a nutshell, experimentalists discover new physical phenomena, while theorists explain them. Lawrence happened to be one of the world's greatest experimentalists. (While still a graduate student, he had made the most accurate measurement of the fundamental constant of quantum physics—Planck's constant.) Two particular attributes made him extraordinary: Lawrence had a remarkable ability to make even the most difficult experiments work, and he was a natural leader who could instill the highest degrees of trust and loyalty in his subordinates.

A dramatic event happened in December 1938 that would change the course of Lawrence's life. Nuclear fission was discovered in a chemistry laboratory in Berlin, then the capital of Nazi Germany. Sparked by that discovery, Lawrence and his cyclotroneers went on to play essential, though little-known, roles in getting the United States prepared for the upcoming nuclear age.

That discovery in Berlin came about because of an event in Rome, where the Italian physicist and future Nobel laureate Enrico Fermi noticed unusual activity when he struck a thin foil of uranium with particles called neutrons. (A neutron is an electrically neutral particle found in the atomic nucleus; it has about the same mass as a proton, an electrically positive particle also found in the nucleus. The English physicist James Chadwick won the Nobel Prize in Physics in 1935 for discovering the neutron.)

Fermi had been striking, in turn, all the elements of the periodic table with neutrons. When the nucleus of an element absorbed these, he often observed a radioactive form of that element, called a radioisotope. With each element, Fermi discovered one new radioisotope after another. But when he reached uranium, he observed a substantial increase in radioactivity apparently coming from multiple radioisotopes. It was a phenomenon he had not seen with any other element. Fermi reported his observations about uranium in the Italian physics journal *Ricerca Scientifica* in May 1934.[3]

This induced the renowned German chemist Otto Hahn to repeat the experiment in his own laboratory in Berlin. Significantly, instead of looking for induced radioactivity from radioisotopes after the neutron bombardment as Fermi had done, Hahn chemically analyzed the remnants of the uranium foil, hoping in that way to find new elements. After bombarding the uranium with neutrons, he found the element barium in the foil, which was perplexing—barium is not even close to uranium in the periodic table. Hahn was an excellent chemist, but he needed a good theoretical physicist to interpret his discovery, so he wrote a letter describing what he had seen to his former partner, the Austrian physicist Lise Meitner.

Although not a well-known household name like Albert Einstein or Marie Curie, Meitner, a world-class physicist, ought to be. She was a prominent physicist, having received with Hahn the prestigious Leibniz Prize for discovering new elements. But she was also Jewish. When Adolf Hitler's Nazi Party came to power in Germany, she was forced to wear a yellow badge in public and was subjected to physical assaults. Meitner could see the coming danger of Nazism for Jews, and Hahn helped expedite her flight out of Germany, giving her a diamond ring, which had belonged to his mother, in case she needed emergency funds. Meitner settled down in the village of Kungalv, Sweden, near the city of Göteborg.

Within days of receiving Hahn's letter, Meitner and her nephew, Otto Frisch, concluded he had observed uranium nuclei split apart—as a parallel to cells splitting in biology, Frisch called it nuclear fission. That she could decipher a complicated chemistry experiment and come up with a theory in nuclear physics in a matter of days is astounding. Aunt and nephew then cowrote an article published in the scientific journal *Nature* that declared, among other things, a nuclear-fission reaction was a million times more energetic than a chemical explosive reaction.[4] (They did this by comparing particle masses after nuclear fission to the uranium nucleus and the neutron mass before the reaction, then equated the difference in masses to energy by using Einstein's famous relation, $E=mc^2$.)

This paper, in a real sense, launched the world into a nuclear age; it also raised a disturbing issue. The discovery of nuclear fission, with its associated great release of energy, occurred in the capital of Nazi Germany. Because of the enormous energies involved, nuclear physicists, including

Lawrence, recognized a danger in the location: Hitler could someday soon possess an atomic bomb.

To a nuclear physicist, Meitner and Frisch's article raised questions. If each fission released a great amount of energy, there should have been a lot of heat generated in Hahn's experiment, so much so one could expect the uranium foil to melt or even disintegrate—but it had not. Apparently, the vast majority of the uranium nuclei in the foil did not fission. There was an ample number of neutrons striking the material, so why were there so few reactions? The answer to this would be found by a Dane and an American.

Within a short time of the discovery's announcement, Nobel laureate Niels Bohr met physicist John Wheeler in New York. They took up quarters in nearby Princeton, where together they wrote a scientific article that appeared in the September 1, 1939, issue of *Physical Review* entitled "The Mechanism of Nuclear Fission."[5] Wheeler and Bohr concluded the nuclear fissions observed in Berlin had not been due to uranium atoms in general; rather, they were due to only one isotope of uranium, uranium-235, composing less than 1 percent of the atoms in natural uranium. (An isotope of an element possesses the same number of protons as other nuclei of the element but differs in the number of neutrons.) As if it were foreboding of catastrophic things to come, their article appeared the same day the Wehrmacht invaded Poland from the west, followed soon by Stalin's Red Army attacking Poland from the east. With these blatant acts, the two Nonaggression Pact partners crushed the country of Poland within thirty days—and initiated World War II.

The Wheeler-Bohr article was profound. It implied, in order to make an atomic bomb, one first had to separate the isotope uranium-235 from natural uranium and then mold enough of it together to form a critical mass that could sustain a chain reaction. Lawrence thought he knew how to do that.

*⫻ ⫻ ⫻*

Once he had digested the Meitner-Frisch and Wheeler-Bohr articles, Lawrence, true to his nature, felt he had to do something. Nazi Germany had an ample supply of world-class physicists who understood the implications of nuclear fission—they would know how to make an atomic bomb.

Someone had to wake up U.S. government officials about a catastrophic threat steamrolling toward the country since the day Hahn had made that discovery in his chemistry laboratory.

His mind made up to act, Lawrence approached an engineer named Vannevar Bush, who fulfilled a role that would later be called the president's scientific advisor. Bush had made his fortune when he and two associates invented a means for a household radio to run off of an electrical outlet rather than a battery. With that invention, he cofounded the American Appliance Company, which became the parent company to Raytheon Corporation. Bush had the ear of the president, and Lawrence pushed him to convince Roosevelt to start an atomic program. Bush, however, was not convinced an atomic bomb could even be built. Disappointed but not defeated, Lawrence returned to Berkeley.

Bush was too busy wrapping his mind around the problem of how the country should prepare itself to enter the war now raging in Europe before he would take on a scientific challenge from Lawrence. His inclination was to seek technology that was readily available and could help win the war. Bush was particularly impressed with British technology, especially radar, which had played a crucial role in England winning the Battle of Britain and staving off a Nazi invasion. The British had developed a means to make radar more effective, and Bush wanted Lawrence to leverage radar technology to develop systems that could provide an advantage in a war he was sure America was about to enter.

Bush reviewed the new British invention, then called a meeting in Washington, D.C., with Lawrence and an influential financial tycoon named Alfred Loomis. The three men discussed how to kick-start radar technology in America. After Loomis encouraged him, Lawrence volunteered to create the Massachusetts Institute of Technology (MIT) Radiation Laboratory—the style of its name and organization were borrowed from the UCRL in Berkeley. Loomis would help him secure the required financing to make the new laboratory viable. Lawrence recruited scientists from around the nation and sent his chief Rad Lab lieutenants, McMillan and Alvarez, to help get the MIT project started.

*// // //*

Loomis was a successful New York lawyer who had had the savvy to secure millions by converting his stocks into cash when he sensed the stock market was about to crash in 1929. He was also a self-made physicist who had built his own science laboratory inside the gated community of Tuxedo Park, located thirty-five miles north of New York City. Loomis was a quiet benefactor who granted scholarships to talented and deserving physics graduate students, and he invited world-famous physicists like Einstein and Bohr to his laboratory. On one such visit during the Great Depression, he met and befriended Lawrence, who afterward made it a practice to visit and stay with Loomis on his business trips to New York.

Lawrence and Loomis complemented each other well, with the professor inventing scientific tools, while Loomis secured grants to fund ever larger and more powerful devices for physicists to use. He had arranged much of the funding for the 184-inch cyclotron that was the basis for a later invention Lawrence called the calutron. Loomis was the kingpin behind the successful launch of the MIT Radiation Laboratory.

Some authors have portrayed Lawrence as a second-rate scientist who spent more time securing funding for projects than conducting research. They quote renowned physicists like Fermi's assistant Emilio Segrè, who claimed Lawrence could not be compared with the likes of his mentor. Such authors apparently never had to create and run a large project—and be successful. Lawrence was that rare kind of individual who can envision a problem, figure out a way to solve it, and have the tenacity to get it done. The successes he achieved would never have occurred without his drive to overcome obstacles, which often meant convincing those with the means to support his dreams with providing him the funding. More often than not, when Lawrence needed support, Loomis was the man he went to.

In addition to financing, Loomis frequently went to the Rad Lab for months at a time to help out with the latest experiments. He took a personal interest in the well-being of Lawrence's young physicists, often showing up when they needed help. Significantly, in a clear indication of just how important he was to those young professionals, two of them,

Alvarez and Johnny Foster, considered Loomis to be like a surrogate father.

∥ ∥ ∥

The MIT Radiation Laboratory was scheduled to open on November 15, 1940. McMillan and Alvarez departed the Rad Lab on November 11, Armistice Day, on the afternoon train out of Berkeley after a going-away party hosted by Lawrence. Oppenheimer provided each of them with a bottle of whiskey as a gift. After arriving in Boston, they checked into the Commander Hotel and prepared for their several months' stay.[6]

After arriving at MIT, Alvarez created a project to develop what came to be known as Ground Controlled Approach Radar (GCAR), a system used to guide airplanes in to the runway and a safe landing. To conduct research, the project needed an airplane with which to practice. So, one of the team members, Ivan Getting, who would later introduce the world to the Global Positioning Satellite (GPS) system, introduced Alvarez to David Griggs, a pilot with a private airplane who also happened to be a first-class physicist. This happy introduction brought Alvarez, Griggs, and Lawrence together for the first time. The three men, who became lifelong friends, would join together again when America had to face the communist threat to its security.

The MIT Radiation Laboratory was a catalyst that connected another individual to Lawrence and Alvarez. While recruiting researchers for the laboratory, the professor had reached out to a renowned Canadian physicist and personal friend, John Stuart Foster, and asked him to help with the radar research. Foster agreed to lend his talent and brought his college-age son, Johnny, to assist. Once settled in Cambridge, Massachusetts, Foster obtained a position for his son at the Harvard Research Laboratory, where Johnny conducted his own radar research. After a year Johnny volunteered for the Army Air Corps and was soon deployed to be a scientific advisor to the Fifteenth Army Air Force in Italy. As had happened to Griggs, Johnny Foster's presence in Cambridge allowed him to establish a relationship with Alvarez and Lawrence. After returning from the Italian theater of war, the younger Foster joined the Rad Lab in Berkeley, where he would play a prominent role in helping make America safe from nuclear threats.

∥ ∥ ∥

Once he had the MIT Radiation Laboratory up and running, Lawrence reignited his passion to get an American atomic program started. On the bitterly cold Boston morning of March 17, 1941, Saint Patrick's Day, he went back to see Bush and told him about a machine he had invented, the calutron, that could enrich uranium—that is, it could extract uranium-235 from natural uranium. Still, Bush remained stubbornly skeptical whether an atomic bomb could be made. But when he read an alarming document from the British government, the top-secret MAUD Report, Bush changed his mind and committed himself to building an atomic program for the United States. The development of the MAUD Report owed much to a physicist named Mark Oliphant.

Born near the city of Adelaide in southern Australia, Oliphant was completely deaf in one ear and needed glasses for a severe astigmatism that left him nearsighted. As if to make up for his physical shortcomings, he developed a deep yearning to study natural wonders discovered through physics. By his late teens, he had won scholarships that allowed him to work for Ernest Rutherford at the prestigious Cavendish Laboratory in Cambridge, England, during the early 1930s. There, he codiscovered an isotope of hydrogen called tritium (hydrogen-3). He progressed in his career to become an assistant director at Cavendish and then went on to become the head of the Physics Department at the University of Birmingham. The developments in radar that eventually led to the creation of the MIT Radiation Laboratory occurred in that department during his tenure.

Oliphant had been intrigued with the power of the cyclotron and used it as a tool to study nuclear physics. In December 1937 he visited Lawrence at the Rad Lab to receive detailed plans for building a sixty-inch cyclotron for research at the University of Birmingham. During his stay in Berkeley, Oliphant became close friends with Lawrence. He later told Lawrence how inspired he was by the hard work of the scientists of the Rad Lab and hoped, before long, their tremendous energy would be directed to help free the world from Nazi domination.[7]

After spending six months with Lawrence, Oliphant returned to Birmingham to build his own cyclotron. That was interrupted in 1939 with the discovery of nuclear fission. After reading the Meitner-Frisch article in *Nature*, he experimentally verified the existence of nuclear fission himself. In a fortuitous coincidence Oliphant had sponsored two expatriates from Nazi-controlled Germany and Austria, Rudolph Peierls and Otto Frisch (Meitner's nephew), to join his academic department. After reading the Wheeler-Bohr article, Peierls approached Oliphant with some calculations he had done with Frisch on the critical mass of uranium-235: they had discovered it was small enough to make an atomic bomb possible.

Oliphant had Peierls and Frisch write a paper outlining the results of their calculations and then presented it to the British government. This resulted in the formation of the MAUD Committee, charged with determining how to build an atomic bomb. The committee wrote a report of its findings and sent a copy to a research organization Bush had created to prepare the United States to enter the war then raging in Europe. It stated the British government believed it feasible to make an atomic bomb, then described the way to do it: "We have now reached the conclusion that it will be possible to make an effective uranium bomb which, containing some 25 lbs. of active material [uranium-235], would be equivalent as regards destructive effect of 1,800 tons of T.N.T."[8]

Oliphant grew puzzled over a lack of response from the Americans, so in late August 1941 he flew across the Atlantic to investigate. He was flabbergasted to learn that members of Bush's organization had not seen the MAUD Report (a section leader had locked the document away in his office safe without reading it). He soon grew despondent believing that getting the Americans engaged in an atomic program was doomed to failure.

In desperation, he wired Lawrence for a meeting. They met in Berkeley, and Oliphant shared the contents of the MAUD Report. Lawrence understood its implications and shared Oliphant's deep concern that the American government was not treating the uranium question with as much attention as it deserved. The professor phoned Bush and arranged for Oliphant to see him. Lawrence tried to reassure his British colleague by briefing him on his own idea to separate uranium isotopes by using a modified cyclotron—this was the calutron. He believed that an Anglo-American effort was still possible, to which Oliphant responded by later returning to Berkeley with a team of British physicists to help develop the calutron.

When he met Bush in New York, Oliphant found him unreceptive. The warm meeting with Lawrence could not overcome his despondency over the cool reception from Bush, who afforded him barely twenty minutes of his time. Oliphant returned to Birmingham, dispirited at the thought the Germans might be the first to build an atomic bomb.[9]

But Oliphant must have had an effect on Bush, who finally digested the facts, understood their implications, and decided to act. Although irritated with theoretical talks couched with degrees of uncertainty from physicists like Lawrence, Bush the engineer understood the British concept that, to make a weapon, all one needed was twenty-five pounds of uranium-235. In Bush's mind the problem had been reduced to an engineering challenge—separating and concentrating uranium isotopes.[10]

While Bush had been dithering, two members of Lawrence's Rad Lab were making discoveries that would drastically affect nuclear research. Before departing Berkeley to join the MIT Radiation Laboratory, McMillan had decided to replicate Hahn's nuclear-fission experiment. He moved beyond the German's observations and found that neutrons were not only causing some uranium nuclei to fission but also were being absorbed by nuclei of the majority isotope, uranium-238, to thereby become a radio-isotope, uranium-239. Then McMillan discovered that uranium-239 decayed into an all-new element, which he called neptunium, named after Neptune, the next planet from the sun after Uranus, for which uranium had been named.

When McMillan departed the Rad Lab for Cambridge, he agreed to let a radiochemist named Glenn Seaborg, working down the hallway from him, take over his experiments. Seaborg discovered that neptunium decayed into yet another new element, which, in keeping with a planetary scheme for naming these elements, he called plutonium. Their discoveries would earn McMillan and Seaborg the Nobel Prize—they were the first of six distinguished Rad Lab physicists and chemists who would earn that international distinction.

On March 28, 1941, one week after Lawrence met Bush in Boston to tell him about the calutron and to promote an atomic program, Seaborg used a Rad Lab cyclotron to expose five micrograms of plutonium to neutrons. As expected, the plutonium readily fissioned. Significantly, plutonium's half-life, the time it takes for half a sample to decay away, was over twenty-four thousand years, which meant it could be stored indefinitely inside a weapon.[11] The military implications were obvious: plutonium was a viable alternative fuel to uranium-235 for making an atomic bomb.

Six months later, on October 9, two months before the attack on Pearl Harbor, Bush finally decided to act. He conferred with President Roosevelt and Vice President Henry Wallace and asked permission to formally begin an atomic program. They discussed its likelihood of success and what little was known of the German uranium project. Roosevelt gave Bush the go-ahead to expedite the U.S. atomic program's progress in every possible way.[12] Bush's options to make an atomic program would principally rely on two technologies given to him by Lawrence and the Rad Lab: using Seaborg's process to produce plutonium, and using Lawrence's calutron to produce uranium-235.

# 3

//////////////

# The Super and the Onset of the Thermonuclear Age

onducting atomic research was one thing, the kind of work well suited for Professor Lawrence and his Rad Lab. Producing an atomic bomb, however, was quite different. Bush could not rely on Lawrence to make an atomic bomb. Instead he would have to partner with a large organization, and he chose the U.S. Army. He met with the Army's chief of staff, General George C. Marshall, and together they agreed to organize a national atomic program. There was little time to spare, for the country had just entered World War II following the Japanese attack on Pearl Harbor.

General Marshall acted quickly. In the months to follow, West Pointers commissioned as engineer officers helped put together the U.S. atomic program. In June 1942 the director of the Syracuse Engineer District of New York, Colonel James C. Marshall (no relation to the chief of staff), took command of a project to produce an atomic bomb. He called his command the Development of Substitute Materials (DSM) Project. His deputy was a thirty-four-year-old lieutenant colonel named Kenneth D. Nichols, who had studied engineering at European universities before completing a doctorate in hydraulic engineering at Iowa State University.

A West Pointer commissioned in the Corps of Engineers, Nichols graduated fifth in his class, one academic rank lower than George A. Lincoln, another engineer officer and a Rhodes scholar then serving as General Marshall's strategic planner. First-class engineer officers in the Army were part of a small but well-connected social group. The two classmates—and friends—played pivotal roles in determining the outcome of the war: Nichols was a key player in the atomic-bomb project, while Lincoln laid out the strategic goals of Allied forces in the conquest of the Axis powers.

The lieutenant colonel was well suited for his new role in an atomic program. Although he had no background in nuclear physics, with his exceptional engineering education, he became an essential conduit to interpret technical requirements for an atomic device into engineering specifications. Nichols was an energetic officer who appreciated professionalism when he saw it—once he was engaged with the atomic program, he thought Professor Lawrence was the most dynamic physicist in the country.[1]

With his program growing, Colonel Marshall moved his headquarters from Syracuse to the Manhattan Engineer District. With the switch of location, he also changed the program's name from the DSM Project to the Manhattan Project. Marshall was a good officer, but he lacked the enthusiasm needed for this important mission. He left much of the work to his deputy, Nichols, who managed to do a remarkable job of moving requisitions through the rank-conscious Washington bureaucracy.

Bush needed to get started producing uranium-235 and appointed a survey team to recommend a location for the uranium-isotope separation plants. Once the site was acquired by the Army, Nichols would be responsible for organizing isotope-separation operations. The site selected was along the Clinch River valley in Tennessee at an area locally known as Oak Ridge. It had a flat topography protected by surrounding hills that added to its seclusion, was adjacent to the Louisville & Nashville Railroad, had access to silt-free river water, and was a twenty-mile drive from Knoxville. Unfortunately, Colonel Marshall was unwilling to acquire the site until he was convinced the proposed processes for enriching uranium had proven themselves. (There were three competing processes: Lawrence's calutron was called the electromagnetic process, Nobel laureate Harold Urey led a gaseous-diffusion process, and finally there was a centrifuge process led by a physicist named Jesse Beams.) At Bush's instigation, and to head off a looming crisis, Colonel Marshall was relieved as project manager and replaced by Colonel Leslie R. "Dick" Groves.

Groves, a native New Yorker and the son of an Army chaplain, was yet another member of the atomic program who had graduated at the top of his West Point class—in November 1918. He was stout, ambitious, and had a contentious spirit that could be annoying, but he got jobs done. Groves, the project engineer who built the Pentagon, was not happy with this new assignment, having wanted to command combat engineers in a theater of war. Nevertheless, he accepted his situation. The colonel had explicit orders: take complete charge of the Manhattan Project, arrange at once for highest priorities to be given to it, and accomplish the immediate acquisition of the Tennessee site.

Groves appeared at Bush's office on September 17, 1942, and formally announced his appointment. Within forty-eight hours, he acquired Oak Ridge; two weeks later he contracted the DuPont Company to build a plutonium production plant in Hanford, Washington.[2] After a month of observing Groves, Bush knew that he had the right leader for his atomic program. Fortunately, Groves kept Lieutenant Colonel Nichols as his deputy; in a coincidence, a decade earlier then second lieutenant Nichols and then first lieutenant Groves had worked to survey a route for a possible interocean canal through the jungles of Nicaragua. Importantly, knowing he had to establish a bond with scientists he could rely on, Groves approached Professor Lawrence, and they soon became trusted colleagues. The two men shared a passion to produce the fuel for an atomic bomb before Hitler's scientists could.

Having already built a prototype calutron in Berkeley, Lawrence transferred the Rad Lab physicists who had developed it to Oak Ridge to help install calutrons into a new compound under construction, the Y-12 Plant. Enough calutrons were needed to produce at least one gram of uranium-235 per day, Lawrence's goal. Each device required an electromagnet weighing 330 tons and used hundreds of feet of wiring, but copper wiring was critically short. Quick-thinking Nichols came up with a solution to this problem by ordering 14,700 tons of silver, an excellent conductor that could replace the copper, to be transported from the national silver repository at West Point, New York, and delivered to the Y-12 Plant. While negotiating with the Treasury Department, Nichols said he would need between five and ten tons immediately. The department official responded to his request icily: "Colonel, in the Treasury we do not speak of tons of silver, our unit is the Troy ounce."[3]

Once the calutrons were emplaced, many of the Rad Lab physicists returned to Berkeley, but the electromagnets still needed much care and attention, as they shorted out and components quit working. Those were not their only problems: uranium-vapor deposits gathered on the inside of conduit walls, and operators recruited from nearby towns proved to be inadequate to keep the machines operational. The calutron project began to look like a disaster. Lawrence ordered the devices torn apart and reassembled in time for a second trial at the end of 1943, reassigning several hundred scientists and technicians from the Rad Lab to work at Y-12. Once operations were running smoothly, the plant was turned over to a new set of local crews. These mostly consisted of young women fresh out of high school, dressed in blue jumpers for uniforms, and proved to be up to the task. (The calutron operators were the young women portrayed in Janet Beard's 2018 book, *The Atomic City Girls*.)

The trust given to Lawrence and his calutrons paid off. While the technical difficulties facing the program were horrendous, Lawrence's perseverance and skill made operations at Y-12 a success. Indeed, the Y-12 Plant provided the highly enriched uranium used to make the bomb dropped over Hiroshima.

*// // //*

Getting the uranium-separation plants operating represented half of the production challenges facing the Manhattan Project. Colonel Groves also needed to produce a plutonium bomb, commencing plutonium production at Hanford, Washington. One reason he was able to act quickly was that the technology to produce and process plutonium had already been developed, thanks once again to a dedicated team that included Rad Lab physicists.

The discovery of plutonium at the Rad Lab was important, but establishing the means to set up a wartime plutonium production line to fuel an atomic bomb required more resources than McMillan and Seaborg could provide. Help came from Enrico Fermi, who had arrived in the United States at a most propitious time.

In 1938 Fermi received the Nobel Prize for his demonstrations of the existence of new radioactive elements produced by neutron irradiation and for a related discovery of nuclear reactions brought about by slow neutrons. He was among the elite of Italian physicists, but he was disenchanted with the Italian government of Benito Mussolini. It began with the rise of

Fascism to power and the subsequent Italian invasion of Ethiopia. He worried about the safety of his family, too, for the Italian dictator had entered into a political alliance with Hitler. Like the Nazi regime, the Fascist government passed laws aimed at Jewish citizens, denying them rights granted to other Italian citizens.

Fermi's wife, Laura, the daughter of an Italian naval officer, was Jewish. The couple realized the coming danger, reluctantly decided they had to leave Italy, and exited their country secretly. (Laura's father was later imprisoned in Auschwitz.) They would use the Nobel Prize money to immigrate to America, where Fermi had an offer to join the faculty of Columbia University in New York City. He and his family departed Fascist Italy in a train, crossed through Nazi Germany, and arrived in Sweden in time for the Nobel ceremonies. During his stay there, he visited the exiled Austrian physicist Lise Meitner. After the pomp and circumstance of the awards ceremony ended, the family boarded an ocean liner for New York. As the Fermis entered New York harbor and glanced at the Statue of Liberty, Laura stood by her husband and heard him say they were about to start the "American branch of the Fermi family."[4]

Within months of his arrival at Columbia, Fermi delved into research on nuclear fission. Following up on McMillan and Seaborg's discoveries at the Rad Lab, he wanted to produce plutonium by inundating a mass of uranium-238 with neutrons, converting it to neptunium, which would then decay into plutonium.

Fermi built what is called a nuclear pile, a lattice of uranium fuel rods encased within a large rectangular structure of graphite blocks. The graphite is needed to moderate, or slow down, neutrons because, as Fermi had discovered, they interact much more readily when they are slowed down. His nuclear pile at Columbia was eight feet square at the base and eleven feet high, but it was a subcritical reactor and could not sustain a chain reaction—once started, nuclear reactions slowed down. To produce the required quantities of plutonium, the Manhattan Project would need a critical reactor, a nuclear pile that could run indefinitely, and Bush would need a competent scientist to manage it.

In yet another coincidence, when Lawrence was a graduate student at the University of Chicago, the laboratory room he used for research was adjacent to one occupied by Arthur Compton. There, the older Compton was scattering X-rays off electrons, from which he noted there was a distinct and predictable change in the wavelength of the x-rays based on the angle they scattered. His observations were called, appropriately, the Compton effect, and his discovery won him the Nobel Prize in Physics in 1927. Lawrence and Compton often found themselves alone in their shared university building at night and helped each other with experiments, becoming good friends in the process. Compton later became the thesis advisor to Alvarez.

Compton was an experimenter—it was for good reason that Bush placed him in charge of the plutonium project. It was just as obvious to Compton that Fermi should lead the effort to design a critical nuclear pile. In the fall of 1941, Lawrence visited his friend in Chicago and urged him to move the plutonium project to the Rad Lab; after all, plutonium had been discovered there. Alvarez happened to be present during the meeting and observed the discussion between the two Nobel laureates was becoming heated as they discussed where Fermi should work. Despite their years of friendship, Compton was not enthusiastic to have his program become a cog in Lawrence's "empire" and instead decided to have Fermi build a critical pile near the Metallurgical Laboratory in Chicago. Disappointed at not having the plutonium project placed at Berkeley, Lawrence bet his friend he would not have a critical pile by the end of the year—a bet the professor would lose.

Compton had just faced a labor dispute in October 1941 that delayed construction of Fermi's nuclear pile, scheduled to be built at a site in the Argonne Preserve. To stay on schedule the pile needed a temporary facility elsewhere.[5] Compton kept things going by locating it in a squash court under the stands of Stagg Field, the University of Chicago's football stadium. He did not confer with Bush on this decision; he dared not. Compton would bear full responsibility if anything went wrong. He had just agreed to build a critical nuclear pile in a structure that was adjacent to one of the densest population areas in North America. Nobel laureate Eugene Wigner observed that Compton was a world-class experimentalist who knew how to evaluate risks; he showed his mettle in handling a critical situation that did not allow for mistakes.[6]

Some doubted the project would work—DuPont engineers released a report suggesting a critical nuclear pile could not be built. When word reached Washington, D.C., Compton repeatedly had to reassure Bush that Fermi knew what he was doing. By midmorning, December 2, 1941, one week before the attack on Pearl Harbor, Fermi raised the control rods of his nuclear pile in an excruciatingly slow process to increase the flux of neutrons until he achieved criticality. Finally, at 3:20 p.m., counters indicated a sustained chain reaction was occurring. A short time later, after the release of a few watts of power, Fermi shut down the pile.[7]

Within a month, Seaborg, still with the Rad Lab, invented a chemical process to extract plutonium from the spent nuclear fuel in a pile (reactor). Thereafter, the nuclear piles in Hanford were built to produce plutonium in quantity. It would be the reactors there that provided the nuclear fuel for the atomic bomb dropped on Nagasaki.

*// // //*

The Manhattan Project had needed a central laboratory to assemble the scientists to design an atomic bomb. Lawrence was the natural choice to lead the effort, and Groves, now a brigadier general, flew out to Berkeley to ask him to take charge. But the professor was too committed to seeing his calutrons at the Y-12 Plant succeed, so he suggested Oppenheimer to lead the new laboratory instead. Groves interviewed Oppenheimer and agreed with the recommendation. Lawrence's next opportunity to create a nuclear-weapons laboratory would occur only a decade later.

Oppenheimer chose Los Alamos, New Mexico, as the location for the Manhattan Project laboratory. He then set about recruiting a staff of physicists, engineers, and technicians while organizing his laboratory into several large divisions: experimental physics, theoretical physics, chemistry, metallurgy, engineering, and others. The task of designing the atomic bomb fell to the Theoretical Division, and Oppenheimer appointed the German American Hans Bethe, a Cornell University professor of physics, to be its leader. Bethe, who would later be awarded the Nobel Prize in Physics for his work on laying out how a star undergoes nuclear reactions during its lifetime, was a good fit to lead the design effort.

In the following years, two designs for an atomic device were developed, a gun-type device and an implosion device. The gun-type design was straightforward. Two subcritical masses of uranium-235 were arranged along a central rod, and an explosive charge propelled one of them into the other, forming a super critical mass. The need for an implosion design arose when developers realized an atomic device using plutonium would not work with a gun-type design.

For the implosion design, the plutonium was fashioned into a subcritical spherical shape and surrounded with a high explosive. When the high explosive detonated, it compressed the plutonium into a much smaller sphere that formed a critical mass roughly one thousand times faster than a gun design could produce, thus circumventing the problems that made plutonium otherwise unsuitable. The gun design was such a stable device, considering the scarcity of highly enriched uranium, it was decided to forego an atomic test of it. A plutonium-implosion design was successfully tested in an atomic test called the Trinity event, held at Alamogordo, New Mexico, in July 1945. Devices of each of the two designs were then dropped over Japan in August 1945, ending the war in the Pacific within days.

⫽ ⫽ ⫽

When Los Alamos opened its gates, two of the physicists who arrived were Fermi and a Hungarian friend of his, Edward Teller. They brought with them an idea for a weapon vastly more powerful than the atomic bomb. While they were on a walk before their departure, Fermi asked, "Do you think it's possible to use an atomic bomb to ignite a fusion bomb?"[8] Teller idolized his friend, so he took his time thinking over the question. Within a week, he had an answer. Teller called Fermi's idea the "Super"; news media would later dub it the hydrogen bomb.

The Super released energy through the collision and fusing together of deuterium ions—deuterium is an isotope of hydrogen (hydrogen-2). Nuclear fission powers the atomic bomb, while the Super is powered by nuclear fusion—a fusion reaction occurs when two ions have enough kinetic energy to overcome their electric repulsion, fuse together, and release energy. Thanks to a relation derived by the Viennese physicist Ludwig Boltzmann, kinetic energy can be expressed as a temperature. (Visitors to Vienna can see Boltzmann's thermodynamic equation prominently displayed on his gravestone.) So, instead of saying ions with high kinetic energy, one can say fusion reactions occur at high temperatures.

Expressing energy in that way led physicists to refer to nuclear fusion as thermonuclear reactions.

When Teller arrived at Los Alamos, he reported to Bethe, leader of the Theoretical Division, responsible for providing designs of the atomic bomb. Bethe organized his division into several groups, appointing Teller to lead the one calculating the physical characteristics of plutonium. The Hungarian balked at the appointment. He thought the task did not match his nature as a "new idea" person, but rather placed him more in the role of a plodding calculator. To use his own words, Teller thought of himself as a brick maker, not a bricklayer. The two argued about the assignment until Bethe gave it to another physicist, Rudolph Peierls, a coauthor of the MAUD Report. The unfortunate interchange began an estrangement between Teller and Bethe. Fueling the disagreement was Teller's resentment that he deserved the appointment as Theoretical Division leader ahead of Bethe.

Oppenheimer interceded and named Teller as a liaison for Los Alamos, but Teller persisted, asking to also pursue thermonuclear physics. Oppenheimer relented and allowed him to form a separate group that would, among other things, design the Super. Early on, a problem with unanticipated energy losses related to the Compton effect seriously impeded the group's efforts in designing the Super. Teller once stormed out of a group-leaders meeting rather than admit to Oppenheimer that his program was experiencing serious troubles.

Fermi noticed his friend's abrupt behavior and came to his aid, laying the groundwork for a more effective design for the Super. Despite Fermi's help, and although Teller remained passionate throughout the war to develop the fusion bomb, his group made little progress. As it happened, Oppenheimer experienced a dramatic ethical reversal after the atomic attacks on Hiroshima and Nagasaki and told him there was no longer a need to develop the Super. Nevertheless, Teller remained passionate to build that weapon.[9]

The Manhattan Project had given Los Alamos a code letter, "Y," but the secrecy demanded during the war had gone away with its conclusion. Afterward, it took on a more formal title, the Los Alamos Scientific Laboratory (LASL, popularly pronounced "lassle"). Oppenheimer having departed soon after the war's end, LASL had a new director, Norris

Bradbury, a mild-mannered physicist trained at Berkeley and Stanford. Bradbury immediately jumped into the controversy over support for the Super program. He called for a conference in the spring of 1946 to "review work that has been done on the Super for completeness and accuracy and to make suggestions concerning further work that would be needed in this field if actual construction and test of the Super were planned."[10]

Most of the presentations at the conference were by members of Teller's group, who outlined their progress to date. Teller ended the conference with a declaration that knowledge of the physics of the Super was sufficient to indicate with reasonable certainty that an operable model could be made. Two months after the conference, he wrote a summary of the proceedings, in part 4 laying out a plan of research and testing needed to make the Super successful. He concluded, "It is likely that a super-bomb can be constructed and will work."[11]

Bradbury was not convinced by the report, commenting it did not mean LASL would build a Super. Besides, he felt it could not happen during his tenure.[12] Bradbury supported research on the Super, but he would not divert substantial resources to develop it. Amid this activity was a singular event overshadowing the conference. One of the participants, Klaus Fuchs, was a theoretical physicist and naturalized British citizen who had been born in Germany. After the conference ended, he shared a patent for a design of the hydrogen bomb with the renowned mathematician John von Neumann. Three years later Fuchs was arrested by the British for being a Soviet spy; he confessed in January 1950 and remained imprisoned for the next nine years. Through Fuchs, the Soviets knew everything the Americans knew about designing a fusion bomb.

To those who knew him well, Teller had become a different man during his time at Los Alamos. Before the war, he freely affiliated himself with the work of others, caring little about how much credit went to whom.[13] Later, as he became more engaging and moodier, he made strong friends and strong enemies. Throughout, he kept one notable trait: he was a visionary who remained optimistic in the face of technical obstacles.[14] Teller was passionate about designing the Super and stopping Soviet aggression, and he linked those two things together. His passion made him intolerant of anyone who did not share his technical or political views.

Despite his feelings about the efficacy of a Super, Bradbury kept the program going. In 1947 he offered Teller, who had rejoined Fermi in Chicago, a consulting agreement, which he accepted, returning to Los Alamos full time to lead the Super program. His new group included a mathematician from his Manhattan Project team, Stanislaw Ulam. Since he was having trouble recruiting members to his team, Teller reached out and asked another friend, George Gamow, a physics professor at George Washington University, to join him. With Gamow's arrival, Bradbury formed an oversight group composed of Teller, Gamow, and Ulam, called the Director's Committee, to become the theoretical core for the Super program. The two physicists and the mathematician were a potent team.

Ulam, born in Poland, had come to America at the behest of the Hungarian-born von Neumann to be a fellow at Harvard, where coincidently he met and befriended David Griggs, the pilot for Alvarez's GCAR project at the MIT Radiation Laboratory. Von Neumann vouched for Ulam to be enlisted in the Manhattan Project. Throughout his early years at LASL, Ulam remained with the Super program. With a droll sense of humor and an easygoing demeanor, Ulam for years longed for the Polish coffeehouses of his youth, where he could chat for hours with members of local mathematics clubs. In the 1950s he started a European-style coffee shop in Los Alamos with another member of the Super team, Nicholas Metropolis; without enough sophisticated coffee drinkers in town, it soon closed.[15]

The third prominent figure of the Director's Committee was Gamow. He was a character—another icon of quantum physics. Gamow was born a Ukrainian in the city of Odessa when it was part of the Russian Empire. Tall and gangly, he had an effervescent sense of humor. He was a visionary in the sense that he could look at an equation and see how it represented reality, and in that way he could formulate a law of physics. His ability to do this was legendary.

Barely out of university, Gamow was able to explain physics phenomena associated with the radioactive elements discovered by Marie Curie. Later, he switched his interest to the cosmos and used his vivid imagination to describe the beginning of the universe as a Big Bang—a phrase since taken up by television and popular culture. He twice attempted to escape the Soviet Union by paddling away in a kayak with his wife, once in the

Arctic Ocean and once in the Black Sea—both attempts were thwarted by adverse weather. Gamow finally succeeded in escaping when, in 1933, he was invited to the Solvay Conference in Brussels. He received permission to have his wife join him, and when the conference ended, Curie offered him employment at her institute in France.

Teller and Gamow were later fellows together at Niels Bohr's institute in Copenhagen, where they became fast friends. When Gamow secured a position as a professor of physics at George Washington University, he procured a physics position for Teller so he, too, could enter America. It was only natural, then, that Teller would call up his friend and ask him to come to Los Alamos to help design the Super.

The members of the Director's Committee, interestingly, all came from Eastern Europe. They had all seen what life was like under a communist regime, which made them ardent anticommunists. They were passionate about developing a thermonuclear weapon before Stalin's Soviet Union could. They were a parallel to eminent Manhattan Project physicists like Oppenheimer, Bethe, and Fermi, who had lived in Western Europe and experienced life under a Fascist regime, and who had been passionate to develop an atomic bomb before Hitler's Nazi Germany could.

As for making the Super practical, to give ions enough kinetic energy to fuse together—or to put it in another way, to get to high temperatures—Teller's team had to design a bomb that could duplicate an environment like that inside the center of a star, where temperatures can reach 27 million degrees Fahrenheit. Almost all of the energy in a star's center is carried by photons—particles of light. High temperatures stay constant because, with thousands of miles of matter blocking their escape routes, photons cannot easily leave the star. (It can take hundreds of thousands of years for a photon created in the center of the sun, for example, to escape and reach Earth.) There is plenty of time for energetic nuclei to collide and fuse.

On the other hand, the Super is vastly smaller than a star, so photons readily escape and carry away energy, which lowers the temperature. As the temperature drops, it falls to levels below what is needed for thermonuclear reactions to occur. The problem facing Teller's physicists was, when an atomic blast raised the temperature of the Super high enough, there would be only millionths of a second to get the nuclei to fuse—a race between nuclei fusing and photons escaping from the device. For guidance on this, Teller often looked to Fermi, who was an expert in this kind of science. Between August 2 and October 9, 1945, Fermi had delivered a series of six lectures at Los Alamos that established the conditions needed for a thermonuclear device to work.[16]

The three members of the Director's Committee dove in and tackled the challenge of designing a fusion bomb. They explored different ideas for starting thermonuclear ignition, with some schemes carrying exotic names, including Gamow's "Cat's Tail" and Ulam's "Jet Fuse." Teller and Gamow cowrote a document in January 1950 in which they laid out in greater detail the design parameters needed for the Super, which became the basis for the design of the Classic Super.[17]

Although he stayed in the background, Lawrence remained a constant presence to the scientists working at LASL. But why was he so interested in their research? He was growing wary of the onset of communist aggression in Eastern Europe and the spread of communism into mainland Asia. Something new stirred within him that he had last felt when he learned nuclear fission had been discovered in Berlin.

*# # #*

Following the war, the Navy Department was intent to see the effects of an atomic blast on naval warships. At nine o'clock in the morning of July 1, 1946, a B-29 bomber dropped a twenty-kiloton atomic bomb over a fleet of seventy-eight ships anchored off Bikini Atoll. At ground zero floated the USS *Nevada*. The old battleship had survived the Pearl Harbor attack, had shelled the beaches of Normandy on D Day, and had been struck by a kamikaze plane off Okinawa. After all of that, it now lay defenseless, anchored in a lagoon and painted a bright orange, the central target for an atomic explosion. Incredibly, the bombardier missed the *Nevada* by about one mile, and the warship remained afloat after the bomb's detonation. Only one destroyer and two transport ships, anchored on the periphery of the fleet, sank immediately after the blast. Unlike America's first atomic test, the Trinity event, which was kept highly secret, the press was invited to witness this one. For all of the spectacular effects associated with a nuclear detonation, the blast was a disappointment to many who observed it. The buildup had been too extravagant. Goats that had been tethered on warship decks were still munching their feed, and the atoll's palm trees remained standing, unscathed. The Bikini test changed public attitudes. Before July 1, the world stood in awe of a weapon that had devastated two cities and forced the Japanese Empire to surrender. After that date, the bomb was still a terrible weapon, but now a limited one.[18]

# Project RAND, the AEC, and the Russians

In an interesting quirk of history, just as the creation of the MIT Radiation Laboratory indirectly helped Lawrence promote an atomic program during World War II by uniting him with David Griggs and Johnny Foster, so, too, did the U.S. Air Force's creation of a think tank after the war help Lawrence promote a thermonuclear program by uniting him and his Rad Lab physicists with prominent political scientists. That relationships that started in a research laboratory in Massachusetts should be somehow connected to an analytic center in California established by the Air Force was not a coincidence; rather, they were consequences of Lawrence's zeal and competence.

The formation of the modern Air Force began during the Great Depression of the 1930s, when a promising U.S. Army Air Corps officer named Henry "Hap" Arnold met and befriended aeronautical pioneer Theodore von Kármán at Caltech. By World War II, Arnold was a general and in command of the Army Air Forces. He asked von Kármán, the man who had created Pasadena's Jet Propulsion Laboratory in 1936, to be his chief scientific advisor. As the war was winding down, Arnold wrote von Kármán a memo asking him to form a committee, to be called the Air Force Scientific Advisory Board, that would study the Air Force's possibilities for future wars.

Von Kármán's committee responded thirteen months later with a report titled "Toward New Horizons," which began with a declaration that scientific discoveries in aerodynamics, electronics, and nuclear physics would open new opportunities for the use of air power. It predicted the advent of the intercontinental ballistic missile (ICBM) and advised the Air

Staff to maintain a permanent interest of scientific workers in problems of the Air Force. To do that, von Kármán suggested the creation of a special organization that connected the service with the sciences.[1]

Arnold made it a virtue to rely on engineers and scientists for advice— he maintained relationships within the aeronautical industry throughout the war. Two of these were with Arthur Raymond, chief engineer of the Douglas Aircraft Company, and Frank Collbohm, Raymond's deputy, who also served as a technical advisor on the general's staff. Early in the war, Collbohm managed a contract with the Royal Air Force for a plane with night-flying capabilities and an ability to land in fog. This resulted in the design of a radar set for the A-20 aircraft, called the Boston.

While searching for technologies to help with his A-20 project, Collbohm went to Cambridge, Massachusetts, to investigate reports of a radar being developed at the MIT Radiation Laboratory that might meet British needs. It turned out to be Alvarez's GCAR project.[2] Impressed with the radar technology, he put it into the A-20 aircraft. He was impressed as well with the talents of Alvarez and the project's pilot, Griggs.

In 1945 Collbohm grew concerned with the lack of analytic thought being given to the strategic bombing of Germany. Staff officers were targeting natural economic resources like coal mines at a time when the Nazi regime was on the verge of surrender. Collbohm warned General Arnold the Air Staff was losing touch with its scientific advisors, something the service could ill afford to do. Arnold agreed and knew it was time to implement von Kármán's recommendations in "Toward New Horizons." He asked Collbohm for an estimate to create a facility for a group of scientists to support Air Force studies.[3]

On September 30, 1945, Collbohm presented Arnold with a proposal to create an analytic research facility. This was sweetened with an offer from Donald Douglas, the owner of Douglas Aircraft, who agreed to provide a site in Santa Monica, California, for the facility. The next day Arnold accepted the proposal and awarded Collbohm $10 million to create the organization, to be called RAND, a takeoff from the phrase "research and development." Organizational work started immediately, and by March 1, 1946, Project RAND was inaugurated. Remembering how impressed he was with the two physicists he had met at the MIT Radiation Laboratory during the war, Collbohm made Griggs the first head of the Physics Division and Alvarez his first consultant. Project RAND attracted several leading intellectuals in America who were motivated to create a national-security strategy for using the power of atomic weapons as a means to deter aggression.

Joining RAND allowed Griggs and Alvarez to maintain their close relationship begun during their stint at MIT. Through that relationship, Griggs also befriended Lawrence and was drawn into his passion for the strategic defense of the country. In the coming years these three physicists would continually support one another in a common campaign to defend the United States against communist aggression.

*// // //*

Although Lawrence concentrated on getting the Rad Lab to return to basic science following the war, he could not totally pull himself away from the nation's atomic program. His wartime relationship with Vannevar Bush stayed alive as the country faced a growing threat from communism. With the end of the war, Bush knew the organizations he had created to build an atomic program, like the Manhattan Project, were not sustainable in peacetime; against bitter resistance, he fought to shut them down. Yet he argued linking the best science to national goals had to endure, and new atomic organizations fitted to peacetime were needed. The challenge was determining how to convert a highly secret wartime program to leveraging the best science for the nation's goals in peace. Bush met with officials of the War Department and with them hatched a plan to create a nine-member commission to oversee atomic research. Four members of the commission would be military flag officers—generals and admirals.

Bush remained actively involved with the War Department plan but then grew wary about the powers being given to the planned commission. For instance, some legacies of the Manhattan Project persisted, such as keeping atomic research secret. That would place restrictions on scientists who were pursuing research in nuclear physics. As plans for the new commission became known to the public, civilian discontent arose. At about this time, at the opening of his Institute of Nuclear Studies, Fermi expressed concerns about the War Department plan, saying this was not because he would not work for the government, rather he could not work for the government. He insisted unless research was free and outside of governmental (military and political) control, the United States would lose its superiority in scientific pursuit.

It was not only the ability to conduct research free from military control that was troubling scientists in Chicago: concern was growing about the effects of nuclear weapons on society. A new publication, the *Bulletin of Atomic Scientists of Chicago*, appeared, and at a suggestion made by Teller, it featured a "Doomsday Clock" to dramatize the danger of future nuclear warfare. Nevertheless, the Pentagon moved forward with its plans for the commission.[4]

In October 1945 the new secretary of war, Robert Patterson, lobbied sympathetic congressmen in the House and Senate Military Affairs Committees to introduce legislation authorizing the War Department plan to control atomic research. The result was the May-Johnson Bill, named after the chairmen of the two committees. Once the public understood its ramifications, the bill drew open opposition. The measure could be interpreted as enabling a military commission to jail a scientist for ten years and fine him $10,000 for violating a security regulation he never knew existed. There was fear of an intrusion of martial law into higher academic institutions.

A campus newsletter from the Woman's College of the University of North Carolina dramatized the effects the bill would have if it became law: "The May-Johnson Bill will permit the Army to go into any university and remove any professor on 'security grounds' and set up military courts in peacetime with precedence over civil courts with power to put civilians in jail. Strong pressure is being exerted in Congress to pass the bill in view of the recent spy scares. Dr. J.R. Oppenheimer is firmly opposed to a plan which would extend Army control and hamper scientific research."[5]

Despite the newsletter's claim, Oppenheimer was not a champion fighting against the May-Johnson Bill; in fact, he tried to persuade Lawrence to support it. But once Lawrence read the proposal, he was clear in his opposition. A movement to gain civilian control over atomic research was growing. While Congressman May held hearings on the bill, Brien McMahon, a freshman senator from Connecticut, succeeded in getting an alternate bill passed by Congress to create an atomic-energy control board strictly under civilian control. On August 1, 1946, President Truman signed the McMahon Act, better known as the Atomic Energy Act, into law.[6]

The McMahon Act established the Atomic Energy Commission (AEC), a panel composed of five fulltime commissioners—one chairman and four members—appointed by the president with the consent of the Senate. The AEC became the government agency responsible for the oversight of the nation's nuclear-weapons program and also held a mandate to foster research in nuclear science. The act also established the General Advisory Committee (GAC), made up of experts in the field of nuclear science, to provide scientific advice to the commissioners. Oppenheimer was appointed to be the first chairman of the GAC.

To keep at least a modicum of military involvement with nuclear weapons, a House amendment required the AEC's director of military applications to be an active-duty military officer. Whoever held that position would play a key role in how U.S. nuclear weapons were developed. The act also established the Joint Committee on Atomic Energy (JCAE), composed of senators and representatives who enacted laws dealing with nuclear weapons and atomic energy. McMahon became the first chairman of the JCAE.

To control the dissemination of atomic secrets, the act created a classification category related to nuclear weapon designs—"restricted data." With the creation of the AEC, the agency had to grant new security clearances to personnel working on nuclear weapons. To organize access on who could see atomic secrets, the bureaucrat responsible for establishing this system borrowed initials from the Personnel Security Questionnaire, a form each applicant filled out to receive a clearance. An applicant given a "P" clearance was not permitted access to classified information and was allowed to perform service duties at AEC facilities. Those given an "S" clearance were allowed access to secret government information related to general national-security topics. A "Q" clearance was needed by anyone wishing to have access to secret or top-secret restricted data information.

*# # #*

While political battles blazed across Washington over passage of the Atomic Energy Act, Lawrence contented himself with getting his Rad Lab involved with making scientific breakthroughs in nuclear physics. Work on the atomic program had been important, and he could look back with satisfaction over the achievements his program had made during the war. That was all fine, but basic physics research remained Lawrence's first love. He looked forward to applying his large cyclotrons, not to separating uranium isotopes, but to digging deeper into the unknown world of the atomic nucleus. Unfortunately, events in the Soviet Union were about to put that dream on hold.

Following the German invasion of the Soviet Union in 1941, a group of Russian physicists led by Peter Kapitza warned the Kremlin the country should pursue an atomic-bomb program. The response was lukewarm; Stalin was uninterested because he could not see how it could make a difference in time to stop the German army. There was one outcome to their initiative, though; the scientists received permission to start a program in February 1943 under the leadership of Igor Kurchatov. The program made modest progress during the rest of the war while it remained a backwater of activity within the Soviet bureaucracy. But the rapid succession of three American atomic blasts in 1945 awakened Stalin to the military implications of the weapon. He set the Soviet atomic program into overdrive, expanding its budget and appointing the head of his secret state police, Lavrentiy Beria, to lead the effort.

The Soviets first achieved a chain reaction on Christmas Day, 1946, in a graphite-moderated pile that looked like Fermi's structure in Chicago— this was no coincidence. Spies working at the Metallurgical Laboratory in Chicago had provided the Soviets with intimate details of Fermi's work. Most valuable was espionage used to gain information about how America produced its special nuclear materials. That kind of information helped Soviet engineers avoid the pitfalls experienced earlier in the U.S. program— they thus had a production reactor operating by 1948. The Russians were ready to test an atomic bomb by August of the following year.[7]

Kurchatov personally directed all the preparations to ensure it was a successful test. He could be seen where bomb components were being assembled and in the concrete bunkers full of electronic equipment. Early mornings in Semipalatinsk, Kazakhstan, even in summer, are cold. The fingers of technicians grew numb as they fidgeted with nuts and bolts to tighten the case around the gadget, so it was easy to drop a part. But

Kurchatov was vigilant; he closely watched the men as they meticulously assembled the final parts of an atomic bomb.

On a Monday morning, as Soviet dignitaries arrived before dawn, the atomic device was lifted atop a metal tower. Kurchatov had to be careful: Beria had warned, if the bomb failed, Kurchatov and his crew would be executed. At 6 a.m. on August 29, 1949, a bright fireball lit up the sky, and the Russians could feel the air heat up inside their bunkers. Kurchatov and his team saw a blinding flash, then a mushroom cloud rose high into the atmosphere—and with it, they gave a sigh of relief.[8] The Soviet Union had just become a nuclear power.

Stalin assumed American leaders behaved the way he did; he feared a test failure would give the United States an opportunity to preemptively strike the Soviet Union to rid itself of an adversary before it became an atomic threat. To avoid that outcome, the Soviets used all the plutonium they had available to make an exact copy of America's first atomic device, which had been tested in the Trinity event.[9]

Four days after the Semipalatinsk test, a B-29 bomber flew over the North Pacific Ocean off the coast of Alaska. It carried beneath its wings filters that collected particles in the air; the crew's mission was part of a new U.S. Air Force program to detect and monitor American and foreign nuclear tests. The plane landed at Fairfield-Suisun Air Force Base, near San Francisco Bay, where the filters were removed and taken to be tested.

The filters usually picked up radioactive particles in the air caused by volcanoes and other natural phenomena. This time, however, they registered eighty-five counts per minute, above the fifty counts per minute that was normal.[10] Following procedure, the Alaska Command sent the filters to a laboratory on San Pablo Avenue in Berkeley called Tracerlab. An examination showed the telltale signs of an atomic-bomb test. President Truman was advised of this a day or two later.[11]

California had an Indian summer in 1949, and on Friday, September 23, the temperature in Merced had reached the 90s by midafternoon. Merced has a road junction that leads to the Highway 140 entrance of Yosemite National Park. Entering the park that way means getting a spectacular view of Half Dome while approaching Yosemite Valley, so it is a popular route for vacationers. On this highway on that day in 1949, Professor Lawrence, then forty-eight years old and on his way to enjoy a weekend at Yosemite, sat in his Cadillac convertible at a stoplight. He noticed a newspaper stand and read the headline on the morning's paper: "Reds Test Atom Bomb." Just below this was a statement by President Truman: "We have evidence that an atomic explosion occurred in the U.S.S.R. Ever since atomic energy was first released to man, the eventual development of this new force by other nations was to be expected."[12]

Many Americans had felt secure with the United States being the sole nuclear power. Now that a communist state had developed an atomic bomb, that feeling of reassurance began evaporating. To make matters worse, two weeks after the Soviet test, a communist government was proclaimed in China under the leadership of Mao Zedong. Mao spent the next month in Moscow, where he appeared in Red Square proclaiming the absolute solidarity of the Chinese government with the Soviet Union. Three years earlier, Winston Churchill had given a lecture at a university in Fulton, Missouri, where he described an "Iron Curtain" coming down along the breadth of Europe, separating the free states in the West from those states dominated by the Soviet Union in the East. With the Iron Curtain now augmented by a "Bamboo Curtain" across the breadth of China's southern border, it seemed to the average American that communism was well on its way to taking over the planet.

A world ruled by communists, especially under the overall direction of a thug like Stalin, was something most Americans dreaded. American journalist and historian William Henry Chamberlin had visited the Ukraine in the 1930s, writing a book about his travels, *Russia's Iron Age*. His visit came during a period known to Ukrainians as the "Holodomor." Chamberlin saw scenes as bad as something from Hitler's Holocaust. He described walking down streets in towns littered with emaciated families, with fathers, mothers, and children dying, looking like skeletons. They had been thrown into the streets for opposing Stalin's land reforms that took away their farms.[13]

Lawrence thought news of a Soviet nuclear test was not totally unexpected; nevertheless, the idea of Stalin having an atomic bomb was a nightmare to him. He thought of how the dictator had helped precipitate a world war by joining Hitler in the invasion of Poland. Now that thug possessed the most powerful weapon known to mankind. Was there any doubt the average American felt a surge of panic knowing that the madman Stalin possessed a nuclear weapon? Lawrence knew he had to do something.

He returned from his weekend in Yosemite to Berkeley and had lunch with Alvarez and Wendell Latimer, a chemistry professor, at the faculty-club cafeteria, where they discussed the Soviet atomic test. The topic of the Super arose, and they agreed the Soviet Union's pursuit of nuclear weapons had to be countered with America's own thermonuclear research. Lawrence and Alvarez were scheduled to depart on a business trip to Washington, D.C., so Alvarez offered to set up appointments with government officials in order to invigorate them to fund new research on the Super. But first he suggested they visit Teller and his group at LASL to get an update on the status of their program.

Alvarez made calls and arranged for meetings in New Mexico. He and Lawrence arrived in Albuquerque at 3 a.m. on a crisp day in early October and caught a shuttle flight to take them the sixty air miles north to Los Alamos. When they arrived, they were escorted to meet Teller, Gamow, and Ulam. Teller told the visitors his team was making progress on the Super, but Ulam warned the project needed a lot more tritium, the isotope of hydrogen that had been codiscovered by Mark Oliphant. Ulam's tip gave Lawrence an incentive to find a way to produce tritium. This was a problem, however, for tritium was expensive to make, and its production would compete with the production of plutonium, which was also in short supply.

That evening Teller joined Lawrence and Alvarez in Albuquerque, and they continued their discussions in Lawrence's room at the local Hilton Hotel. Teller had been a vociferous advocate for thermonuclear research, but Lawrence wanted him to take his message about the Super outside Los Alamos. To get this point across, Lawrence demonstrated in his hotel room how to wash a shirt while on travel, a subtle hint to Teller he needed to go to Washington. The next day Lawrence and Alvarez headed east to the nation's capital to garner support for the Super while Teller prepared to recruit more scientists to his project.[14]

Several days later Lawrence and Alvarez met with Senator McMahon, the author of the Atomic Energy Act and the chairman of the Joint Committee on Atomic Energy. McMahon, too, was strongly affected by news of the Soviet atomic test. In order to get a better technical understanding of its implications, he had called for a hearing of the JCAE with the AEC to assess Soviet nuclear capabilities.[15] Before that happened, he welcomed the chance to meet with someone like Lawrence, who could speak with authority on the topic.

Lawrence warned the senator the Russians were just as capable of developing a hydrogen bomb and were probably pursuing that end. (In fact, they were doing just that. By June 1948, a thermonuclear group had been set up at the Soviet Academy of Sciences [FIAN] under the leadership of Igor Tamm. It had recently brought in a young physicist named Andrei Sakharov.[16]) The meeting had its desired effect on McMahon, who scheduled an additional hearing with Pentagon officials to explore if the Soviet test warranted a new military requirement for the United States.

Lawrence and Alvarez next visited AEC chairman David E. Lilienthal and found him to be cool, if not outright belligerent, to their suggestions. As Lawrence spoke about the need for a vigorous effort in thermonuclear research and the production of special nuclear materials, Lilienthal sat in his chair and looked out his office window. He later recorded the meeting in his journal and described Alvarez and Lawrence as "drooling with the prospect [of the Super] and bloodthirsty."[17]

The two Berkeley physicists next met with Major General Nichols, the same engineer officer who had supported Lawrence's calutron operations at the Y-12 Plant during the Manhattan Project, and who had succeeded General Groves as director of the Armed Forces Special Weapons Project. Lawrence suggested the Joint Chiefs of Staff make a thermonuclear weapon a military requirement, to which Nichols was receptive and promised to raise the issue at the Pentagon, which he did. The chief of staff of the Air Force, General Hoyt Vandenberg, soon announced the Super should be developed as quickly as possible.[18]

# 5

////////////////

# The GAC Rejects the Classic Super

While Lawrence and Alvarez garnered support for the Super, others sought to achieve the opposite effect. Oppenheimer, still chairman of the GAC, and Lilienthal, the AEC chairman, shared a common aversion to thermonuclear research, and they grew concerned about the flurry of activity in its support following the Soviet atomic test. Lilienthal felt he needed more technical information to respond to mounting inquiries from government officials, so he bade Oppenheimer to call a special meeting of the GAC to assess the Super. Gathering quickly, the committee assembled two months after the Soviet test, on October 28, 1949, convening in five sessions over three days.

On the second day the GAC meeting was opened to AEC commissioners and senior military officers from the Pentagon. Since the Soviets had produced an atomic bomb, the military assumed they would go on to develop a hydrogen bomb—if it could be done. They asked members of the committee how the United States should respond.[1] By the end of the third day, the GAC provided an answer in a report written by Oppenheimer.

His consistent argument was for the country to rely on its atomic bombs for strategic defense rather than to start a new program for a bigger weapon. In part 2 of the report, Oppenheimer wrote the GAC had considered whether to pursue with high priority the development of the fusion bomb. He said no member of the committee was willing to endorse such a proposal. His predominant message was that it was immoral to develop such a weapon. In part 3 Oppenheimer stated unequivocally that, although members of the GAC were not unanimous in what should be done with regard to the Super, they all hoped its development could be avoided.[2]

Oppenheimer admitted the Russians could develop the Super, but he felt America's development of it would not deter the communists from acts of aggression. He said if the Russians developed a hydrogen bomb, the U.S. stockpile of atomic weapons should be a sufficient deterrent, so he proposed improving the performance of atomic bombs.[3] The October GAC meeting could not be kept quiet for long; within two months, it was brought out to the public in a front-page article published in the *New York Times*.[4]

The recommendation of the GAC to stop the Super made Teller more adamant to push the program. The technological uncertainties troubling the GAC did not dissuade the ever-optimistic physicist. As he said to Lawrence and Alvarez several months after the committee's report was issued, "We still don't know if the Super can be built, but now we don't know it on much better grounds."[5] Teller traveled east and continued to recruit physicists to join his group. He asked Fermi to take over the project, but his friend declined and instead volunteered to come to Los Alamos as a part-time consultant.

Then Teller telephoned John Wheeler, an American physicist he had met while at Bohr's Institute for Theoretical Physics in Copenhagen and with Bohr coauthor of a renowned article on nuclear fission, and asked for his help. Wheeler was on sabbatical in Europe to conduct research in France and to write a scientific paper on the atomic nucleus with Bohr.

Teller's request put Wheeler in a quandary. He felt it his patriotic duty to help, but he also felt obligated to complete his research funded through the Guggenheim Foundation's fellowship. While in Copenhagen working with Bohr on their new paper, Wheeler told his mentor about his indecision. As they discussed it at breakfast, Bohr said to him, "Do you imagine for one moment that Europe would now be free of Soviet control if it were not for the Western atomic bomb?"[6] That settled it for Wheeler; he moved with his family to Los Alamos.

Wheeler was one of the greatest U.S. physicists of the twentieth century. A pioneer with Bohr on the theory of the atomic nucleus, he had been Richard Feynman's thesis advisor and helped lead his student to win a Nobel Prize. Later in his career Wheeler switched physics fields and wrote a classic work on general relativity, which became one of the country's more popular physics textbooks. He coined the term "black hole" to describe a star so massive even light could not escape its gravitational field.

When he arrived in Los Alamos in the spring of 1950, Wheeler was given a sober briefing on the status of the program. He thought the Super as then conceived had fatal flaws. Wheeler questioned whether even an atomic bomb could produce a temperature high enough to assure ignition. Then, once ignited, he questioned whether there was enough energy to keep the thermonuclear flame alive. At the temperature required to sustain fusion, most of the energy is contained not in the material but in the photons (light). If that radiation was allowed to escape, he feared there would not be enough energy left to heat the thermonuclear fuel, just as a coal fire that is not banked will die out because too much of its energy radiates away.[7]

Teller was aware of Wheeler's concerns, but confident he could overcome them, he continued to recruit new talent for the project. He went to Cornell University to enlist his old friend Hans Bethe and thought he was succeeding. As the two discussed the work, Bethe received a call from Oppenheimer, who asked that he come to Princeton to meet with him. On hearing that Teller was present, Oppenheimer extended the invitation to include him as well.

The two went together and met with Oppenheimer, who ridiculed the Super. What concerned him was not the technical problem so much as that the Super itself appeared to have caught the imagination of both congressmen and military officials as the answer to the problem posed by the Russians' advances in atomic weapons.[8] A few days later Bethe called Teller to say he was not joining his team to develop the fusion bomb.

While still on the East Coast, Teller scheduled a meeting with Senator McMahon. As he arrived at the railway station in Washington, he was met by the deputy director of LASL, John Manley, who asked him to cancel the meeting with McMahon. Manley felt Teller was out of line and did not want the senator to get a slanted impression of the physics community's views about the Super.[9] Manley was hardly objective about the subject; he had written a letter to the GAC opposing development of the weapon.[10] Teller refused to cancel the meeting.

When Teller reached the senator's office the next day, they discussed the GAC report. McMahon was furious; he felt if Congress adopted the

GAC's recommendations, it would lead to a catastrophic situation with the Soviets in sole possession of a thermonuclear weapon. He wondered what could be done and discussed the merits of moving the Super program to a new laboratory so competition might spur LASL to greater effort.

Creating a second weapons laboratory had crossed McMahon's mind earlier; a few months before the GAC report, he directed his chief of staff, William Borden, to research the issue of nuclear weapons. Borden, a B-24 bomber pilot in the Eighth Air Force who had flown thirty combat missions to drop commandos and supplies behind German lines, was passionate about the topic.[11] He saw the Soviet Union's possession of an atomic weapon as a threat to the country. As a law student at Yale immediately after the war, he wrote a book, *There Will Be No Time*, in which he lamented, in the United States, the notion still persisted that weakness promotes good will. He felt that fallacy was at the heart of America's long record of unpreparedness.[12] Borden agreed with the senator that the nation needed to develop a thermonuclear weapon before the Soviets could, even if it meant creating a second laboratory that competed with Los Alamos.[13]

McMahon urged President Truman to order the AEC to develop a thermonuclear weapon. The senator argued if the Russians produced the hydrogen bomb first, the results would be catastrophic, whereas if the United States produced it first, there was at least a chance of protecting the country through deterrence. Karl Compton, Arthur's brother and who had left MIT and was the chairman of the Research and Development Board of the Defense Department, advised the president if a U.S. decision not to develop a hydrogen bomb would ensure a similar attitude on the part of all other governments, then he would agree with the GAC recommendation. Failing a strong international agreement backed by adequate inspection, however, the Soviet Union could proceed to obtain a fusion bomb regardless of any altruistic decisions made by the United States. Declaring there was no reason to believe Russian scientists were incapable of developing such a weapon, he concluded it was in the best interest of the country to develop the hydrogen bomb with all haste.[14]

To get additional opinions, Truman asked a subcommittee of his National Security Council to determine whether or not to develop the Super. The subcommittee members, Secretary of Defense Louis Johnson,

Secretary of State Acheson, and AEC chairman Lilienthal, met in December 1949. Lilienthal alone backed the GAC report rejecting development of the Super, while Johnson recommended stepping up a thermonuclear program. Acheson did not accept the GAC logic calling for "maintenance of ignorance or the reliance on perpetual goodwill," which he deemed an untenable policy, and sided with Johnson.[15] Acheson's view was that a country that uses nuclear weapons is going to be so badly hurt in return it is not wise for it to do so. That did not dispose of the relevancy of power in foreign affairs, nor did it mean the United States had to use such a weapon to make it relevant. It meant that to give up either nuclear or conventional power altogether would allow the Russians to engage in policies the United States could not meet, and that would be disastrous.[16]

Truman accepted the advice of his two senior cabinet members and made his decision on January 31, 1950: "It is part of my responsibility as Commander-in-Chief of the Armed Forces to see to it that our country is able to defend itself against any possible aggressor. Accordingly, I have directed the Atomic Energy Commission to continue its work on all forms of atomic weapons including the so-called hydrogen or super bomb."[17]

Among those who opposed Truman's decision, Oppenheimer and Lilienthal were the most vocal. Bethe expressed his views in a letter to the editor in the April 1950 issue of *Scientific American*, arguing that he agreed it would be better to lose our lives than our liberty. But in a war fought with hydrogen bombs, Americans would lose not only many lives but also all their liberties and human values as well. Overall, those in the U.S. physics community who agreed with Bethe's sentiments tended to be more vocal in expressing their views than those who disagreed. Ad hoc groups formed at universities, and petitions against a thermonuclear weapon circulated among physics students.[18]

Those like Wheeler who disagreed were in the minority and risked social stigma for their views; they were often snubbed at professional gatherings. Wheeler remained adamant in his view that work on the Super was important, unavoidable, and had to be done. He understood the revulsion felt by some of the Manhattan Project physicists over the effects of their work at Hiroshima and Nagasaki, but he noted men who had personally experienced the killing in the war did not share those feelings.

Wheeler's brother Joe, a driven young man who had earned a doctorate in history, served in the U.S. Army in World War II, fighting in Italy. He was smart enough to realize his older brother was involved with making a nuclear weapon, and he saw it as something badly needed. In a postcard written to John a few months before he was killed in combat, Joe wrote, "Hurry up."[19]

Wheeler later revealed his feelings that, if the government had not dithered for months after President Roosevelt had ordered an investigation of the uranium question, his brother might not have died. He had no doubt the atomic bomb had stopped the war in its tracks and therefore saved countless American and Japanese lives. He could see no difference in situation between the threat from Nazism before World War II and the threat from communism then facing America. In his mind the best way to avoid a war with the Soviet Union was to have a weapon that could deter it.

*⧸⧸ ⧸⧸ ⧸⧸*

Remembering Ulam's warning during his visit to Los Alamos that the Super program needed tritium, Lawrence committed himself to finding a way to produce it. Tritium could be produced by placing lithium-6 inside a nuclear reactor; this would cause the lithium to absorb neutrons and transform into tritium and helium gases, which were collected and separated. Since AEC reactors were dedicated to producing plutonium, then also in short supply, Lawrence sought another method for tritium production. The plutonium-production reactors were moderated with graphite, like Fermi's nuclear pile. Lawrence thought he could avoid taxing AEC reactors by building another reactor moderated with heavy water, which uses deuterium (hydrogen-2) rather than the abundant hydrogen-1 to form the water molecule and thus could produce tritium efficiently.

Alvarez accepted responsibility to lead this effort. He assembled cost estimates while Lawrence selected a site for the reactor in Suisun Bay, northeast of Berkeley. With his proposal prepared, Alvarez discussed it with AEC commissioners and the GAC. When meeting with Oppenheimer, he became aware how much the GAC chairman opposed the hydrogen bomb. Oppenheimer reiterated his belief that, if the country built the weapon, the Russians would build it too, but if the United States did not build one, then the Russians might not build one either. Alvarez told him he might think such an argument reassuring, but he doubted if there were many Americans who would accept it. He soon realized he could not dissuade Oppenheimer, and if the GAC chairman opposed building the hydrogen bomb, he would certainly oppose building a reactor to furnish tritium for it. Alvarez returned to Berkeley and dropped the proposal.[20]

Lawrence was not so easily dissuaded and came up with an alternate plan. He ordered calculations done on the feasibility of using an accelerator to make tritium. These showed that striking practically any heavy metal from an accelerator with the nuclei of high-energy deuterium (hydrogen-2) atoms created the large number of neutrons needed for tritium production. Lawrence's idea thus seemed plausible, and Alvarez accepted responsibility to run the program. Lawrence also tasked one of his Rad Lab physicists who had returned from the Y-12 Plant, Herb York, to measure the efficiency of producing neutrons that way. York was assigned a newly arrived twenty-two-year-old physicist from Columbia University named Harold Brown to help him. Tall and slim, Brown looked like he had nothing in common with the shorter, stockier York. In fact, they complemented each other well as they set about designing accelerator targets and measuring results.[21]

To produce suitable amounts of tritium, Alvarez calculated the drift tubes for the accelerator had to be three feet in diameter. This was a staggering estimate since his design for an earlier accelerator had two-inch-diameter drift tubes, which had to be surrounded by a vacuum chamber three feet in diameter. The newly calculated accelerator would require a vacuum chamber an astonishing sixty feet in diameter. Lawrence tagged Johnny Foster, who had returned from service with the Army Air Corps in Italy and was now a member of Alvarez's research group at the Rad Lab, to design an ion-pump vacuum system to evacuate the cavernous volumes. (Using an ion pump to create the vacuum came from a suggestion made by Lawrence—Foster was designing an instrument that was very much unprecedented. The result of this research became Foster's doctoral dissertation.[22])

To get construction support, Alvarez used the California R&D Corporation, a subsidiary of Standard Oil of California. A tritium project in Idaho featured a nuclear reactor called the Materials Testing Reactor, and copying the name, Lawrence called his device the Materials Testing Accelerator (MTA). Neutrons produced by the accelerator could also be used to produce plutonium, or uranium-233, another fissionable material; Lawrence used this as an additional reason to fund his concept.

Lawrence took the MTA concept to Washington and, over the objections of Isidor Rabi, a member of the GAC, presented it to Kenneth Pitzer, the director of research at the AEC. In February 1950 Pitzer approved the project and directed construction to begin. Now came the decision on where to locate the MTA. The project was too large for the Berkeley campus of the Rad Lab, so Lawrence asked officials in Washington for a list of possible sites. Most were abandoned military bases. One at Livermore, California, a square mile in area, offered a mile-long runway, barracks buildings, a gymnasium, and a huge indoor swimming pool. As soon as he and Alvarez saw it, Lawrence said, "Well, Luis, this is it."[23]

Having a former naval air station close to Berkeley worked well for Lawrence's plans. In the winter of 1942, the Navy had purchased 629 acres of ranchland (at $120 an acre) two miles east of the town of Livermore. Within months they had built the Livermore Naval Air Station, a training ground for many fighter pilots during the war. The Navy mothballed the site after the war, but as Lawrence had discovered, the infrastructure needed to operate a research laboratory remained. He saw in its one square mile of land an opportunity to expand facilities for Rad Lab projects.[24]

In 1950 California R&D Corporation started construction of the MTA, enclosing the accelerator in a voluminous corrugated-steel building. Newly welded joints could arc as electric voltages reach high levels, which either cleaned away the rough spots or made them worse; Alvarez was not sure which way the MTA would respond. Lawrence was usually reserved when he visited projects, but he uncharacteristically lost his temper on one occasion as a technician brought the MTA up to full power and it started arcing, leaving a smell of ozone in the air. Lawrence snatched the controls away from the technician and yelled out, "Slower, you've got to raise the power much more slowly."[25]

The MTA was intended as a prototype machine. A full-sized plant would be a one-thousand-foot-long accelerator built at Weldon Spring, Missouri, but it never came to be. The special nuclear materials the MTA was supposed to produce had become more abundant, as uranium ore, once scarce, had been discovered by prospectors lured by its high value. More plutonium had been produced now, making it easier to share reactors to produce tritium. By the time the MTA came online, the critical production shortage motivating its creation was gone.[26]

Despite the morass of technical difficulties with the MTA and other programs, Lawrence was determined to keep the Super project going. With the newly acquired campus in Livermore, he had room to conduct more research, and he asked Alvarez to consult with Teller at Los Alamos to find out what the Rad Lab could do to help. Teller requested help with upcoming nuclear tests, so Alvarez assigned two Rad Lab physicists, York and Hugh Bradner, to lead a project to lend support to Los Alamos. They visited Carson Mark, the Theoretical Division leader at LASL, who asked for assistance with experiments to detect thermonuclear reactions. Mark was keen to field diagnostics in the upcoming George event, a test of Teller's notion an atomic explosion could generate fusion reactions in hydrogen.

The George event was part of Operation Greenhouse, a series of four nuclear tests in April and May 1951 at the Pacific Proving Grounds, an area in the South Pacific that included the Marshall Islands. Two atolls in the Marshalls, Bikini and Eniwetok, became epicenters for American nuclear testing. The last two tests in Greenhouse, George and Item, featured events in which Teller had predicted thermonuclear reactions.

York and Bradner organized a team of physicists to build experimental equipment to detect thermonuclear reactions, calling themselves the Measurements Group. They needed a lot of space, more than was available at the Rad Lab, so they occupied a barracks adjacent to the MTA site in Livermore. Once they organized themselves, their activities became known as Project Whitney. With construction of the diagnostic equipment underway, York left for the South Pacific and prepared for the George event.

At Eniwetok, Teller arrived one evening and met with York in a Quonset hut. He went to a blackboard on the wall and drew a design for a thermonuclear device based on a paper he had written with Ulam the previous month. York saw how it worked and began thinking about how he would design such a weapon, ideas that would surface later; his focus was now on Operation Greenhouse. After two months of hard work, the

Measurements Group arrived at Eniwetok and installed sensors in time for the George event, scheduled to occur on May 8, 1951. This, their first experience with a nuclear test, was a success.[27] They detected thermonuclear reactions and verified Teller's idea that an atomic blast could ignite nuclear fusion.

Brimming over with joy at the successful experiment, York went back to the Rad Lab while Lawrence secured a position for him to begin a new career teaching physics at the University of California in Berkeley. York started with an introductory physics course and was assigned a graduate student, Mike May, to be his teaching assistant. Throwing his energy into a new career, he then created a graduate-level class in nuclear physics, an experimental-research course that concentrated on the transformation of matter. After seven years at the Rad Lab, York was at last feeling secure about his life's work and looking forward to a quiet and fruitful career as a college professor.

# 6

////////////////////

## *Computers and the New Super*

W
hen Lawrence took up the challenge of engaging the country in a thermonuclear program, it was quickly apparent the problem of actual production would be much more complex than anything he had faced when he helped start an atomic program during a world war. It is one thing to configure a heap of fissionable fuel into a critical mass; it is quite another to figure out how to raise the temperature of thermonuclear fuel to approximate the center of the sun and then maintain it long enough for nuclei to release fusion energy. To design a thermonuclear warhead, one had to have the ability to create and then use mathematical models. Looking back at the relatively primitive mathematical tools available in postwar America, that was a daunting task.

Fortunately, the United States was home to the world's greatest mathematician of the twentieth century and one of the most influential intellectuals to usher in the thermonuclear age: a Hungarian-born Jew and Roman Catholic convert who hated Nazis and communists and who was a patriot. John von Neumann had a passion for mathematics, having published his first mathematics paper at the age of seventeen, while he was still in high school. In 1928 he wrote the textbook *Mathematical Foundations of Quantum Mechanics*, which is still in print. The next year he and fellow Hungarian Eugene Wigner received invitations to join the faculty of Princeton University, then in 1930 they joined Einstein at one of America's most influential institutions, the Institute for Advanced Study.

Von Neumann had a brief experience of living in a totalitarian state after World War I, when communists under Béla Kun took over Hungary, an episode that made him an ardent anticommunist. In 1937 he became a U.S. citizen and tried to enlist in the Army but was turned down because of his age. Instead, the Army hired him as a consultant, and his involvement with the military continued for the rest of his life. In 1938 he returned to Europe and married Klári Dán, a talented athlete who had won the national figure skating championship of Hungary when she was fourteen. The couple left Europe after their wedding, bearing an unforgiving hatred for the Nazis, a growing distrust of the Russians, and a determination never again to let the free world fall into a position of military weakness.[1]

Von Neumann's role in helping usher in the thermonuclear age had to do with a fascination he had to use machines to do mathematical calculations. In the spring of 1936, Alan Turing, a twenty-four-year-old British mathematician, wrote an article for the *Proceedings of the London Mathematical Society* titled "On Computable Numbers, with an Application to the Entsheidungsproblem."[2] In the first section, titled "Computing Machines," Turing lays out the principles needed for a machine to do mathematical calculations. That paper helped launch computer science.[3]

Von Neumann read the article and invited Turing to join him at Princeton. Turing left England from Southampton in September 1936 on the liner *Berengaria*, after buying a sextant from a London merchant presumably to learn navigation at sea. He arrived at Princeton, where von Neumann helped enroll him as a doctorate student in mathematics. Turing could not wait to see an electronic computer become a reality. He designed an electric multiplier and built its first three or four stages to see if it could function. He machined relay-operated switches and wound them; to his delight, the calculator worked.[4] Even now, a mechanical device that applies the principles from his 1936 article makes it a "Universal Turing Machine," a label applied to practically all modern digital computers.

Turing turned down an offer to stay at Princeton as an assistant to von Neumann and returned to England, where he instead devoted himself to the field of cryptology. In World War II he was a central figure in the successful British effort to crack the German military's Enigma code, a service to the Allies that was portrayed in the popular movie *The Imitation Game* (2014). Turing and von Neumann left lasting impressions on each other, and their collaboration in 1937–38 led both to devote a substantial portion of the rest of their lives to developing computer science.

Sometime in August or September 1944, von Neumann witnessed a demonstration at the Aberdeen Proving Grounds of the Army's Electronic Numerical Integrator and Computer, or ENIAC, a product of John W. Mauchly and J. Presper Eckert. Mauchly was an electronics instructor at the Moore School of Electrical Engineering at the University of Pennsylvania in Philadelphia. There he met Eckert, a native Philadelphian whose first job while in high school had been at the television-research laboratory of Philo Farnsworth, a job that left him with an excellent understanding of electronics. Mauchly and Eckert worked together to develop an analog computer to help guide antiaircraft gunners in aiming at enemy bombers. Mauchly afterward had an idea to use electronics to digitize the analog computer and made a formal proposal to the Army. This was submitted in April 1943, and the result was the ENIAC.

The ENIAC could add five thousand numbers or do 357 ten-digit multiplications in one second. But it was not easy to set up. The machine was programmed by setting a bank of ten position switches and connecting thousands of cables by hand, a process that could take hours or even days to complete.[5] Yet, as von Neumann watched Mauchly and Eckert demonstrate their machine, he understood how valuable it could be to the Super project.

For all its sophistication, the ENIAC did not have all the attributes of a Universal Turing Machine. Von Neumann hoped to address that by building his own computer at the Institute for Advanced Study. The result was a machine that could do fast, electronic, and completely automatic all-purpose computing. He called his device the Mathematical and Numerical Integrator and Computer, or more familiarly, the MANIAC. The computer stood six feet high, two feet wide, and eight feet long and weighed one thousand pounds. Von Neumann hoped to see his machine used to help design a Super, but he was uncertain how to configure a computer program to do that. The solution would come from a member of Teller's group at Los Alamos.

*# # #*

Stan Ulam, that illustrious member of the Director's Committee, had an inspiration. While Ulam recovered from a bout of encephalitis in 1946, his doctor told him to lie still and not think. To the Polish mathematician, that was like asking him not to breathe. He passed his time playing solitaire and, despite his doctor's admonition, began to calculate the probability of winning a game. To do that, however, he needed statistics based on random distributions of cards in the deck.

The number of card combinations was too great to deal adequately with a mathematical formula; Ulam came to realize it would be easier to get statistics by playing the game repeatedly with random starting cards and recording the results. He then applied that reasoning to the Super. Perhaps instead of keeping track of randomly distributed playing cards, he could keep track of how random neutrons behaved inside the Super.[6]

Ulam imagined he could randomly select a neutron and, by applying appropriate probable outcomes, could track it to its fate. If he repeated the process for thousands of neutrons with randomly selected starting values, he could build up a statistical basis on which to determine the outcome for a flow of neutrons in a real problem. One member of Teller's group, Nick Metropolis, dubbed Ulam's methodology a Monte Carlo calculation because it resembled a game of chance.

Applying a Monte Carlo method to a fluence of neutrons traveling through the Super required millions of calculations, so it seemed Ulam's idea would be impractical—except that the digital computer had been invented. Doing Monte Carlo simulations became a major driver for involving the digital computer in thermonuclear research. A duplicate of von Neumann's MANIAC was constructed at Los Alamos to do thermonuclear calculations using, among other things, the Monte Carlo methodology.

In January 1950, after Teller and Gamow had published their design paper for the Super, Ulam decided to use his Monte Carlo method to see if their scheme would work. Amid the confusion of getting a computer to Los Alamos, Ulam recruited a mathematician he had met at the University of Wisconsin, Cornelius J. Everett, to assist him with the calculations. Since they did not yet have full access to a computer, these calculations followed a mathematical schema worked out by Ulam in which intelligent estimates were used to compute nuclear reactions. The work was painstakingly slow and laborious, and Ulam had to bring in an army of human "computers," including his wife, Françoise, to do much of the arithmetic.

By early March 1950, Ulam published his report. In the introduction he said it was the product of hand calculations; using a computer to make Monte Carlo calculations would have to follow at a later date. One unorthodox feature of his results was the use of guesses or estimates of values of multidimensional integrals. Several paragraphs later he dropped his bombshell: "The result of the calculations seems to be that the model considered is a fizzle."[7] In other words, after months of mind-numbing arithmetic, he concluded that ions in the Super did not retain energy long enough to ignite fusion.

When Teller read the report, he was livid. For years he had been extolling his design of the Super, and now Ulam was telling him it was flawed. The Polish mathematician wrote to von Neumann that Teller was "pale with fury . . . literally—but I think he is calmed down."[8] In a classic example of shooting the messenger, Teller was angry enough to persuade Bradbury to disband the Director's Committee, which did not please Gamow. A dramatic reduction of intellectual power followed: Bradbury replaced the Director's Committee with a "Family Committee" of ten or so physicists and engineers to review the family of fission and fusion devices then undergoing development.

Teller tried to debunk Ulam's work, but there were no obvious ways he could scientifically disprove its conclusions. Suggesting there may have been a mathematical error, Everett, who was renowned for his ability to perform calculations flawlessly, responded simply there were none. Bethe visited Los Alamos a short time later and, after reading Ulam's report, agreed with its conclusions.

That summer Fermi went over the calculations with Ulam. To be sure he understood the mathematician's approach to the problem, Fermi asked him to review his methodology one more time, which he did. Fermi and Ulam cloistered themselves and redid the calculations, this time looking at how the Super would propagate thermonuclear reactions once it was ignited. They repeated the earlier time-step calculations in a sort of competitive environment, with Ulam and Everett working as one team, and Fermi working in parallel, assisted by Miriam Planck, a LASL employee who made many of the calculations on a desktop electric calculator.

This time they used "intuitive estimates and marvelous simplifications introduced by Fermi."[9] Ulam took the opportunity to employ his Monte Carlo technique by literally tossing dice at critical phases of the calculation to decide what courses of action a neutron, photon, or nucleus would take. The numerical work was done on Monroe, Friden, and Marchant electric calculating machines used for arithmetic operations rather than with slide rules to ensure the accuracy of digits in the answers. By the end of the summer, Fermi was satisfied that Ulam's earlier conclusions were correct.

Von Neumann as well decided to check Ulam's results himself. He duplicated Ulam's schema on the MANIAC at Princeton but with finer calculations, including Monte Carlo simulations. A key programmer for the Monte Carlo calculations was his wife, Klári, who had worked with the Census Bureau during the war and had gained an appreciation for building algorithms for statistics. Slowly, as May and June went by, the results began to come in. The computer calculations also confirmed Ulam's original finding.[10]

While the MANIAC crunched out thermonuclear calculations at Princeton, a crisis struck America. In June 1950 Communist North Korean leader Kim Il Sung's ground forces bolted across the 38th parallel and invaded South Korea. The North Korean army came equipped with Soviet T-34 tanks as they brushed aside resistance offered by the South Korean military. U.S. Army units were rushed over from Japan, but they were inadequately armed and ill prepared and had to retreat down the Korean peninsula to the seaport of Pusan. After an amphibious assault made at Inchon, the Americans, as part of an overall United Nations military command, pushed the North Koreans back north in short order. Then, just after the Thanksgiving Holiday in November 1950, soldiers of three Communist Chinese armies launched massive "human wave" attacks that drove the U.N. forces headlong to the south. The American Eighth Army barely held on and suffered staggering losses. In December Truman said he would consider using atom bombs in Korea unless communist forces fell back.

The communist aggression in Korea made Ulam even more determined to succeed. He may have concluded that the Super, as originally designed by Teller and Gamow, would not work, but that did not mean he had given up on the project. Quite the contrary, he insisted thermonuclear research should continue at all costs and redoubled his efforts to devise a working design. One morning he had an inspiration. His wife, Françoise, found him at home at noon, staring intensely out of a window with a very strange expression on his face. She heard him say, "I found a way to make it work." When she asked what he was talking about, he answered it was the Super. Ulam believed his idea would change the course of history.[11]

His idea was similar to Teller's original concept for the Super, but with a few important distinctions. Ulam suggested using one atomic bomb, which he called a primary, to compress another atomic bomb, called a secondary, placed adjacent to it. So, instead of using an atomic bomb to initiate fusion reactions, as Teller had suggested, Ulam wanted to use an atomic bomb to compress another fission device. His point was that imploding an atomic bomb with high explosives was shown to be a means to achieve an atomic explosion, but the amount of compression garnered from high explosives was limited. The much greater energy from an atomic blast could conceivably compress a secondary atomic device much more, which meant greater nuclear fission. This was not the classic Super as Teller had envisioned, but a means to achieve more yield from an atomic device.

Ulam brought his idea to Teller, who at first hesitantly took it up, but then he saw a parallel version, an alternative. The physicist and the mathematician discussed the problem several times, then drew a sketch for a new idea. Teller made some changes and additions, and then they wrote a joint report. This contained engineering sketches of the possibilities of starting thermonuclear explosions.[12]

Teller's conversation with Ulam made him rethink his earlier ideas about compressing the deuterium in the Super. He had thought compression did not matter since the increase in the rate of nuclear reactions that would come with compression was offset by the increased rate at which radiation escaped from the device. It was not only Teller who held to this idea: Fermi, Bethe, von Neumann, and Gamow all had not suggested compressing thermonuclear fuel.[13] Perhaps Ulam's depressing news that the Super did not work as originally conceived made Teller reconsider the physics behind its design, which also opened his mind to alternative ideas.

Teller had considered compression to be a linear effect: there was a one-for-one tradeoff between reaction rates and escaping photons. According to Fermi's calculations during the Manhattan Project, that is true to first order, but there are subtle second- and third-order effects favoring fuel compression. For instance, a compressed fuel offered a smaller volume to be heated, making energy losses more manageable. Once Teller understood Ulam's concept, he transformed it into an idea of using the radiation from the atomic primary to surround, not another atomic bomb, but a thermonuclear secondary and thereby compress it. The physicist and the mathematician eagerly explored ideas, then agreed to jointly write their collective thoughts into a paper. It was March 1951.

Their article was twenty typewritten pages long, double-spaced, with four figures. In their introduction they laid out their message: "By an explosion of one or several conventional auxiliary fission bombs, one hopes to establish conditions for the explosion of a 'principal' bomb . . . a thermonuclear assembly." [14] They offered two alternative approaches to applying the new idea. Over the decades to come, both approaches were found to be useful.

In the years following, however, a controversy arose about who had invented the hydrogen bomb—was it Teller or Ulam? Teller later claimed it was the work of many people, but certainly they were the two main collaborators. [15] Teller and Ulam needed each other. Their joint paper was remarkable in that, having been written by a mathematician and a theoretical physicist, it had surprisingly few mathematical equations. Written in clear and distinct language, it became a landmark publication and in one stroke pushed aside an obstacle stalling development of the Super almost to failure.

While Teller and Ulam established the concept of a workable Super, Teller's assistant, Frédéric de Hoffman, solidified the idea into a reasonable design. One month after the Teller-Ulam article was published, de Hoffman wrote a document that laid out the characteristics of a new Super, a device he called the "Sausage." He insisted on using Teller's name as the sole author, saying that all the ideas in this second paper owed their origin to him. [16]

The exact materials, dimensions, shape, and densities that made up an actual device still had to be determined. The year before, Fermi had sent Teller one of his graduate students, Richard Garwin, to help during the summer months. A greater level of design emerged three months after the Teller-Ulam article when Garwin wrote a paper that gave more precise physical characteristics for a thermonuclear test device. Teller claimed that Garwin thus became the essential link between the design physicists and the engineers who were responsible for manufacturing a thermonuclear device. Wheeler's assistant Ken Ford thought Garwin's paper set forth an actual workable design of a thermonuclear weapon.[17]

*⁂*

April 1951 marked one year since Wheeler had arrived at Los Alamos. He longed for more stability for his family and wanted to return home to New Jersey. He suggested a contract with the AEC to create a laboratory at Princeton to do calculations of a thermonuclear device based on the newly written Teller-Ulam article. To make his proposal more attractive, he collaborated with a fellow member of the university's physics faculty, astrophysicist Lyman Spitzer. Spitzer's portion of the contract involved producing energy with a fusion reactor, using an invention he called a stellerator, a so-called star-making machine. Later, the stellerator evolved into a Russian invention called the Tokomak.

Spitzer, a mountain-climbing enthusiast, suggested the name Matterhorn for the project. Subsequently, the project was split in two, with Spitzer's part called Matterhorn-S, the "S" standing for stellerator, and Wheeler's part called Matterhorn-B, the "B" standing for bomb. Bradbury accepted Wheeler's proposal and agreed to support Matterhorn-B, and the AEC granted him the contract. Spitzer's portion of the program eventually led to founding the Princeton Plasma Physics Laboratory.

The Matterhorn-B Project found a home in a small metal shack on property newly acquired by Princeton, and Wheeler set about recruiting physicists. He wrote and called 120 prominent theoretical physicists around the nation. Some were astrophysicists who were important to him because they were specialists in radiative-transport calculations (essential for understanding the Super). Only one colleague responded to Wheeler's request for help, Louis Henyey, a professor of astrophysics at Berkeley.[18]

Henyey, born in Pennsylvania, was the son of Hungarian immigrants. He arrived at Princeton with two of his graduate students, Richard Levee and Bill Grasberger.

For the rest of the Matterhorn-B crew, Wheeler recruited physicists who had not yet had a chance to establish themselves. Among them was his assistant Ken Ford, who wrote a radiative-transport computer code to calculate reactions for the Teller-Ulam thermonuclear model, the New Super. Ford wrote this code on a primitive machine created by IBM Corporation called the card-programmed calculator, or IBM-CPC.[19] To use it, the programmer fed the computer punched cards, which were read at a rate of about one per second. Wheeler procured permission to use an IBM-CPC at the IBM offices in New York City during off hours. Ford took the train from Princeton to New York in the evening and returned to New Jersey in the morning with the results of the night's work. His calculations looked promising.[20]

Despite having written a well-received paper with Ulam, Teller was agitated. He felt the leadership of Los Alamos did not enthusiastically support the Super program. Bradbury had expanded the role of the Theoretical Division to devote more time to thermonuclear research, but that did not satisfy Teller. Frustrated, on April 4 Teller took his case to Gordon Dean, the new chairman of the AEC. He complained of being frustrated working at Los Alamos and turned in his resignation. Teller now wanted to create a separate and independent laboratory and staff it with fifty senior scientists, eighty-two junior scientists, and 228 engineers and technicians, establishing it in Chicago, where he could recruit scientists from a nearby university—and he could be close to Fermi. Dean convinced him to postpone his resignation and offered to mediate his differences with the management of LASL.[21]

Dean was now curious about developments in the Super program and scheduled a meeting of the GAC with AEC commissioners to discuss thermonuclear research. Oppenheimer arranged for it to take place at the Institute for Advanced Study at Princeton. Dean was clear about what he expected: a recommendation from the GAC whether to proceed with a test of a thermonuclear device.[22]

The meeting began on June 16, 1951, a Saturday. Theoretical Division leader Carson Mark gave a progress report on LASL research. He made no mention of the Teller-Ulam breakthrough with the Super, and Teller became disheartened. On the second day Henry Smyth, an AEC commissioner, asked Teller to give a fifteen-minute review of the article he and Ulam had written three months earlier.[23] Following this report, Wheeler prepared to brief the GAC on the feasibility of the Teller-Ulam principle.

Ford's calculations during the previous week had been encouraging, so he made a final run with the most realistic assumptions that night. He brought the data back on an early train the next morning and went to the Matterhorn building, where he made graphs of the principal results on sheets of paper about two feet by three feet in size. Then, with only minutes to spare, he rolled up the graphs and sped to the institute. He approached the first-floor conference room where the GAC was meeting and tapped on a window. He caught Wheeler's eye just as he was starting his presentation. Wheeler opened the window and accepted the roll. He unrolled the graphs, taped them to the blackboard, and explained their meaning.

The reaction was electric. Here, for the first time, the GAC saw convincing evidence that a thermonuclear device based on the Teller-Ulam principle would burn up a significant fraction of the fuel. Once he had seen the calculations, Oppenheimer called the design for the New Super "technically sweet." The sense of the scientists present was there was a sure route to success—there was no technical reason to delay the program.[24]

In a dramatic reversal from its findings in October 1949, the GAC recommended a thermonuclear device should be tested. Bradbury would have to organize LASL to quickly develop a device based on the Teller-Ulam document. Its test would be called the Mike event. Teller was a visionary, not a manager, so Bradbury assigned responsibility of day-to-day activities for the test to his W (Weapons) Division, led by a no-nonsense engineer named Marshall Holloway. Teller was not a happy man. Holloway was a member of the Family Committee and had crossed swords with him continually over the Super program. Teller now felt more estranged from Bradbury than ever, convinced he did not care whether Teller worked on the project or not.[25]

Bradbury did not share that sentiment. If he placed Teller in charge, then LASL would have spent time doing computational work in a field it was not well equipped. They would have spent time exploring, by inadequate methods, a system that was far from certain to be successful. Bradbury could not see how they could have reached their objectives in a more rapid fashion.[26]

In a series of meetings, Teller and Bradbury had heated exchanges, and LASL scientists made acrimonious remarks directed at Teller and his wild accusations.[27] Teller's disenchantment with the management at Los Alamos was complete, and he resigned from LASL a second time. By November 1951, he was back in Chicago.

⫻ ⫻ ⫻

The Mike event was part of Operation Ivy, a series of nuclear tests scheduled for the fall of 1952. The test of a thermonuclear device occurred without Teller, the man who had championed it for years during the Manhattan Project. The Matterhorn-B program supported the effort with calculations, as Wheeler and his physicists made regular trips back to Los Alamos by train in reserved Pullman cars—a two-day trip. Those travel days were filled with Wheeler interacting freely with his charges, who in turn got to enjoy highly rewarding experiences. The train from Chicago to New Mexico was called the Chief, and not surprisingly, Matterhorn-B computer codes carried names from the Old West, "Chief" and "Squaw" being two examples.[28]

The Mike device was not a usable weapon—the size of a small house, it could hardly be carried by a bomber. Nevertheless, it was a thermonuclear device, the first to ever exist, and Bradbury felt a sense of accomplishment about it. Despite Teller's warnings to the contrary, the LASL-Matterhorn team completed its work on schedule.

The Mike event occurred on Halloween, 1952, American time (November 1, Western Pacific time), at Eniwetok Atoll. To anyone observing the detonation, it must have seemed as if Armageddon had arrived. A radiochemist named Gary Higgins was at Bikini Atoll at the time of the test and saw a flash of light, then a fireball that grew over the horizon.[29]

The yield of a device is the amount of nuclear energy it releases—the yield of the Mike device was about ten megatons (10MT), some seven hundred times more powerful than the Hiroshima bomb. After the atomic blasts of the 1940s, the military services had thought that an atomic bomb was just a new, albeit powerful, weapon in their fighting arsenal. After the Mike event, they had to rethink what nuclear war meant.

America's feat of being the sole country in the world with a thermonuclear weapon did not last long. On August 8, 1953, Soviet premier Georgy Malenkov announced that, just as the United States had no monopoly on the atomic bomb, it no longer had a monopoly on the hydrogen bomb either. In the Soviet Union's fourth nuclear test, dubbed by U.S. intelligence as "Joe 4" in reference to Josef Stalin, Soviet weapons scientists detonated their first hydrogen bomb.

Although the blast was larger than any of America's early atomic bombs, the Russian version only had a fraction of the yield of the Mike device. It also did not share the sophistication brought out by the Teller-Ulam article. Even so, it was clear the Russians were intent on developing a thermonuclear weapon and had made a significant start. It had taken Soviet scientists only four years, compared to the seven years for those in the United States, to develop and test a thermonuclear warhead once they had successfully tested an atomic bomb. To anyone associated with America's nuclear program, it was clear the Soviets had an excellent nuclear-weapons program of their own.[30]

# 7

////////////////

# *The Second Laboratory*

O nce Frank Collbohm got things started, Project RAND did very well. Its analysts pumped out position papers on national secu- rity, which always drew a lot of attention from government poli- cymakers. It was fortuitous that Collbohm had hired David Griggs when he created RAND, for Griggs proved to be a significant asset for the think tank. He was also a natural fit with the U.S. Air Force.

After working with Luis Alvarez on GCAR, Griggs left the MIT Radiation Laboratory in July 1942 and volunteered to be a technical advi- sor to the Army Air Corps in the European theater of war—just as Johnny Foster had done. While flying on a combat mission with Eighth Air Force on a flight over Bremen, Germany, the bomb-bay doors of his aircraft became stuck. Griggs kicked the doors open, falling through as they sud- denly unhinged. He caught himself with one hand and was pulled back into the bomber by the crew.

Lieutenant General Jimmy Doolittle, commander of Eighth Air Force, ordered Griggs grounded for fear of losing his scientific advisor, but Griggs was adamant to keep flying combat missions, so he transferred to Fifteenth Air Force. In a mission over northern Italy, a Messerschmitt fighter fired its 20-millimeter cannon at the bomber Griggs was in; he was struck by a shell and awarded the Purple Heart. When the war ended in Europe, he transferred to the Pacific to help with the Hiroshima mission. On April 15, 1946, President Truman presented him with the Medal for Merit, the highest award the country gives to a civilian for service during war.[1] Early in 1948, Collbohm formed a physics division at RAND, appointing Griggs its leader. It did not take long for Griggs to make his mark.

RAND attracted some of the leading political scientists of the nation, drawn by the opportunity to affect U.S. national-security policy at the beginning of the nuclear age. One was Bernard Brodie, who, as a member of the Yale Institute of International Studies, wrote a landmark political analysis, *The Absolute Weapon* (1946), soon after the atomic bomb had been dropped on Hiroshima. Other influential political thinkers included a protégé of Brodie's named William Kaufmann; a political scientist named Andy Marshall, who would later become an icon at the Pentagon; and a young aspiring physicist named Herman Kahn. With intellectuals like these, Collbohm's think tank was destined to have a profound influence on world events as it developed a national deterrence strategy to ward off nuclear war.

Since the Air Force controlled most of the country's atomic weapons, RAND's contributions to its policy had significant consequences for national-security policy. To be pertinent, RAND analysts had to have access to nuclear-weapons data, but they could not see that information because the AEC granted Q clearances only to those working under AEC contracts. The Air Force deputy chief of staff for research and development, General Curtis LeMay, put pressure on the commission to grant Q clearances to analysts at RAND, his persuasive powers proving adequate to the task. By 1951, physicists in Griggs' division had begun regular visits to Los Alamos, where they were astounded to learn about the Super project.

With that, thermonuclear research became a major concern for Griggs. Among other things, he had a member of his division, Ernie Plesset, assemble a team to assess the political ramifications of developing the Super. Plesset recruited Brodie as well as economists and missile experts to assess a thermonuclear weapon. Within a short span of time, the RAND team concluded the Super would have a profound effect on national-security strategy.

Brodie was a strategic thinker. He understood that the famous dictum of Carl von Clausewitz, "war is a continuation of policy by other means," had profound implications for nuclear warfare: any use of a nuclear weapon had to have a political rationale. Brodie concluded it would be irrational to initiate conflict with a nuclear strike inside the Soviet Union; that would only spark Soviet retaliation with monumentally destructive effects in the

United States. He observed, "Thus far the chief purpose of our military establishment has been to win wars. From now on its chief purpose must be to avert them."[2] Brodie recognized that the *threat* of a nuclear strike was a powerful deterrent, which presented a classic conundrum: with a thermonuclear weapon representing the ultimate deterrent against aggression, how do you configure a strategy of deterrence around a weapon you cannot use?

Albert Wohlstetter, a renowned RAND analyst, gave a sober assessment that deterrence was not automatic, emphasizing that one of the most disturbing features among political thinkers was an underestimation of how difficult it was to achieve. This was due partly to a misconception of the technological race as a problem in matching striking forces, partly to a wishful analysis of the Soviet ability to strike first. Since thermonuclear weapons give an enormous advantage to the aggressor, Wohlstetter noted it takes great ingenuity and realism at any given level of nuclear technology to devise a stable equilibrium.[3]

According to Wohlstetter, it was not so much the size of a nuclear force that mattered as much as how well it was structured that determined whether it was an effective deterrent—that is, building a credible deterrent would take great ingenuity and realism by political and physical scientists. Brodie and his fellow RAND analysts understood this explicitly and strove to get an answer to deterrence in time for the United States to face the Cold War. Plesset and his team finished their studies and wrapped up their work in a briefing entitled "Implications of Large-Yield Nuclear Weapons."[4]

It was time for von Kármán to retire as chief scientist of the Air Force, and he recommended Griggs replace him. Griggs accepted the appointment, left RAND, and took his post in Washington, D.C. This did not mean he had lost interest in studies going on at Santa Monica, nor did it mean he had lost interest in thermonuclear research. Griggs continued to maintain a close relationship with Alvarez and Lawrence.

In 1951 the most important policy question facing the Air Force was how to effectively integrate atomic weapons into the country's arsenal. The major arm of the Air Force most concerned with nuclear integration was the Strategic Air Command (SAC), a fleet of large nuclear-armed bombers capable of conducting intercontinental missions. As might be expected, a proper and effective role for SAC became a dominant feature for Air Force strategic planning. To make it an effective force, Griggs became convinced the hydrogen bomb had to be developed quickly, which made him an ardent opponent to Oppenheimer and the GAC.

While the Air Force concentrated on large-yield nuclear weapons, the other services drew their own conclusions about small-yield weapons, called tactical nuclear weapons. The Army had been rudely awakened to its fragility when the Eighth Army had almost been annihilated early in the Korean War. Tacticians saw low-yield nuclear weapons as being valuable options to possess on a battlefield. They argued if an Army unit had such a weapon system, say nuclear artillery, an enemy would avoid concentrating forces into large masses to make human-wave attacks, as the Chinese had done in Korea, lest a single nuclear artillery shell destroy large formations of soldiers. The Navy saw advantages with tactical nuclear weapons as well. Fighter-bombers launched from aircraft carriers carrying small-yield bombs could augment nuclear artillery.

General Lawton Collins, the dynamic commander of U.S. Army VII Corps in World War II, was Army chief of staff in 1951. He lauded the development of tactical nuclear weapons, especially artillery, as opposed to strictly developing strategic atomic bombs. In an interview with *U.S. News & World Report*, Collins said military leaders were confident that Western Europe could be defended against communist "hordes" without having to match Russia's army division for division. He claimed the military leadership of the Pentagon thought that atomic bombs were considered mainly a strategic weapon—for use against the enemy's cities and industrial centers—because they must be dropped from planes. That did not permit the great accuracy necessary on the field of battle.[5]

In his comments Collins reflected a view held by influential military leaders: atomic bombs counterbalanced the enormous conventional military strength of the Soviet Union, which was wielding a heavy hand of dominance over the governments of Eastern Europe. That view was at variance with those RAND analysts like Brodie, who felt the only proper role for a nuclear weapon was deterrence. Brodie would have thought the general reflected a naïveté about how destructive a nuclear war could be to the United States.

As the Army placed demands on the AEC for tactical nuclear warheads, it competed with the Air Force, which favored large bombs, and this taxed the commission's limited resources, especially at Los Alamos.[6] General LeMay, who had assumed command of SAC, saw Army demands as a threat to the well-being of his command. Many Air Force planners believed it was strategic bombing in World War II that brought Germany to seek surrender. To them, it was still the only way to deter the Soviet Union, and they did not tolerate disagreement. LeMay's philosophy reflected his wartime experiences: when hostilities broke out, strike the Soviet Union with the entire nuclear force of the nation in one massive strike.

As chief scientist, Griggs became an avid devotee of the Air Force position, and his attention was drawn to a threatening study called Project Vista. The project had started in 1951 under Caltech president Lee DuBridge to examine the usefulness of nuclear weapons against a Soviet invasion of Europe. It had grown out of a visit to Korea by General James Gavin, who had led the 82nd Airborne Division through World War II, and Caltech physicist Charles Lauritsen. There they investigated the feasibility of deploying tactical nuclear weapons to support the Army.

To help with the study, DuBridge invited Oppenheimer, who readily accepted; it gave him a chance to reiterate, since the nation had atomic bombs, weapons such as hydrogen bombs were unnecessary. Predictably, the Vista report emphasized the importance of atomic weapons used against tactical targets and downplayed a possible role for hydrogen bombs. Especially disturbing to Air Force planners was a chapter implying a secondary role for a strategic air offensive, suggesting tactical atomic weapons could be the decisive factor in the defense of Europe.[7]

Air Staff officers agreed tactical nuclear weapons were useful; they even proposed them for fighter-bombers. But to them the primary purpose of nuclear weapons was strategic deterrence, not tactical combat. They saw a pattern in Oppenheimer's actions: One year earlier he had called for refinement of atomic weapons while relegating thermonuclear research to a lesser priority. Now he was proposing to split up the national allocation of fissile material equally among the three services rather than allocating an adequate amount of it for strategic weapons.

Griggs saw those actions as evidence of Oppenheimer's disregard for Air Force strategy. He accused Oppenheimer of being a member of a cabal he called "ZORC"— Z for Zacharias, O for Oppenheimer, R for Rabi, and C for C. C. Lauritsen, all members of the Manhattan Project who were actively opposed to thermonuclear research—which was engaged in what Griggs considered to be nefarious anti–Air Force schemes.[8] Oppenheimer's participation in the Vista study caused Chief of Staff Hoyt S. Vandenberg to take him off the Air Force's secret access list in the fall of 1951.[9]

Oppenheimer's attempts to forestall development of the hydrogen bomb struck the Defense Department (as the War Department was now called) as being outside the GAC's charter. His use of the GAC as a platform to promote a political agenda was too much to bear. For those at the Pentagon, the AEC was supposed to develop and produce nuclear weapons; nuclear policy should be within the purview of the Defense Department. The secretary of defense felt no agency should come between the president and the Pentagon concerning the use of nuclear weapons, and he asked Truman to clarify the issue.

As passions rose in the Air Force against Oppenheimer, LASL began to feel the effects. As the former director of Los Alamos, Oppenheimer was a respected figure there, and his opinion still counted. The Air Staff judged LASL as being guilty by association and even contemplated creating another nuclear-weapons laboratory. They considered establishing it in Chicago and reached out to the University of Illinois for support. Meanwhile, the Army felt LASL was devoting too much of its attention to the Air Force at the expense of the needs of the other services. Both it and the Navy believed if LASL was being overwhelmed by its commitments to the Air Force, perhaps it was time to create a second laboratory for the other services.[10]

Griggs was not the type of individual to stand by passively and allow events to overtake him. He discussed ways to support the Super program with friends, among them Lawrence and Alvarez, and came up with a plan. He appointed Teller to the Air Force Scientific Advisory Board and sent him to a conference at Cape Canaveral, Florida, where Griggs introduced him to General Doolittle, the chairman of the Science Board. Doolittle had a doctorate in aeronautical engineering from MIT and understood technical briefings about nuclear weapons; indeed, he had had conversations with von Neumann about the hydrogen bomb.[11]

Teller told Doolittle about a recent experience he had addressing the GAC and AEC commissioners on the morning of December 13, 1951, on the need for a second laboratory. He had argued that, while LASL made good use of limited resources, it was not enough to exploit thermonuclear research. A second laboratory could concentrate on developing the hydrogen bomb and, for good measure, added in one of his favorite causes dating back to discussions he had had with Bohr: a second laboratory could develop uranium hydride as a fuel for an atomic device.[12] (Uranium hydride is discussed in a later chapter.) The GAC, led by Oppenheimer, listened but remained unconvinced. Teller said the committee denied his request to create a second nuclear-weapons laboratory. Doolittle was impressed with his passion and agreed there was a need for a second such facility.[13]

In mid-February 1952, Griggs and Doolittle arranged for Teller and RAND's Plesset to brief Secretary of the Air Force Thomas Finletter about the Super program. After the briefing, Finletter asked them to give the briefing again to the new secretary of defense, Robert Lovett, and to the other three service secretaries. After that briefing on March 19, 1952, the service secretaries urged Lovett to have Teller and Plesset address the National Security Council about the need to create a second nuclear-weapons laboratory.[14]

On April 1 Teller and Plesset briefed three members of the National Security Council: Deputy Secretary of Defense William Foster, Secretary of State Acheson, and AEC chairman Dean. The meeting took place in Foster's office at the Pentagon. Although Dean was not against the development of the hydrogen bomb, he was not in favor of creating a laboratory to compete with Los Alamos. He also feared he was losing control of the situation; there was a chance the Defense Department would dictate its will upon his civilian agency.

Dean captured the meeting in notes from his daily journal on April 1, 1952: Teller explained the early thinking on the Super and the very slight thermonuclear effort at Los Alamos during the Manhattan Project. He said LASL's objection to the Super was based on moral grounds, but after the president resolved the question in January 1950, Los Alamos had

engendered considerable enthusiasm. Teller paid tribute to LASL generally but said there was not sufficient effort being placed on the project. He
emphasized the competence of the Russians to develop thermonuclear
weapons. In closing, Teller referred to the importance of getting additional
people into the project and establishing an additional laboratory.[15]

After the briefing, Dean shared with Foster and Acheson his disfavor
in creating a second laboratory, but he did not get a sympathetic response.
Foster said he had been out to discuss the thermonuclear program at LASL
with Bradbury in September 1951 and had come away feeling the director
resented having to discuss the program with him. He had also discussed
the issue at Berkeley with Lawrence, and that conversation made a far different impression on him. Lawrence admitted LASL lacked having a passion for thermonuclear research and a second laboratory was needed.[16]
Secretary of State Acheson agreed with Foster.

As rumors at the Pentagon surfaced about the need for a second weapons laboratory, Dean had to consider the ramifications a second laboratory could have on Los Alamos. Would it affect recruiting? Were there
enough special nuclear materials to meet the needs of two laboratories?
And the Pentagon was not the only place stirring the pot to establish a second laboratory, as Senator McMahon expressed frustration over the lack
of enthusiasm for thermonuclear research. Dean grew agitated. The last
thing he wanted was for AEC internal matters to come before the president
or Congress.

*/// /// ///*

Carl Helmholz, a faculty member at Berkeley, held a New Year's Eve
party in 1951 at his home in Orinda, a small picturesque town in the hills
east of the city. Herb York was enjoying the socializing when Lawrence
approached him and asked if he would come by his office soon; he had
something important to discuss.

Always eager to chat with his boss, York called in two days later.
Lawrence said one of the AEC commissioners, Thomas Murray, a good
Irish Catholic New Yorker, had visited to tell him that when Teller had gone
before the GAC, most AEC commissioners were sympathetic to the committee's rejection of a second weapons laboratory. Murray, disenchanted

with the negativism he witnessed, urged Lawrence to create a second laboratory anyway.[17] Taken by Murray's passion, Lawrence wondered, "Is there enough government interest to create a second nuclear weapons laboratory?" He wanted York to learn the answer, so York set out on an extended trip around the country to discuss the matter with those who might have helpful views. He met with LASL management at Los Alamos, Teller in Chicago, Wheeler at Princeton University, and finally Griggs, Doolittle, and AEC commissioners Dean and Murray in Washington, D.C.

York returned to Berkeley after a few weeks. He told Lawrence he thought it was a good idea to start a second laboratory; the competition with Los Alamos would benefit the nation, and the new laboratory could expand our knowledge of thermonuclear reactions. With that, Lawrence asked him to take the lead in creating the new laboratory and to go see if Teller would work under the plan. But he warned him that Teller had earlier expressed reservations about working in the Rad Lab because he objected to the loyalty oath the University of California required from its staff and faculty. Teller had also disliked the idea of placing himself within Lawrence's "empire." He had been encouraged in that notion by Fermi, who insisted Teller needed to stay in Chicago.[18]

Why did Lawrence reach out to York to lead the laboratory instead of Alvarez, who must have been Lawrence's natural choice? While it is likely Lawrence did approach him first, Alvarez was burned out after managing the MTA Project and wanted to get back to doing fundamental research. He had arguably the most innovative mind at Berkeley, or anywhere else for that matter, and was happiest doing experiments to explore the unknown. This was what Alvarez finally got to do and, in the ensuing years, devoted himself to exploring the inner workings of the atomic nucleus as well as discovering new subatomic particles outright. He helped develop the bubble chamber and made it a practical tool to study subatomic particles, work for which he won the Nobel Prize in Physics in 1968.

Later, Alvarez joined his son Walter, a geologist, to propose the theory a meteor had collided with Earth 65 million years ago and caused the extinction of dinosaurs. He defended his hypothesis by finding a worldwide distribution of iridium, an element associated with meteorites, in a boundary layer of the crust marking the end of the Cretaceous period. With this, Alvarez provided a classic lesson to the next generation of physicists on how to build a theory and defend it.[19]

Meanwhile, York laid out an organizational plan for the new laboratory. He split physics responsibilities between two divisions: the Theoretical Division, dedicated to weapons research and led by Teller, and the Sherwood Project, dedicated to basic research in controlled fusion for energy production and led by physicist Dick Post. To these organizations York added the Chemistry Division, the Experimental Division, and the Mechanical and Electrical Engineering Division to provide general support. This new laboratory would be a branch of the Rad Lab, which would provide administrative support. The entire operation would fall under Lawrence's leadership.

In the late spring of 1952, York paid Lawrence a visit to his office in Berkeley, only to find Brigadier General Kenneth Fields, the AEC deputy director for military applications, already there. Fields had been sent by Chairman Dean to discuss how a second weapons laboratory could fit within the AEC. Lawrence asked York to show the general his plans for the new laboratory's organization, and York reminded him that they had not yet had a chance to talk it over themselves. Lawrence replied that this was okay: "Show General Fields what you're planning."[20] And that is what he did.

York's proposal was based on two assumptions: First, UCRL would be asked to support the LASL weapons program, particularly in the field of diagnostic experiments; and second, UCRL would design and test thermonuclear weapons. Taking York's notes, Fields returned to Washington with a blueprint for a fully fledged nuclear-weapons laboratory. Members of the GAC had come around to seeing the benefits of a second laboratory, but they wondered what its explicit charter would be and where it would be located.

The location was the easier question to answer: near the Rad Lab. That was where Lawrence was, and most of those who had a stake in the decision thought him to be the only person who could assemble another facility capable of designing nuclear weapons. The new laboratory would be too big for Berkeley, but the Rad Lab had run operations for the MTA and Project Whitney at Livermore for a while, and that site offered plenty of space. So the new laboratory should be located in Livermore.

The stickier question was its charter. On May 27, 1952, the AEC formally tasked the Rad Lab to perform instrumentation and component testing for a thermonuclear program. This was the commission's first official step to establishing a second laboratory. Lawrence was receptive to the proposal. But Teller, when he heard the details, was adamant the second laboratory needed to be given a charter to conduct independent research. There was a short period where some thought his attitude looked like a deal breaker, and Lawrence told York to be prepared to start the new laboratory without Teller.

York recalled that tense period in negotiations with the AEC. Teller was concerned the plan was not certain enough. At a party one evening, he got morose and said he was not going to have anything to do with the new laboratory. Lawrence told York it was okay, the laboratory could survive without him. But Captain Chick Hayward, the new AEC deputy director for military applications, was there and told York that Teller had to stay. With that, Lawrence talked with Teller and changed his mind.[21]

Chairman Dean did not want Teller excluded from the second laboratory; the process had moved too far, and Teller had grown a coterie of admirers within the Pentagon that Dean did not want to antagonize. That is when he decided to allow UCRL to participate in a thermonuclear program.[22] The stage was set for the regents of the University of California to amend their contract with the AEC, the same contract they had signed to join the Manhattan Project, to provide the nation with a second nuclear-weapons laboratory.

Even then, there was no formal declaration about a role for the Livermore site, whether, for instance, it would constitute a permanent weapons laboratory or whether it would even conduct its own nuclear testing. "It would be impossible for the Commission to write out a specific charter for the Livermore Laboratory," was Dean's assessment on September 8, 1952.[23] But within a short span of time, a general charter did take shape, and the Livermore site emerged as a fully functional and independent laboratory.

Dean's concerns became the basis for an unwritten obligation for the laboratory: Livermore should not compete with Los Alamos for staff and scarce material resources, and it had to avoid duplicating Los Alamos designs.

# 8

///////////////

# The Legacies of Lawrence, von Neumann, and Wheeler

The second U.S. nuclear-weapons laboratory opened on September 2, 1952, the day after Labor Day. Physicists with their doctorates were offered a starting salary of about $4,000 per year—hardly competitive with commercial companies like General Electric that were offering annual salaries in the range of $6,500 to $7,000. A sign posted on the front gate of the former Livermore Naval Air Station proclaimed the site to be the University of California Radiation Laboratory (Livermore), but to most it was simply called the Laboratory. The Livermore adjunct to Lawrence's Rad Lab, the Laboratory was, in a sense, ready to proceed with thermonuclear research with a young but experienced staff of technical personnel. Most of the scientists and engineers pulling up to its main gate that first day had commuted from Berkeley.

The hour-long commute was an invigorating drive, where one left a temperate climate with breezy neighborhoods along San Francisco Bay and arrived in a sun-drenched valley east of Oakland. Within a few weeks, some grew weary of the forty-mile jaunt and took up residence in the town of Danville, about midway between Berkeley and the Laboratory. Still others, Herb York among them, avoided commuting altogether and purchased or rented modest duplex homes in the town of Livermore. There was a shared excitement in the air; they were embarking on an adventure, a new beginning in their lives. For those accustomed to the urban neighborhoods of Berkeley, Livermore was a stark contrast.

Just as much as the Rad Lab and the MIT Radiation Lab were products of Lawrence's leadership and energy, so too, was the Laboratory his creation. With its establishment in Livermore, there was a passing of a baton of sorts to a new generation. Lawrence still led the Laboratory; truly, for the first two years of its existence, he was the director. But handling the day-to-day challenges facing these young scientists and engineers fell to York and his lieutenants. They were upstarts, not in the sense of causing disruption, but in setting out on a new course to help the nation defend itself against a grave new threat to its security, indeed its very existence. York and his upstarts were inspired to accomplish that challenge by the example Lawrence set in leading research and development through a world war— this was his legacy.

Summer days in Livermore are hot and dry, with the sun shining unremittingly and not a hint of a cloud in the sky. The weather on the Laboratory's first day was even warmer than normal, with temperatures reaching 112° Fahrenheit by midday. York wanted a workspace appropriate for running a top-secret laboratory, so he placed himself in the former infirmary x-ray room, which had lead-lined walls that drowned out sound and facilitated classified discussions. He soon regretted this, for like many good ideas, it had its unforeseen consequences. While lead-lined walls may dampen sound, they also hold heat; the intense outside heat essentially baked the insulated room. When Harold Brown stepped into York's office later in the day, he found his boss sitting at his desk, his shirt soaking wet, with perspiration pouring down his face.[1] The Laboratory was located in Livermore Valley, about two miles east of the namesake town. It and the town were connected by a single two-lane road, East Avenue, which ran from a flagpole in the heart of Livermore to the Laboratory's front gate. Instead of Berkeley's bustling streets lined with shops catering to practically any taste or need, Livermore offered a few antique stores and saloons reflecting a cowboy culture.

The look and feel of Livermore stayed much the same for years, quite unfazed by the progressive and offbeat culture of nearby Berkeley, Oakland, and San Francisco. But the pioneers of 1952 would hardly recognize it today. The town is now a thriving East Bay community, with an abundance of vineyards and a culture that has coalesced into something new. Its downtown has tree-lined streets, fine restaurants, retailers, and a public 520-seat theater that hosts musical groups, symphonies, operas, and plays. Many of the saloons have become upscale ale houses. Those Berkeley pioneers could not have known it, but their adopted town would become an epicenter where some of the greatest intellectuals in the nation gathered to help counter an aggressive Soviet Union.

The Laboratory's accommodations were rather austere. It had no cafeteria, just an "industrial canteen" servicing those MTA workers from California R&D Corporation who remained on site. The former air station's morgue was converted into a classified-documents vault, and the old drill hall became an auditorium and makeshift machine shop. Even the drill hall was inadequate for well-attended gatherings, so Teller used Livermore High School's auditorium to give lectures on nuclear weapons. The physical plant was a shamble. Building 161, a wood-frame structure that had been the base infirmary, became the home for the Theoretical (T) Division and weapons-design teams; most rooms had only a single light bulb. Likewise, Building 162, next door to T Division, housed experimental physicists who designed diagnostic equipment for nuclear tests.[2] For everyone, there was inadequate air conditioning on summer days, when temperatures hit the 90s or 100s, and in winter there was little in the way of heat. Draftsmen working in the printing shop in summer often had to make two copies of blueprints, the first draft often soaking wet from the draftsman's perspiration. AEC inspectors refused to allow the purchase of air conditioners, feeling it too extravagant an expense for taxpayers. Finally, the director of engineering cleverly arranged for an hours-long meeting with the inspectors in the drafting room in August. That worked, and soon thereafter the Laboratory was permitted to purchase air conditioners.

Working conditions on site were not the only challenges; driving back to Berkeley or Danville at night could be risky. The route followed an unlit two-lane highway that crossed over the busy four-lane Route 50. Employees were urged not to drive home late at night and were allowed to stay in a barracks furnished with Army-style bunkbeds. Other furnishings were sparse: some chairs, a desk or two, and often only a single light switch in a room; there were no closets or even nails in the walls to hang up clothing. After some loud complaining, Spartan quarters were provided in another building that had individual rooms and a lamp by each bed.[3]

York focused on recruiting students from Berkeley so much it seemed as though he was hiring the graduate class of 1952. He recruited Johnny

Foster from Alvarez's group at the Rad Lab and assigned him to the Sherwood Project. This endeavor satisfied Lawrence's insistence that part of the Laboratory's budget be devoted to basic science. York then enlisted Harold Brown to lead the Megaton Group, which designed thermonuclear warheads.

Mike May, York's former teaching assistant, arrived a week after the gates opened and was assigned to the Theoretical Division. On his first day he walked into a barracks and was briefed by a mathematician, Chuck Leith, who said the Laboratory was going to work on thermonuclear weapons. May's jaw dropped; he had no idea he was volunteering for that, and he did not particularly like it. Although not much of a pacifist—he had been a paratrooper in the war—he was not crazy about nuclear weapons. Nevertheless, May reasoned the country had to know how to manage them. He soon associated with great intellectuals like Herman Kahn, John von Neumann, and John Wheeler, who came in once in a while, visiting the Laboratory for weeks at a time. And so he became caught up in the physics.[4]

May was exceptional in every sense of the word. Born in 1925 in Marseilles, France, he lived with his mother's relatives while his father studied at medical school. After graduation, his father started a medical practice in a suburb of Paris, Paris-en-Fleck, before accepting a position to teach surgery in Hanoi, then part of French Indochina (Vietnam). With the onset of World War II, the family left Hanoi and immigrated to the United States using some connections with American relatives. Having befriended a Seventh Day Adventist missionary in Hanoi named Winton who had extolled the wonders of the American Northwest, they relocated to Walla Walla, Washington. May became Americanized and fluent in English, but he retained a distinct French accent, which gave a very distinguished elegance to his speech.

Drafted into the Army, May spent a couple of years in the service and volunteered to be a paratrooper. He was an airborne infantryman in a regiment training to drop by parachute into Japan, but the atomic blasts over Hiroshima and Nagasaki ended the war before he was deployed into combat—events that probably saved his life. After his discharge, he went to Berkeley, where he worked as a teacher's assistant to York. In 1952 May earned his PhD, got married, and accepted a position at the Laboratory.

By the time May left Berkeley for Livermore, his wife, Mary, was pregnant. Some realtors, seeing an opportunity with the opening of the Laboratory, built several cardboard duplexes along East Avenue. The Mays rented one of them for about eighty dollars a month, as did many others. Whenever von Neumann visited the Laboratory, York assigned a coterie of physicists, usually led by May, to escort him. After a few weeks, May invited the great mathematician to his duplex for lunch. Telling his wife that evening that the great Hungarian mathematician was going to be their house guest the next day, she wondered what to serve. After thinking it over for a while with her husband, she finally decided, "Well, since he's Hungarian, we'll have liverwurst sandwiches."[5]

May's office was next to one occupied by Kahn, a RAND analyst who often commuted to the Laboratory from Santa Monica. Since he was devoted to studying deterrence theory, Kahn closely observed the thermonuclear research going on at Livermore, coalescing his ideas into a coherent national strategy. He introduced the concept of the "Doomsday Machine" to the national jargon through his book *On Thermonuclear War* (1960); he won notoriety as the person the eponymous character "Doctor Strangelove" was based on in the Stanley Kubrick movie.

Years later, May explained Kahn had done a singular service for the country. Despite the madman reputation he had gained from the satirical Hollywood portrayal of him, Kahn had done the difficult but necessary task of forcing the American government to think about nuclear weapons and what role, if any, they played as a strategic deterrent. May and Kahn developed a close working relationship at Livermore, trading ideas with each other as they shared their experiences with thermonuclear research.

Kahn created the Hudson Institute in 1961, a think tank located in upstate New York in the town of Croton-on-Hudson. A popular intellectual, he led seminars there. Kahn lectured a generation of West Point cadets about how military power should properly deter aggressive armies, and he could often be found at the institute in the evening socializing with visitors and analysts, sipping his favorite drink, Grand Marnier.

The dominant presence of analysts from a national think tank like RAND at a nuclear-weapons laboratory was a unique arrangement. It placed political scientists in close contact with physical scientists in an environment where both benefited from each other's contributions. The analysts guided physicists to design weapons to fit the needs of deterrence strategies, while the physicists kept the analysts abreast of technological breakthroughs.

*# # #*

Teller, because of his special status, was given veto authority over design decisions involving nuclear weapons—he never exercised it throughout his years at the Laboratory—but otherwise had no formal authority. He was not interested in being a manager, so York had to appoint a T Division leader to handle administrative duties. Richard Latter, a RAND physicist on loan four days a week, was made acting head of the division for about a year, after which York replaced him with a physicist named Mark Mills.[6]

York wanted Laboratory positions to be valid for a few years only, after which scientists were expected to change assignments. He included himself in this, expecting to run the Laboratory for one or two years and then head back to Berkeley. A flexible organizational climate existed in which professionals flowed from Berkeley to Livermore and back. Lawrence's philosophy was "no one was too good to do any job that needed doing and, conversely, no job was too hard or too esoteric for anyone to do, if only he tried hard enough."[7] He did not believe in organization charts but just got the best person for the job, had them do the work, and, when that was done, had them do something else. Lawrence believed that handing scientists titles, then asking them to do something else, would make them think they had been demoted, which was not the case.[8]

For Lawrence, the key to organization was to identify a leader responsible for a task. His was a style of leadership called "matrix management," wherein a professional with a special type of background, such as chemistry or mechanical engineering, was assigned to a parent division consisting of like-trained professionals. When a program with specific goals was created, a program leader was chosen. The program leader drew experts from parent divisions to form an eclectic group of professionals, then assigned them into positions best meeting program needs. York adopted Lawrence's management style, which gave an unanticipated benefit to the Laboratory: The RAND analysts became just more "matrixed experts" to weapons programs and were readily accepted as members of the team.

Matrix management can easily bruise the egos of ambitious persons seeking individual recognition. But when professionals are properly brought together in this way, it forms an environment that breeds a spirit of innovation into an organization. This is exactly what happened at Livermore. The system worked because each program leader grasped that he or she was responsible for a specific task. The quality of work depended on the talents of the leaders, so the key to success was making good selections. Strong investment into matrix management characterized the Laboratory as different from other scientific establishments of the time.

Duane Sewell, who worked for Lawrence at the Rad Lab, was York's deputy. Lawrence wanted him at the Laboratory and told him not to worry about getting a degree. Sewell's influence in guiding matrix management there is hard to overestimate. In an environment that could have become dominated by sectarian politics, he defined responsibilities for program leaders and made sure they exercised the appropriate authority to get projects done.[9]

York unashamedly managed projects the way he had learned from his mentor. Lawrence regularly came out to the Laboratory every week and toured every nook and cranny. York made it a habit to tour the facility too, often at night and on weekends.[10]

A comparison of management styles between the Laboratory and its sister in New Mexico became inevitable. LASL matured as an organization created at a feverish pace during World War II; it operated in a traditional organizational way, with professionals working together in groups. The Los Alamos structure featured a mixture of Oppenheimer's freewheeling style and General Groves' rigid military style. Many of the physicists originally brought to Los Alamos were educated in Europe, where there was an emphasis on theoretical physics. They were accustomed to proceeding from theory to calculations and finally to experimentation.

At its start, Livermore scientists were predominantly American-trained experimentalists, less wedded to starting with theoretical calculations and more comfortable pursuing designs for which it was "hard to make advanced calculations of expected results."[11] Livermore's roots in the Rad Lab shaped the way it pursued programs. One physicist noted his habit of meticulous care, which he developed to perform cyclotron experiments, served him well when he arrived there in 1955.[12]

This is not to say that everyone at the Laboratory was an experimentalist. Livermore also had its fair share of theoretical physicists and mathematicians in T Division. Their role was to aid design groups by "thinking out of the box." This, too, was an important legacy of Lawrence, for under his management system, theorists were intimately embedded in design groups. They were active participants in the design process, a setup that made design groups highly creative. This matrixed organizational arrangement was so effective, scientists were often only vaguely aware of their parent organization. Los Alamos had its share of excellent experimentalists as well, as is evident from their successful atomic tests. Importantly, its scientists and engineers helped their Livermore counterparts from the beginning. Bradbury instructed his staff to give their California colleagues all assistance available. Indeed, Livermore scientists could not have succeeded in testing their earliest warheads without the active organizational support of LASL staff.

*// // //*

Lawrence's management system was not the only aspect that kick-started the Laboratory, for von Neumann introduced scientists there to the world of computers. Leith, a mathematician and early disciple of computer science, recalled how von Neumann persuaded Laboratory leaders they could never understand what was going on with fusion if they did not start working on numerical methods—computer techniques.[13]

Computers allowed a designer to explore multidimensional problems more readily than a theorist could envision the same complex problem in the mind. This point is important, for it explains a lot about how Livermore was able to progress rapidly in the 1950s. To do a calculation on a computer, a program—or code as it was called—was written to instruct the machine how to do the calculation. When the first computers arrived, there were no codes, so everything had to be done from scratch.

A computer culture took root at Livermore and became an important avenue for physicists to get their ideas accepted. It was von Neumann's habit to encourage those engaged in weapons designs to write a computer code, and many Laboratory leaders who would emerge in its first twenty years had a similar event linking their careers: their first assignment was to write a computer code. This emergence of a computer culture was a legacy of von Neumann, his profound influence on the role the Laboratory later played in the Cold War. May's early experiences in Livermore were a prime example of this. Once he arrived at the Laboratory, von Neumann asked May to write a radiative-transport code for a thermonuclear device. Radiative transport is the science born from studying stars. When astrophysicists, physicists who study stars, do research, they learn how a star creates energy and how it efficiently radiates away that energy. They become experts in how heat is transported through matter, and that science carries the catch phrase "radiative transport." The way a thermonuclear weapon works is for an atomic device to raise the temperature of a mass of thermonuclear fuel and compress it to induce fusion reactions so the fuel releases more energy. Knowing how energy—or thanks to Ludwig Boltzmann, heat—transports itself from the atomic device to the thermonuclear device is a prime example of radiative transport. May was too young to be overwhelmed by the task of writing a radiative transport code; he thought writing complicated codes must be what PhD physicists were expected to do. After leaving von Neumann, he went to his office and pulled down from his bookshelf a physics textbook on radiative transport and wrote a code by directly applying principles of physics from the text.[14] It speaks volumes about May's abilities that his work became a bedrock for the radiative transport codes following it.

The Laboratory's first computer, an IBM-CPC, arrived in November 1952. This was the same type of machine used by Ken Ford to make the Matterhorn-B calculations the year before. It was soon supplemented with an IBM 650 Magnetic Drum Data-Processing Machine. This was the world's first mass-produced computer, with two thousand units created. These early IBM machines lacked features that are standard today, especially memory space, so from the beginning, there was a plan to procure a more robust computer.

Teller's response to von Neumann's call for a computer was to order the purchase of a Universal Automatic Computer, or UNIVAC. When the purchase order went out in September 1952, one physicist and four mathematicians went to the Eckert-Mauchly plant in Philadelphia for training. In November eight more Laboratory mathematicians joined the first group. UNIVAC No. 5 came under the jurisdiction of the Laboratory on November 22, 1952, after it was used by CBS television to predict that Dwight D. Eisenhower had won the presidential election.[15]

The UNIVAC had a large console housing a series of switches set to address the machine's one thousand words of memory. Its data system was a set of ten tape units designed to write data with the tape running forward; for it to read data, the tape was run backward. These served as an expanded main memory for the computer. With its 5,200 tubes, kilometers of wire, and the Laboratory's demanding schedule, the UNIVAC needed constant maintenance.

The UNIVAC had an unusual method of storing information temporarily—a mercury acoustic line. To do an arithmetic calculation—for instance, to add a number from a select location to a number in the register—the result of the calculation often had to be temporarily stored while other operations continued. Later, the computer had to recall the stored number to use it again. The UNIVAC did this by changing the digital representation of a number, a series of 1s and 0s, into a sound pulse started at one end of a five-foot-long tube of mercury vapor. As the pulse traveled down this length, which took two-thousandths of a second, the computer performed other operations. Then the pulse was picked up at the other end of the tube and translated back into electronic data. It was a bizarre system, but adept operators like Leith learned to use it effectively.

Leith did all three functions of code building: developing the physics, working out mathematical solutions, and programming the resulting code. As he developed his skills, he became one of America's most influential computer scientists. Years later he made a three-dimensional computer model of the earth's atmosphere, partitioning it into five-by-five zones of 5° latitude by 5° longitude. He was recognized as a world leader in climate modeling, in 1970 helping found the National Oceanic and Atmospheric Agency, headquartered in Boulder, Colorado.[16]

An effective programmer like Leith had to have the patience of Job to write computer codes, for in those days codes were written in machine language, which is much more difficult than writing a code while using a compiler, like Fortran. For instance, to perform even a simple arithmetic operation in machine language, Leith had to state precisely which memory location a fetch instruction was to occupy and then identify the exact memory address of the datum to be retrieved.

To enter computer codes into the computer, the UNIVAC used a Unityper, a modified typewriter console that transferred typed data directly onto a metal magnetic tape. The tape's contents were then read into memory. This was not like texting on a smart phone: for one thing, the Unityper did not signal back to the typist what character had been input—it was like typing with your eyes closed.[17]

The first person hired by the Laboratory to specifically prepare input for the UNIVAC was Cecelia Larsen. She came up with a method for checking typed input for mistakes, creating two tapes and then comparing one with the other. A single mother and the daughter of Portuguese immigrants, Larsen was born and raised in Livermore, getting a job first at the Rad Lab in Berkeley. Once the Livermore site opened in 1952, she took advantage of the opportunity to work closer to home and, even though she had no experience with computers, won a position in the new computations group as a data-input specialist.[18]

Larsen was good at it, extraordinarily good. She was promoted to lead a group of data-input specialists, and her team, all of whom she hired, were extraordinary in their ability to master the critical function of accurately and swiftly preparing tapes for the many impatient users of the UNIVAC.[19] Larsen became legendary among Laboratory physicists for her propensity to have a conversation with a computer user while she continued to unerringly type computer codes onto the Unityper.

*# # #*

Another important source of support to the Laboratory was John Wheeler, that icon of nuclear physics. When his contract with the AEC was fulfilled, Wheeler dismantled the Matterhorn-B program but continued to work with physicists in Livermore, helping them tackle the enormously difficult challenges they faced. Other Matterhorn veterans followed him to the Laboratory, including astrophysicist Louis Henyey, who came along with two graduate students, Dick Levee and Bill Grasberger.

While with the Matterhorn-B Project, Grasberger had been introduced to radiative transport codes. Once back in Berkeley he completed his PhD requirements and Teller recruited him into T Division. There Grasberger joined May's radiative transport group and resumed his work with codes, although at a deeper level than anything he had done at Princeton. Henyey and Levee, meanwhile, became consultants to T Division.[20]

Another recruit from the Matterhorn-B Project was an Army captain named Carl Haussmann. He had graduated from West Point in 1946 and went to graduate school at Pennsylvania State University, where he received a master's degree in physics. Wheeler heard about him from an Army officer already working at Princeton, then called him up and offered him a position. As Matterhorn-B wound down, Haussmann approached Sewell and York to see if they would accept him if the Army assigned him to Livermore; they did.

Haussmann arrived at the Laboratory in 1953, was assigned to T Division, and matrixed into Brown's Megaton Group. Two years later he resigned his Army commission but stayed on at the Laboratory as a full-time physicist. The managerial skills he developed in the Army made Haussmann especially valued by Brown, who eventually appointed him to be his deputy.[21] May thought if Haussmann had had a PhD, he would have been director of the Laboratory.[22]

The "Matterhorn veterans"—Wheeler, Henyey, Grasberger, Levee, and Haussmann—became invaluable to the Laboratory in its earliest days. Physicists there eagerly sought out the highly respected Wheeler. They surrounded him inside renovated World War II barracks and absorbed tidbits of advice he might share with them, which became an important part of his legacy to the Laboratory. The Matterhorn veterans helped introduce the untested Rad Lab veterans into the world of thermonuclear research.

Wheeler was only one of several world-class physicists who mentored these young and eager professionals. The Rad Lab scientists who had arrived on that September day in 1952 were coached by some of the best scientific minds in the country. This injection of intellectual power soon made itself felt. In addition to von Neumann, Wheeler, and Henyey regularly coming to Livermore, an organizational chart of the Laboratory, dated February/March 1954, listed the following eminent scientists as consultants: David Griggs, Gregory Breit, Richard Courant, Charles Critchfield, George Gamow, and Emil Konopinski.

# 9

//////////////////

# *An Inauspicious Start*

Y ork may have had his hands full recruiting, organizing, and putting the physical plant together, but more importantly he had to move the Laboratory toward its primary mission of designing nuclear weapons—and that had to happen quickly. The creation of the Laboratory had been a hard fight in Washington; now it was time to deliver.

Being the sole member of the Laboratory with experience as a nuclear-weapons designer, Teller's views were highly regarded. He was not shy about expressing them either, which had not changed since he went before the GAC in December 1951 to argue for a second weapons laboratory. With Livermore operational at last, he felt it should concentrate on thermonuclear research and hydride weapons. Work on the hydrogen bomb was self-evident, although no one thought it would be easy. It was Teller's interest in hydrides, compounds of uranium mixed with deuterium, that was curious, for their use had never achieved prominence at Los Alamos.

Teller's interest in a uranium hydride atomic bomb had to do with using the heat from nuclear fission in an atomic device to cause embedded deuterium nuclei to fuse together. His passion for this had started with a discovery made by Fermi that had helped win him the Nobel Prize. Fermi had discovered that slowing down neutrons made them more likely to stimulate nuclear reactions—like causing nuclear fission. Adding deuterium to the nuclear fuel slowed down neutrons. The physics logic went like this: with slower neutrons causing more fissions, less uranium-235 was needed to form a critical mass. Teller called this symbiotic relationship—getting more heat from a smaller critical mass—an autocatalytic interaction.

Reducing the critical mass of uranium-235 had been a hot topic in the Manhattan Project when it was discovered Lawrence was having problems at the Y-12 Plant. It took all of his gifts to keep that calutron project going. (Lawrence once ordered the local fire department to douse the calutrons with water to keep them from overheating.) Scientists at Los Alamos wondered whether enough enriched uranium could be produced at Y-12 to make a critical mass. One can imagine Teller and Fermi arguing the case for using uranium hydride since less uranium-235 would be required. Teller pressed his argument for a hydride bomb to Oppenheimer, who assigned the problem to a Theoretical Division group leader, Richard Feynman.

Feynman, who would later win the Nobel Prize, conducted five series of calculations using various combinations of deuterium with uranium to see which one offered the most promise for a weapon. The results were sketchy. He said the explosion would be small but sharp and concluded more needed to be known about the physical characteristics of a hydride. By that time, the calutrons at Y-12 had produced the needed enriched uranium, the crisis had passed, and Los Alamos physicists kept with a design using pure uranium metal. Some hydride research continued after the war, but a panel of physicists thought the concept held limited value and recommended LASL abandon it. Bradbury accepted the recommendations and terminated the hydride program in 1946.[1]

Nevertheless, Teller steadfastly pushed for a hydride device long after weapons using uranium metal were successfully tested. Likely, he thought a hydride fuel would induce fusion reactions, thus making a hydride device a hybrid atomic/hydrogen bomb. In a paper written in 1947, he suggested a design for a hydride device, addressing obstacles to creating such a weapon and suggesting ways to overcome them.

York needed to conduct a nuclear test quickly, and if Teller advocated hydride devices, a test of a fuel seemed to be as good an idea as any other. The next series of nuclear tests, Operation Upshot, was scheduled to take place at the Nevada Test Site in the spring of 1953, so participating in that series became the target. Designing a device, manufacturing and testing components, and transporting the experiment to Nevada within a seven-month period were ambitious goals.

*# # #*

As Livermore physicists tackled the design of a hydride device, unforeseen challenges of the Cold War began to shape the political climate of the country. Eisenhower took office as president of the United States in January 1953. The Korean War by then was two and a half years old, and one of Eisenhower's election promises was to find a way out of that Northeast Asian quagmire. As a former Army general, the new president might have been expected to support large defense budgets. Instead, he believed the foundation of military strength was economic strength, and a bankrupt America was prone to fall victim to Soviet aggression. It was a rude awakening for Eisenhower to learn that the nation's debt was five times greater than it had been before World War II; his budget director forecast it would exceed the congressionally set limit within the next two years. The president stated his political goals emphatically, "the first order of business is the elimination of the federal deficit."[2]

That attitude made Eisenhower amenable to accept arguments that nuclear weapons provided a more economical means of defending the country. (Hypothetically, an atomic bomb could replace an armored division, which cost millions of dollars a day.) After reviewing a national-security study titled "New Look," he adopted a strategic defense policy called "Massive Retaliation." This was announced in a speech by Secretary of State John Foster Dulles before the Council of Foreign Relations in New York. Dulles said the Soviets were planning to gradually divide and weaken the free nations of the world by overextending them into efforts that were, in Lenin's words, "beyond their strength."

Dulles said crises like the Korean War were sapping the military strength of the United States and feared there would come a time of economic and military weakness when it would be, as Stalin called it, "the moment for the decisive blow." Dulles concluded, if the country went about the world committing troops to stave off piecemeal communist aggression, as it had in Korea, it would soon be exhausted to the point of bankruptcy, leading ultimately to the decay of its true security: "The way to deter aggression is for the free community to be willing and able to respond vigorously at places and with means of its own choosing." Coming to the point of his lecture, that meant reinforcing conventional forces with the massive retaliatory power of the country's nuclear arsenal.[3]

The Massive Retaliation speech enhanced the role of the Strategic Air Command; indeed, it bolstered official Air Force strategy as stated in the *Doctrine of Atomic Air Warfare* in 1948.[4] That strategy was a legacy of the bombing campaigns of World War II, when massive air strikes by Eighth and Fifteenth Air Forces were directed against the heartland of Germany. With the advent of massively destructive nuclear weapons, atomic bombs could replace fleets of aircraft to accomplish the same purpose against the Soviet Union.

Massive Retaliation was meant to avoid engaging soldiers in regional conflicts, so the Army's budget declined. This laming of conventional military capability became so bitter an issue that General Matthew Ridgway, the man who had salvaged Eighth Army from destruction by Chinese armies in Korea, resigned as Army chief of staff. Ridgway predicted such a policy opened the door for the Soviet Union to engage in foreign adventures at a level lower than would prompt the United States to use its nuclear forces. With the budgets of conventional forces strictly limited, there was little the country could do to respond to such foreign adventures, so, the general argued, Massive Retaliation simply encouraged them.[5]

Nevertheless, Eisenhower was adamant—despite Ridgway's objections, the United States would rely on its nuclear arsenal to counter whatever acts of communist aggression emerged in the world. The chairman of the Joint Chiefs of Staff, Admiral Arthur Radford, told officers at the Naval War College the president's Massive Retaliation strategy meant nuclear forces were now the country's primary forces. Conventional forces were relegated to a secondary role—nuclear weapons, atomic and thermonuclear, would be used in the next major war.[6]

Eisenhower's strategy got LASL heavily engaged in developing nuclear warheads, especially for the Air Force. If the United States had to engage in actual massive retaliation, it would primarily have to be carried out by SAC bombers. This raised a troublesome issue that led to countless debates about the nature of America's nuclear deterrent force. RAND had conducted a study that concluded SAC airbases could not withstand a massive

Soviet air attack.[7] If so, then Massive Retaliation rested on a bed of sand, its deterrent force vulnerable to being destroyed in a surprise attack.

// // //

The scientists and engineers at Livermore probably had little inkling their work would soon be center stage in the political debates emerging over the country's future. At the moment they were concentrating their collective energy to seeing their institution become a nuclear-weapons laboratory. Before they could deal with how they fit into the national-defense structure, they had to design a nuclear weapon that worked and see it successfully tested.

The opportunity to test in Nevada was a new capability. The impetus to create a proving ground there came from a need to better prepare for large tests in the Pacific. In late 1950, after construction and procurement orders were well along for Operation Greenhouse in the Pacific in 1951, the desire for accurate yield measurements led to a decision to launch a series of low-yield nuclear experiments, called Operation Ranger, to test and calibrate diagnostic equipment.

The time required to arrange nuclear tests overseas was excessive, so the AEC searched for a suitable place within the continental United States to conduct land-based nuclear tests. There was concern about nuclear fallout on American soil, but AEC scientists felt they could control radioactive fallout either by limiting the yield of the weapon and hoisting it onto a tower, or by dropping an atomic bomb from an aircraft and detonating it at altitude.

A survey team led by Los Alamos test director Alvin Graves recommended a location sixty or so miles northwest of Las Vegas, Nevada, known as Frenchman Flat, a portion of the Air Force's Nellis Bombing and Gunnery Range. On December 18, 1950, two days after declaring a state of emergency during the Korean War, President Truman authorized the AEC to establish a nuclear test site at Frenchman Flat; in 1951 it became the Nevada Proving Ground.[8]

On July 8, 1951, the AEC officially renamed the continental nuclear testing site the Nevada Test Site (NTS). Devices having yields of about fifty kilotons (50kt) or less, roughly three times the yield of the Nagasaki bomb, could be detonated in Nevada while saving effort and funding compared to the massive operations in the Pacific.[9] Public fears about atmospheric testing persisted, and the AEC later had to quell a rumor that nuclear tests would contaminate the water supply of the city of Los Angeles.[10]

Livermore was assigned two nuclear events in the upcoming Operation Upshot, and preparations proceeded to test devices with hydride fuels. The yields for the UCRL tests were supposed to be small, around one kiloton, to make the work of diagnostics easier. The deuterium composition of the two devices varied slightly; otherwise they were identical.

The Laboratory's head of engineering, Jim Bell, gave one of his engineers, Wallace Decker, the job of drawing up the blueprints for the devices. Decker recalled getting the assignment: "Within a couple of days Bell had started me on the design drawings, and I must say he started me on them, because I didn't know how to draw a nuclear device."[11]

The leader of the Small Atomic Device Group, Art Biehl, led the design team. The general attitude of his team was that the hydride would be a more adventurous experiment than most of those done previously. Lawrence took an active interest in the experiments. He usually listened in briefly on many of the design discussions, encouraging everyone to do the best they could but not to worry excessively about the chance of failure of the device to give a significant yield.[12]

The two Livermore tests were called Ruth and Rae, named after two administrators—Edward Teller's secretary, Ruth Brockett, and Jim Bell's secretary, Rae Duffus. In October 1952 York gave a rationale for the tests in a preoperational report. He said since Teller suggested a hydride fuel was desirable for a hydrogen bomb, they had to know how the material behaved in a thermonuclear environment. Monthly Laboratory progress reports to the AEC emphasized how uncertain physicists were in the compressibility of hydride fuels because, as Feynman had discovered during the Manhattan Project, adequate equations of state for hydrides did not exist. (An equation of state describes, among other things, how a substance will compress when it is subjected to shockwaves from an implosion.) Further, a hydride device will create a burst of neutrons with energies different than previously experienced, so a test was needed to see how well uranium nuclei fissioned in such conditions.[13]

Officials wondered how high to make the tower for the Ruth event. The designers talked about a yield of one or two kilotons, so test officials thought a fifty-foot tower would do. When the test director asked what the maximum yield could be, one field engineer gave a figure of thirty kilotons, which would have been incredible. Nevertheless, the official decided on a three-hundred-foot tower. Firing the device on a higher tower minimized the entrainment of ground debris by the fireball, reducing fallout.

The Ruth and Rae devices were assembled in Albuquerque and transported to NTS. Ruth was set to go off the morning of March 31, 1953. Typically, the Nevada desert in March is windy and cold. Conditions the day before the test were just that; there was a dust storm, then rain, and finally snow. The Ruth device was hoisted to the top of the three-hundred-foot tower, and Laboratory engineer Wallace Decker led a crew of men up to do final assembly. The tower elevator did not reach to the top of the platform, so they had to climb up the final thirty feet on a staircase carrying his tools. Decker suffered from acrophobia—as he rattled along inside the elevator cage, he could feel his symptoms erupt. To control his vertigo on the staircase, he kept his eyes glued straight ahead, not daring to look down as he clambered up the steps.

Unfortunately, the construction worker who had put the staircase together secured the next to last step with two bolts rather than four. When Decker placed his boot on the step, it rotated and he lost his balance, falling forward against the railing and staring at the ground three hundred feet below. His heart felt like it was in his throat. Decker steadied himself, riveted his glance straight ahead into the horizon, and waited for the dizziness to go away. Then he straightened up, turned toward the top of the tower, stepped onto the platform, pulled out a wrench, and started to secure an atomic bomb to the top of the swaying metal tower.[14]

The wind caused the platform at the top to shake, giving the crewmen trouble as they tried to fit tiny screws into place. It took them several hours to complete the task and allow the arming crew to go up and do their work. Duane Sewell was on the scene with the arming crew. This was his first nuclear test. It was cold and black outside (around 2 a.m.) as he went up in the elevator to the top of the tower. The wind was thirty-five knots, and lights mounted on loose joints were swinging much like chandeliers in an earthquake.[15]

In the early morning darkness after the arming crew had finished, the high-explosive charge in the Ruth device was detonated, but there was only a small flash of light. The test was a "fizzle"—a failure—the device's yield was so small the lower parts of the tower remained standing. The Livermore engineers took a lot of joshing from a Los Alamos test team about the pile of debris left on the desert floor at ground zero; it was supposed to have been incinerated.

Army officials were annoyed because they had planted tanks, trucks, and other military equipment around the tower that were supposed to have been destroyed. Instead, the small blast had barely caused them to move. That was not so bad, but the equipment had become contaminated with radioactive residue and needed to be cleansed. The weak shockwave had barely registered on the sensors embedded in the trucks and tanks, so no data were collected.

Philosophically speaking Laboratory managers argued the poor results vindicated the decision to conduct the test since it confirmed they were dealing in a nuclear regime in which the behavior of the nuclear fuel was unknown. York said as much in a telegram to Captain Haywood at AEC headquarters that revealed the best interpolations and estimates of experts were flat wrong. That was good enough reason, he insisted, to continue with the Rae event, which was scheduled to occur less than two weeks later. Last-minute changes were instituted in an attempt to raise the projected yield of this second device.

Because of the poor performance of the Ruth device, the height of the tower for the Rae event was reduced to one hundred feet. This meant there was no elevator in the tower, so the components for the assembly had to be carried up a staircase. Some items weighed over one hundred pounds, requiring two men to carry them. When the device was finally secured to the tower the night before the test, it was covered with a canvas tarp. Written on the cover was the title of a popular Jerry Lee Lewis song, "Great Balls of Fire," to honor a fellow mechanical engineer, Bill Twitchell, who was terminally ill and always sang it at work.[16]

The Rae event occurred on April 11, 1953. It, too, fizzled. Decker, who was still in charge of the assembly crew, thought the explosion was sickeningly small as he turned with some embarrassment to a Los Alamos crew standing nearby, who grinned knowingly. Some of the LASL engineers teased the Livermore men, saying they should not have put the canvas on the device because it blocked the light from the explosion. At that time there was a strong feeling that the Livermore folks should not have been there—who needed another laboratory?[17]

Both tests suffered from a basic flaw. Teller was fixated on developing a hydride warhead, perhaps to save fuel or perhaps to induce fusion reactions inside an atomic device. That was all very good, but he failed to fully consider unintended consequences. As the hydride imploded and approached a critical state, nuclear fissions heated up the mass, causing it to expand. The neutrons released by nuclear fissions, moderated (slowed) by the deuterium in the fuel, were not fast enough to cause further fissions. That meant the fuel expanded at a rate greater than the rate energy was produced until the fuel was no longer a critical mass. The device gave a sudden, but small, burst of energy, then stopped.

Before the tests, Laboratory physicists did not think to question Teller and the path he was taking them down. That changed after these tests. Biehl, the physicist who had led the Ruth and Rae design teams, had had enough. He later announced he was leaving the Laboratory to take a job in Los Angeles, so York had to replace him quickly with someone who could lead and inspire a group of disheartened physicists. After getting recommendations from Lawrence and Alvarez, he offered the position to Johnny Foster, still doing basic science research in the Sherwood Project. Foster accepted, taking responsibility for running the atomic-weapons group. Keeping with the Greek prefix motif of Brown's Livermore Megaton Group, York called Foster's new organization the Livermore Hectoton Group (hectoton meaning one hundred tons).

At first there seemed to be some self-denial that the twin tests had failed. A post-test report stated, "The Upshot program was quite successful in that almost everything worked reasonably well. The bombs were small, as planned." The incongruity of this statement came out two sentences later: "The first explosion left about 125 feet of the 300-foot tower still standing." A subsequent report suggested it was a good thing the devices had fizzled, for if the devices had delivered yields exactly as predicted, Livermore would have been criticized for conducting unnecessary tests. It seemed as if Laboratory management was trying to put a silver lining on events. Teller thought starting operations and conducting two nuclear tests within seven to eight months of the Laboratory's creation was a considerable achievement in itself.[18] But this self-denial did not last long.

Having accepted the results of the Hydride Shots, as they were called, the Laboratory staff prepared for the next series of tests, Operation Castle. This would present them with an opportunity to test a thermonuclear weapon, which after all was the reason for creating the Laboratory in the first place. Teller showed no sign of changing the experimental path they were on. The Hydride Shots were setbacks, but they were not such devastating blows as to cause him to deviate from his plans.

The Hydride Shots presented an opportunity for critics to comment. LASL director Bradbury had been a vociferous critic of UCRL, stating how hard it would be for the new laboratory "to make progress in a field [thermonuclear research] beyond its current frontiers."[19] He made it clear he disagreed with the decision to create a laboratory at Livermore. Echoing AEC chairman Dean's concerns, he said Livermore competed for limited material resources needed for nuclear research and needlessly drew talent away from Los Alamos. Seizing on the Livermore fizzles, Bradbury questioned the rationale for creating a second laboratory, claiming it was constrained by the limitations of its staff and confirming his prediction that recruiting an adequate scientific staff would be a problem.

Since the AEC stated its rationale for creating the Livermore laboratory was to concentrate on a more fundamental level of nuclear research than was being pursued at LASL, Bradbury argued the Hydride Shots were hardly fundamental experiments. He said the AEC should restrict Livermore scientists to simply supporting LASL's nuclear-test program with diagnostics, just as they had been doing since the George event two years earlier.[20]

This was not an auspicious start for the Laboratory, as York later admitted:

> The two devices that we did in Nevada were not conceived as weapons but had as their purpose exploring intimate mixtures of uranium and deuterium, wherever that might lead. The fact that they gave small yields was something of a disappointment, but not a great one. In retrospect it may not have been a very smart thing to do. But they were conceived of as a way to get started: something to do, something to calculate, something to make, something to take out there and test, leading in a possibly interesting direction. Regardless of their performance, they were a remarkable accomplishment for an organization which started from zero; zero staff and zero facilities.[21]

# 10
///////////////

# *Hitting Rock Bottom*

O peration Castle was the fifth series of nuclear tests conducted in the Pacific Proving Grounds that lasted from February to May 1954. This was during a period of heightened tensions in the Cold War as French troops were fighting for their survival at Dien Bien Phu in Vietnam. With the success of the Mike event in November 1952, the Defense Department's objective for Castle was to task the AEC to demonstrate that a one-megaton hydrogen bomb could be dropped from a strategic bomber. LASL planned to test five devices, while UCRL planned to test two.

These were all prototype devices, so none of the tests actually involved a bomber dropping a hydrogen bomb. Instead, four of the devices were to be placed on platforms standing a mere seven feet above ground level, while the remaining three were mounted on barges. All but one of the Castle events, including the two Livermore devices, were to take place at Bikini; the lone exception would test at Eniwetok. This was Teller's opportunity to finally demonstrate his design of a thermonuclear weapon.

Livermore assembly teams arrived early at Bikini to prepare for their tests, which would occur after several of the Los Alamos events. On the day before Castle's first nuclear test, called the Bravo event, the teams exited Bikini's lagoon aboard Navy landing boats and approached the MSTS *Ainsworth*, a military sea transport ship, where they climbed up Jacob's ladders and scampered onto its main deck. The *Ainsworth* had four decks reserved for transporting personnel. Higher-ranking officials berthed in A Deck, up in the superstructure. Wally Decker, who would lead the assembly of Livermore's two devices, was on B Deck, which housed midlevel supervisors, four to a cabin. Most of C Deck was taken up with a galley and mess hall. That left D Deck, below sea level, where physicists, engineers, and contract workers were berthed twelve per cabin. The plan was to observe a test the next morning and disembark in the afternoon.

Early the next morning, passengers mustered onto the main deck to witness the Bravo event. This LASL device had some of its thermonuclear fuel replaced with an inert material so its yield would not exceed Pacific Proving Grounds limits. The personnel put on dark glasses and faced toward ground zero, located some thirty-five to fifty miles away. The Bravo device was detonated on March 1, 1954, and its yield, fifteen megatons, greatly exceeded expectations. The material placed inside the device was not inert after all but contributed energy to the explosion. Decker's first sensation was heat, like an oven door opening in his face, "then I watched the fireball growing, and this one kept growing and growing and growing. I felt, My God, it's filling the whole horizon."[1]

Bravo's fallout cloud of radioactive particles, ranging from about one-thousandth to one-fiftieth of an inch in diameter, contaminated an elongated area extending over 330 miles downwind and varying in width up to 60 miles. It covered populated sections of the Marshall Islands, and over 250 Marshallese, as well as American servicemen stationed on the islands, experienced enough radiation to cause beta burning of their skin.[2] A Japanese fishing vessel, the *Daigo Fukuryu Maru*, which ironically translates as "Lucky Dragon," was caught in the fallout plume, and one of the twenty-three fishermen on board later died of radiation sickness.[3]

Aboard the *Ainsworth*, the captain became confused and headed the ship toward the fallout cloud, entering it about ninety minutes after the event. Everyone was confined to quarters, and ventilation systems, including air conditioning, were shut off. Temperatures inside cabins reached 118° Fahrenheit, and men in D Deck, where temperatures were even higher, were stifled by the heat. The ship cleared the cloud after several hours, and hazards-material teams washed down the deck. They then cordoned off areas so the men could leave their quarters and assemble on deck. By six in the evening, they felt human again. The next morning the personnel would be back on Bikini preparing for their own tests.

Livermore's scientists had been tasked to measure fusion reactions in several of the Castle tests, including the Bravo event. Stirling Colgate, a physicist trained at Cornell and Berkeley, led this team. He designed a diagnostic called, appropriately, the Gamma-Neutron Experiment, or GANEX, which measured gamma rays and neutrons emitted by thermonuclear reactions. An heir to the Colgate fortune associated with toothpaste, Colgate loved physics and the challenges it brought him to solve. He thrived with designing a diagnostic instrument to measure radiation from a thermonuclear device, all while shielding the instrument from an atomic blast.

For the Bravo event, the GANEX used a mile-long pipe, one end of which pointed at the device, while the other end led to a bunker holding instruments. An array of oscilloscopes recorded signals coming from the detectors: observing the intensity of reactions told physicists the number of neutrons going down the pipe, while measuring the amount of time it took neutrons to reach a detector provided their speed and energy. Knowing neutron energies, they could conclude what types of reactions were taking place. For instance, if they detected neutrons with energies of 14MeV (MeV stands for "Million electron Volts," a unit of energy commonly used by nuclear physicists), they deduced those neutrons were created by the fusion of deuterium with tritium—a sure sign thermonuclear reactions had occurred. By contrast, neutrons released by nuclear fission have energies that often differ from neutrons released by nuclear fusion.

In the weeks leading up to the test, Colgate examined photographs of previous atomic tests. He noticed that surges of electrons poured out of a nuclear explosion along the guy wires holding up the test towers. After some consideration, he realized his metallic pipe could suffer from the same effect. He calculated about one kiloton of energy would surge down the GANEX pipe and strike his bunker, so material was placed atop the structure to withstand the energy surge. When the test was conducted, the expected surge struck Colgate's bunker, which barely survived. Even so, GANEX worked remarkably well, obtaining signals needed for a measurement of the thermonuclear activity of the device.[4]

In the following weeks LASL tested its other devices, and all performed well, a vindication of LASL's scientific abilities. Unfortunately, Lewis Strauss, who had replaced Gordon Dean as chairman of the AEC, instituted a news blackout about details associated with these events. News reporters had to figure out the facts on their own. Since Teller was the most vocal advocate for the hydrogen bomb, they credited him and the new laboratory in Livermore for the successful string of tests. Senior Los Alamos officials were livid. This championing of UCRL over what should have been a resounding LASL success story strained already tense relations between managers of the two weapons laboratories.[5]

*// // //*

Livermore's turn to test arrived, and its two entries in Operation Castle seem like anomalies. It is ironic, given the successful Los Alamos devices were based on the Teller-Ulam concept for the new Super, that Teller went back to the classic Super for the two UCRL tests. Los Alamos had an experienced professional staff that could challenge Teller about slipping back to his earlier ideas. But at Livermore no one was prepared to question his judgment.

The reason Teller would revert to an old design might be summed up in a single word: Fermi. Like other physicists of his time, he idolized Fermi and unabashedly accepted anything the Italian scientist said as being the product of genius. Fermi had suggested the Super concept to Teller in the first place and, during the Manhattan Project, had done the calculations that laid out the basic principles for the classic device. Teller stayed true to his friend and mentor, keeping his original ideas.

Despite the mediocre performances of the Ruth and Rae devices, Teller remained confident and saw no need to make changes to his plan for the Castle event. His thermonuclear device was called the Ramrod, and it was truly a classic Super. Teller thought measuring the performance of a complete Super was too complicated an affair, so as 1954 approached, he decided not to test his entire concept, just part of it.

Brown's Megaton Group calculated every aspect of the device without the benefit of having a precedent to draw on. They had help: RAND physicists, including Albert and Richard Latter, David Griggs, Ernie Plesset, and Herman Kahn, lent their support. They had to decide how far to place the Ramrod from an atomic device, the primary, and what size the primary should be. Their determinations relied on calculations done on radiative-transport codes written by Mike May's group.

At a biweekly meeting of the Megaton Group, May sketched his calculations for segments of the experiment on a blackboard. Bill Grasberger, formerly with the Matterhorn-B program and now a member of the group, used a Matterhorn-B code to calculate other select parts of the problem. By April 1953, they had enough data to request a specific Los Alamos atomic primary to drive the Ramrod. (Because of the Ruth and Rae fizzles, Livermore at the time had no successful primaries that they could use.)

As calculations progressed, it became evident segments of Teller's concept for the Ramrod had to be changed. More calculations brought more changes, with one of the more exotic being an alteration suggested by Herb York that made the device resemble a mace, a Medieval weapon. Teller was concerned the purity of his original Ramrod design was getting lost, so a compromise was offered and designs for two devices were pursued. The Echo event in Castle would feature the Ramrod without significant changes, while the Koon event would test the device with features dictated by code calculations.

The Koon device went through one reconfiguration after another. What stymied designers was their inexperience in dealing with radiative transport calculations. How did x-rays coming from an atomic device react with the channel material positioned between the primary and secondary? The situation became a double-edged sword: the designers' confidence grew as the quality of their calculations got better, but the improved calculations revealed greater uncertainties about the performance of the device.

A minor crisis over the design of the Koon device erupted in July 1953 when they found the choice of materials for the radiation channel was not ideal for the distance they had chosen between the primary and the secondary. Teller recommended changes, and Brown proposed a solution requiring smaller alterations. The matter was settled when additional calculations suggested the problem had been overstated, and the design went back to its original configuration. Finally, by January 1954, designs for Livermore's two devices were finalized, and blueprints were issued to engineers to begin manufacturing parts.[6]

Deputy Laboratory Director Sewell was learning lessons about the economics of conducting a nuclear test featuring original research: costs greatly exceeded the budget. An estimate for material had been $10,000, but the actual cost ran up to $80,000. Rental costs for an IBM-CPC computer overran estimates as well. There was a fear the Laboratory would use up its resources, its annual budget being about $2 million to $3 million, before the nuclear test even occurred.

The Koon device was transported to Bikini aboard the USS *Curtis.* Military aircraft flew in other nuclear components separately. The experimental device was a substantial affair, being the size of a railway car and weighing forty-five tons. The final assembly was placed on railroad tracks and consisted of the Los Alamos primary mounted onto one end and the Livermore secondary mounted on the other end; the radiation channel was mounted on its own rolling stock in the middle. The GANEX, the same diagnostic instrument designed by Colgate for the Bravo event, was set up to look directly into the secondary.

Original plans had called for the Echo event to take place in early March, followed two weeks later by the Koon event, but then things changed. The unexpected size of the Bravo blast contaminated the area around the Echo device, so that event was rescheduled for late April. This meant the Koon device would be tested before its simpler cousin, the Ramrod.

The day before the Koon event, assembly crews went aboard the *Ainsworth*. That afternoon the men of the arming crew, technicians who armed the device by connecting an electrical power source to it, were helicoptered back to ground zero. They completed their work in time for the event to take place early the next morning, April 6, 1954. The resulting test was a bust. From what anyone could tell, practically nothing associated with the Livermore portion of the event worked correctly. Considering this sad outcome, York, in consultation with Brown, Sewell, and Teller, canceled the Echo event.[7]

The failure of the Koon device brought a short, intense period of gloom to the scientists of Livermore, even though most were too junior to worry about all the ramifications it could have on their careers. Grasberger walked into a lecture hall for a post-shot briefing, seating himself toward the rear of the hall. He was getting comfortable when a man came in and sat beside him, introducing himself with a smile, "Hi, I'm Ernest Lawrence." Grasberger, who knew perfectly well whom he was talking to, introduced himself and told Lawrence what his job was and the role he had played in the Koon event.

The two discussed the test briefly, then Lawrence rose and went to the front of the hall to address all those gathered. He told them not to be discouraged over the results of the test. Having a perfect string of successes was not important, he said; what was important was what one learned from the experiment. The strongest memory Grasberger took from the meeting was reassurance, the feeling Lawrence was with them and they were all in this campaign together. It was classic Lawrence, displaying his leadership qualities at their finest.[8]

Montgomery Johnson, a distinguished physicist at the Laboratory and the same age as Lawrence and Teller, led a team to examine the data from the Koon event. His conclusions about what went wrong have stood up to the passage of time. He determined the calculations of energy flowing throughout the device had been wrong. May agreed with him, saying comparisons of the radiative transport calculations with measurements of the output of the Los Alamos primary had shown they differed by a factor of two. The device's design had been based on those calculations, so it was not optimal and contributed to its failure.[9] Dealing with failure was difficult enough for the Livermore team, but events in Washington, D.C., were making things worse.

*# # #*

The 1950s included the era of McCarthyism, fueled by an aroused public wary of communism. Dramatic episodes like the British arrest of Soviet agent Klaus Fuchs for espionage and the spy trial of Julius and Ethel Rosenberg in 1953 made newspaper headlines. This was the background in which a drama involving Oppenheimer played out.

Oppenheimer himself set the stage: for years he had associations with communists and communist causes. Most significant in the events to come, he had lied to investigators about attempts of the Communist Party to obtain atomic secrets from him. Oppenheimer could be an arrogant man, and those with whom he disagreed, especially about the hydrogen bomb, had felt his sharp wit and acerbic tongue. It now led some to question his motives.[10]

This episode started with a letter written to FBI director J. Edgar Hoover by William Borden, former chief of staff of the Joint Committee on Atomic Energy. Borden said Oppenheimer had made monetary contributions to the Communist Party and noted that the physicist's wife, younger brother, mistress, and many friends were communists. He added that Oppenheimer had recruited known communists to work on wartime projects and had made contacts with Soviet espionage agents. Finally, Borden said Oppenheimer used his position as chairman of the GAC to oppose research on the Super.

Eisenhower had recently issued Executive Order 10450, which required government agencies to review personnel files to identify those who might be security risks. Borden's letter made it plain Oppenheimer's file warranted review. On December 3, 1953, the president met with AEC chairman Strauss and ordered him to suspend Oppenheimer's Q clearance until a commission hearing could be completed to determine whether he was a security risk.[11]

Acting on the president's order, Strauss called in Kenneth Nichols— the same Army engineer officer who had helped Lawrence during the Manhattan Project—who was then the AEC general manager. Strauss directed him to have the AEC general counsel draft a letter to suspend Oppenheimer's Q clearance. Nichols acted immediately and ordered the counsel to write the letter, then reviewed the draft himself.

The gist of the document said Oppenheimer had lied about a man named Chevalier, who had asked him to pass Manhattan Project information to the Soviet Consulate in San Francisco. It also brought out Oppenheimer's opposition to the Super. Nichols told Strauss he thought mentioning that opposition was a mistake and should be removed, but he had no qualms noting Oppenheimer's cavalier attitude toward the secrecy of the atomic project. The chairman disagreed, and the clause outlining Oppenheimer's opposition to thermonuclear research stayed in the letter.[12]

Strauss met with Oppenheimer on the afternoon of December 21, with Nichols present, and informed him the president had ordered his clearance revoked. Oppenheimer could either resign as chairman of the GAC or demand a hearing to have his clearance restored. Nichols showed Oppenheimer the letter written by the general counsel. It would be sent to him officially if he declined to resign. Strauss asked for his reply within a day.[13]

Oppenheimer recruited Lloyd K. Garrison, a great-grandson of the famous abolitionist William Lloyd Garrison, to be his chief counsel. After discussions, Garrison notified the AEC that Oppenheimer would not resign. Nichols then set a hearing for mid-April 1954, which coincidentally was the same period the Laboratory would be testing its first thermonuclear device in the Koon event. A panel of three judges was chosen to hear the case. Their findings had to be based on their judgment of Oppenheimer's character, his associates, and his loyalty.

Strauss appointed Isidor Rabi to be interim chairman of the GAC. Rabi sought to avoid a hearing by proposing the AEC wait until Oppenheimer's contract expired on June 30, 1954, and not renew it. But Oppenheimer would still have to agree to have his access to classified documents restricted immediately. Nichols brought Rabi's suggestion to Strauss, and the chairman agreed to delay the hearing until Oppenheimer decided what he would do. Two days later, on March 2, Garrison replied that his client had decided not to go with Rabi's plan and wanted his clearance immediately restored.[14] Oppenheimer had made an unfortunate choice. His hearing began on April 12, six days after the Koon event.

The hearing started off well enough for the "prosecution," as the government provided evidence Oppenheimer had lied to security investigators. Oppenheimer admitted he had given an Army security investigator a "cock and bull story." When asked why he had lied, he could only say, "because I was an idiot."[15] If the hearing had stopped then, his security clearance would have been permanently revoked, and the affair would have ended. That would not do for Strauss, who wanted Oppenheimer branded a Soviet agent committed to stalling development of the hydrogen bomb.

To make that case, the prosecutor needed witnesses knowledgeable about the country's thermonuclear-research program. So he approached Griggs, Lawrence, Alvarez, and Teller to testify. It did not matter that none of these men thought Oppenheimer was a Soviet agent. What mattered to the prosecutor was they had each been set back, dismissed, or otherwise thwarted by the "defendant." In a planning meeting among the perspective witnesses, emotions over years of frustration poured out, and they all agreed to testify about Oppenheimer's obstruction of thermonuclear research.

Lawrence departed for Washington, D.C., to give his testimony but stopped on his way to attend a meeting of the AEC's laboratory directors. As he entered the meeting hall, Rabi, who was still the acting chair of the GAC and adamantly opposed thermonuclear research, confronted him and angrily asked what he was going to say at the hearing. A moment later AEC commissioner Henry Smyth appeared in front of Lawrence and was barely civil to him. Lawrence began to realize that his participation in the hearing could jeopardize the Laboratory. In a panic he called Alvarez and told him what had happened. It was obvious to Alvarez that Lawrence had been badly shaken by the experience, something he had never seen happen to his boss. Then, toward the end of the phone call, Lawrence recovered his composure and his resolve returned.

Lawrence may have recovered his composure, but his health was compromised. The stress of his meeting with Rabi and Smyth took a toll on him, for that evening he came down with an attack of colitis. He left his table at a formal dinner to go to a restroom, where he spit up blood. Lawrence called his physician brother, John, and told him about his symptoms; John ordered him back to Berkeley. Lawrence once again lost his nerve and called Alvarez, telling him it was not a good idea to appear at the hearing. With the recent setback of the Koon event, the idea of having Livermore's thermonuclear program shut down before it even had a chance to begin was eating at him.

Alvarez called Strauss to say he was going to follow Lawrence's lead and not appear as a witness. The chairman had heard about Lawrence's withdrawal and asked Alvarez how he could look in a mirror knowing he had given in to the intimidation of his peers. Alvarez hung up the phone, thought about what he was doing, and decided Strauss was right. He took a stiff drink, went to the airport, and purchased a ticket for the TWA redeye flight to Washington.[16]

On April 28, 1954, Teller testified before television cameras; he was a colorful figure. His ability to forcefully bring out points made his testimony stand out above the others. Lawrence, the other bigger-than-life witness, had regained his composure and decided to testify, but he was spared the national glare of the cameras—since he could not travel, he made do with a deposition. Teller's testimony caught the drama of the moment, and film producers made sure the footage was shown widely on television and movie newsreels. For that performance, Teller was ostracized by almost all of America's physics community.[17]

After a lengthy two-month hearing, the panel voted 2 to 1 to revoke Oppenheimer's security clearance. They found his character and associations did not meet government standards, remarking he "was less than candid" with investigators but finding no evidence of disloyalty. Nichols reviewed the hearing, agreed with its findings, and recommended Oppenheimer's Q clearance be permanently revoked. The AEC commissioners had to vote whether to accept the panel's decision; all but Smyth did.

Oppenheimer's counsel released an answering brief. Garrison stressed that if his client was a security risk because he had opposed the hydrogen bomb, then that kind of reasoning would discourage scientists from candidly advising the government in the future. Garrison made no mention of, nor did he apologize for, Oppenheimer having lied to security officers about events concerning the atomic secrets of the nation. Nichols' interpretation was that Oppenheimer's past and continued association with communists made it impossible not to consider him a security risk under existing atomic-energy law and Executive Order 10450. To decide otherwise would require an adaptation of the concept that if someone is sufficiently distinguished, rules should be waived.[18]

Most of the news coverage of the hearing was sympathetic to Oppenheimer, a national war hero. A feeling of empathy ran especially high within the American physics community. Those physicists who had testified against Oppenheimer were vilified in universities and science laboratories across the nation. High among the list of villains were Teller, Lawrence, Alvarez, and Griggs.[19]

Amid this Washington drama, news came that Fermi was fatally ill: an exploratory operation revealed he had a malignant tumor in his stomach that had metastasized. Spending his last days in the hospital with his wife Laura, at his side, Fermi died on November 29, 1954. He was buried in Chicago not far from the institute on nuclear physics he had helped create and not far from Stagg Field, the site of the world's first critical nuclear pile.[20]

When the world's scientific community learned of Fermi's death, its reaction could be described by one word: stunned. Fermi was a dominant figure in twentieth-century science; it was difficult to imagine modern physics without him. He had described some of the most fundamental laws of nature and had provided a better understanding of the mysteries of the new quantum theory. He played a central role in some of the most important events of World War II, helping usher in the thermonuclear age. Fermi was a friend of decency and freedom, and he enjoyed living vigorously. The world would miss him.

⫻ ⫻ ⫻

The year 1954 had been a low point for the Laboratory. For Los Alamos, with its string of successful tests in Operation Castle, it was a golden age. Comments about the failure of the Koon event did not take long to appear. In a letter to the AEC, Bradbury once again suggested UCRL be made subordinate to LASL on matters of nuclear-weapons design. He observed Livermore scientists obviously needed to be better guided since "brilliant new ideas have not appeared." Likewise, as Lawrence had feared, the failure of the Koon event gave Rabi a chance to get back at Lawrence for the Oppenheimer affair. The GAC chairman judged the Livermore effort in Operation Castle to be "amateurish," and he too thought the Laboratory ought to play only a supporting role to Los Alamos. Rabi wondered aloud at meetings of the GAC whether Livermore would ever "really be an important laboratory." He later instigated an investigation by the AEC general counsel on how UCRL had become involved in the nuclear-weapons program in the first place.[21]

The combined stress of a failed nuclear test and testifying against a former colleague had taxed Lawrence to his limit, and he was hospitalized. The same stress worked its way into Teller, who suffered his own attack of colitis and also ended up in a hospital. A short while later York began to experience sudden, inexplicable fevers, which caused him to be absent from the Laboratory for long periods at a time. Brown thought he suffered from Valley Fever, a malady caused by a fungus found in the soil of the dry-climate regions of the American Southwest. Whatever the cause of York's illness, the stress coming from the failure of the Koon event could not have helped his health.

The Oppenheimer hearing's physical effects on Lawrence and Teller, occurring as it did in the same time period as the Koon debacle, had an indirect and underappreciated influence on events at the Laboratory that would lead to profound ramifications later in the Cold War. With the three Laboratory leaders in hospitals or laid out in bed, the leadership of the weapons program now rested on the shoulders of twenty-seven-year-old Harold Brown and thirty-two-year-old Johnny Foster. To paraphrase Winston Churchill, never had so much responsibility fallen on two young individuals.

Having failed in its first three nuclear tests, the stakes for the Laboratory were such that, literally, failure was no longer an option. There were far too many influential people in Washington and elsewhere who would gladly shut down the Laboratory if they could, and one more failure could be all the reason they would need to act. The two young upstarts took over the helm of the Laboratory's weapons program as they figuratively tightened their belts to prepare for their new challenge. Within a few months of taking charge of weapons development, Brown and Foster coauthored a document to the Laboratory's scientists and engineers announcing they were going to pursue a new direction in nuclear-weapons research—and departing from the path set by Teller.[22]

# 11

////////////////

## *The Upstarts Take Over*

I t would be easy to imagine that anyone working at the Laboratory in the fall of 1954 would feel depressed. Yet the upstarts there were anything but. Despite having fielded three successive absolute failures in Nevada and the Pacific, they dove into their work with energy. Now was the time of the upstarts, followers of Lawrence, to make their mark.

When Lawrence had created the MIT Radiation Laboratory during World War II, he sought the help of the McGill University associate professor and renowned Canadian physicist John Stuart Foster, whom he had befriended while they were both at Yale, to help him get the MIT facility started. When he received the call from Lawrence, Foster was happy to oblige his friend and departed Montreal for Cambridge, Massachusetts, with his son John Jr., known as Johnny. The elder Foster enrolled his son into the Harvard Research Laboratory, and after a year of doing his own radar research, the younger Foster volunteered his services to the U.S. Army Air Corps. Johnny was sent to Foggia, Italy, where he was assigned to the 16th Air Reconnaissance Squadron of the Fifteenth Air Force.

With persistence and a bit of luck, young Foster got his hands on a captured German radar unit, took it apart and studied it, and, once he knew how it worked, developed tactics for bomber crews to outwit German radar units that guided air defenses to shoot them down. Putting his thoughts together, Foster went out into the Italian countryside to nearby airbases and gave survival talks to bomber crews—young men, half of whom were still teenagers, and who had one of the most dangerous jobs in the European theater of war. Within months, Foster helped reduce casualties among those airmen by one-half. A grateful Fifteenth Air Force commander, Major General Nathan Twining, started a process to award Foster the Army's third-highest combat award, the Silver Star, but the war ended before the paperwork was completed. After the war Johnny Foster graduated with honors from McGill University, and Lawrence returned a favor to John Foster Sr. by accepting his son as a physics graduate student in the Rad Lab, where he joined a research group led by Alvarez.

Like the man who was his group leader at Berkeley, Johnny Foster had an extraordinary ability to design experiments. He had a characteristic trait to face obstacles and tackle them directly, as he once demonstrated after he had returned from a war-ravaged Italy. As he was departing the Rad Lab after a full day of work, Foster walked along a security fence toward a guard shack and noticed his motorcycle parked on the other side. Rather than walk another one hundred yards to the guard shack as required, he held up his badge toward the security guard and then bolted over the barbed-wire fence. Then he went directly to his motorcycle and drove home. Foster was reprimanded the next day, but that did not quell his tendency to unabashedly tackle problems the best and most direct way he saw.

Foster excelled in competition. He was a champion ski jumper for McGill University, having made the longest jump at a North American championships held at Dartmouth University in 1946. He was also the captain of the university's gymnastics team and had been chosen to represent Canada in the 1948 Olympic Games, though a shortfall in funding forced the Canadian Olympic Committee to eliminate gymnastics that year.

He owned a Vincent HRD motorcycle and used it to transport himself and his new bride, Barbara, from Montreal to Berkeley. One day, as Foster was entering the Rad Lab on his motorcycle, he saw Lawrence in his Cadillac convertible. Lawrence stopped him and asked him who owned "that thing" he was riding. Foster said it was his. When Lawrence asked how many miles he had driven on motorcycles, the young man replied he had driven them for about 100,000 miles. Lawrence grumbled, "Well, you've already gone through too many mean free paths for your own safety. Get rid of it." (A "mean free path" in physics is the average distance a particle will travel before a collision.) Foster's adventures with motorcycles were over.[1]

Soon after he took over the Livermore Hectoton Group in July 1953, the thirty-year-old Foster set out to get past the poor performance of the

Hydride Shots. Success in designing atomic devices greatly depended on computer modeling, and much of the group's computer-code support, especially with hydrodynamic codes, came from Bob LeLevier, who shared an office with Chuck Leith, the man who first programmed the UNIVAC. LeLevier and his hydrodynamics team would become experts in writing hydrodynamic computer codes, which predict how matter reacts to energy.

To get theoretical support, Foster relied heavily on Jim Wilson, a physicist matrixed into the Hectoton Group from T Division. Wilson was a formidable theoretical physicist and loved mountain climbing—he was not just a good climber, he was world class. In their book *Fifty Classic Climbs of North America*, Allen Steck and Steve Roper describe Hummingbird Ridge, Mount Logan, Canada: "The peak is striking. But the full line hasn't seen a second ascent, and four people have died attempting it."[2] That first successful ascent was in 1965, accomplished by Wilson and five companions.

Later in life, a grizzled-looking Wilson turned his attention to astrophysics, using his computer skills to write a code that modeled a collision between two black holes. Jumping from black holes to neutron stars, he joined Colgate and Bethe to formulate a theory of how supernovae occur. In the 1980s he improved a stellar model of Colgate's, which led to a publication describing the first successful model of a Type 2 supernova. Nobel laureate Bethe called Wilson the "grand champion of supernova modeling."[3]

With his first-class team, Foster tackled the challenge of designing one of the world's smallest atomic devices. He could have replicated a successful Los Alamos device to assure he got a yield on his first try, but that was not Foster's way, and he never considered it. A fission device (the primary) that drove a fusion device (the secondary) in a thermonuclear warhead was one role for atomic devices, but Foster was not inclined to devote his attention to perfect a primary for a secondary that did not yet exist. With the Ruth and Rae events still fresh in his memory, he had to create an original atomic device that worked.

With the absolute failure of the Koon event receding into the past, Foster announced the thrust areas his Hectoton Group would pursue: Hy-Ball (also called Celeste) was yet another hydride device suggested by Teller; Geode was a futuristic concept that had first been proposed by Foster's predecessor, Art Biehl; and Gun was a small fission device that, despite the name, was not a gun-assembly weapon. The Geode and the Gun initiatives were new ideas, each something revolutionary.[4]

Work proceeded on the Hy-Ball, and "improved" versions of the Ruth and Rae devices soon appeared. The Chemistry Division chipped in, figuring out how to better compress a hydride compound. The Physics Division at RAND did calculations for the equations of state of hydrides, but hydrotests attested to the fact that the Hectoton physicists still did not understand how a hydride compressed. (A hydrodynamics test, or hydrotest, is an experiment that usually involves using a high explosive to inject energy onto an object to observe how it reacts.) Foster soon quit development of the Hy-Ball, a significant show of independence. He saw testing yet another hydride device as an invitation to failure, and despite Teller's fascination with hydrides, Foster went with his instincts. And to his credit, Teller supported him in the new direction he was about to take.

The Geode concept went to the heart of designing a small atomic device, but it required computational and diagnostic tools that did not yet exist and experience the Hectoton designers did not have. Von Neumann was intrigued by the Geode concept and assisted with design calculations on his MANIAC at Princeton. Foster sorely wished to pursue the idea, but there was not enough time to adequately develop the Geode before the next series of tests in 1955, Operation Teapot. (Foster did not know it, but a LASL team of engineers and technicians had by this time invented a diagnostic tool called a pin dome, which could exquisitely measure how a fission device imploded. He later claimed if he had known about the pin dome earlier, he would have used it to immediately design and test a Geode device.)[5]

His love for challenges and his lifelong ethic to be relevant to the needs of the country led Foster to focus on making a tactical nuclear warhead; he was passionate to give the Army a weapon that could deter massive attacks. So given the circumstances, he focused his energies on the Gun device, which was given the nickname Cleo. There are good government regulations that prevent presenting to the reader a thorough description of what Foster was proposing, but the Cleo was an unprecedented design, promising to be one of the smallest atomic devices yet developed.

U.S. President John F. Kennedy meets with Soviet Premier Nikita Khrushchev in Vienna, Austria, in June 1961 for a summit to discuss the status of West Berlin. *John F. Kennedy Presidential Library photo*

RAND analyst Herman Kahn, author of *On Thermonuclear War*, giving a lecture (circa 1963) at the Livermore Laboratory. *Lawrence Livermore National Laboratory photo*

Cavendish Laboratory deputy director Mark Oliphant (*left*) meets with Ernest Lawrence in Berkeley in 1937 to study the cyclotron. *Lawrence Berkeley National Laboratory photo*

Created in 1955, Site 300 in the Altamont Hills was a high-explosives testing facility used to conduct hydrotests. *Lawrence Berkeley National Laboratory photo*

Radiochemist Glenn Seaborg and physicist Edwin McMillan, discoverers of plutonium and neptunium, at the University of California Radiation Laboratory, circa 1940. *Lawrence Berkeley National Laboratory photo*

Ernest Lawrence (*left*) and Enrico Fermi seen together in 1940 in Chicago. *Lawrence Berkeley National Laboratory photo*

Sign placed at the entrance of Lawrence's new laboratory in Livermore, California, on September 2, 1952. *Lawrence Livermore National Laboratory photo*

Aerial view of the Livermore Laboratory in 1953 with the Altamont Hills in the background. *Lawrence Livermore National Laboratory photo*

Operators in the Livermore Laboratory's computer center running the IBM 701 mainframe computer that arrived in 1956. *Lawrence Livermore National Laboratory photo*

Physicists who helped create the Livermore Laboratory in 1952: Glenn Seaborg, Edwin McMillan, Ernest Lawrence, Donald Cooksey (Lawrence's deputy), Edward Teller, Herb York, and Luis Alvarez. *Lawrence Livermore National Laboratory photo*

The Livermore Laboratory's leaders in 1953: Ernest Lawrence, Edward Teller, and Herb York. *Lawrence Livermore National Laboratory photo*

The Upstarts take over: Johnny Foster, thirty-two years old, and Harold Brown, twenty-seven years old. *Lawrence Livermore National Laboratory photo*

The lower 120 feet of the tower that held the device tested in the Ruth event on March 31, 1953. *Lawrence Livermore National Laboratory photo*

The Cleo being escorted to the Nevada Test Site during Operation Teapot in 1955 by a Livermore Laboratory summer intern as he eats a sandwich. *Lawrence Livermore National Laboratory photo*

The Cleo, packed into two suitcases, is delivered to the Nevada Test Site. *Left to right*: Summer intern Tommy, Walt Arnold, and Navy commander Art Werner. *Lawrence Livermore National Laboratory photo*

Soldiers and Marines observing an atomic test at the Nevada Test Site in 1957 as part of Project Desert Rock. *Lawrence Livermore National Laboratory photo*

Rows of Polaroid cameras attached to oscilloscopes in a diagnostic trailer at the Nevada Test Site during Operation Teapot in 1955. *Lawrence Livermore National Laboratory photo*

Members of Johnny Foster's B Division relaxing in the evening at Eniwetok in 1956. *Lawrence Livermore National Laboratory photo*

Water lashed to steam after the blast of the Antler Event and instantaneously generated a high-pressure geyser; the steam can be seen escaping from the ridge. *Lawrence Livermore National Laboratory photo*

Members of the Polaris warhead design team, including Jim Frank and Jack Rosengren (*third and fifth from left, respectively*) and Mike May (*far right*), celebrate with a Polaris banner. *Lawrence Livermore National Laboratory photo*

Photograph taken through a periscope of a submerged submarine of the detonation of a Polaris warhead in the Frigate Bird event in 1962. *US Navy-Special Projects Office photo*

Livermore Laboratory director Mike May escorts California governor Ronald Reagan at the Laboratory in 1967. *Lawrence Livermore National Laboratory photo*

President Kennedy stands before the entrance to the Rad Lab with (*left to right*) Norris Bradbury, Johnny Foster, Edwin McMillan, Glenn Seaborg, Edward Teller, Secretary of Defense Robert McNamara, and Harold Brown. *Lawrence Berkeley National Laboratory photo*

President Kennedy addresses a crowd of 85,000 enthusiasts at the UC Berkeley football stadium on March 23, 1962: "I have come to an uncomfortable truth that the New Frontier owes more to Berkeley than to Harvard." *Lawrence Berkeley National Laboratory photo*

Wilson performed calculations to help design the Cleo, but despite his talents, computer codes were primitive affairs in 1954, and his calculations proved inadequate. Foster could not hope to have the computational ability he needed in the time he had available. Instead, he relied on hydrotests in which a model of the Cleo was subjected to shockwaves generated by high-explosive detonations.

Before the Cleo design could undergo a hydrotest, a model of it, using substitute materials, had to be made. A part was cut into a prescribed shape on a lathe by guiding the cutting blade with a metal template. The lathes could cut to within one or two thousandths of an inch of specifications, but Foster wanted tolerances reduced by an order of magnitude. This was for a good reason: LeLevier's hydrocode calculations required the shapes and thicknesses of the Cleo's various layers of metals to be exact.

Mechanical engineers saw the smaller tolerances as a challenge and teamed with electrical engineers to design a new generation of digital metal-working machines. This kind of work broke ground in areas usually reserved for universities—the engineers won several patents a year. Afterward, some returned to Berkeley as professors and created academic courses in advanced mechanical and electrical engineering. As a result, the campus became a center of excellence in advanced tooling.

Foster was adamant to involve the veterans in Los Alamos in his design work. He visited LASL once or twice a month to meet his New Mexico counterparts, especially Theoretical Division leader Carson Mark. It was a good, quiet form of collaboration that benefited both laboratories. Through Mark's intercession, Foster received hydrotesting support from Duncan MacDougall, LASL's GMX-6 Division leader. That proved to be critically important.

The Los Alamos hydrotests gave MacDougal a window into Livermore's warhead designs, and he was intrigued enough to send a message to Bradbury: unless Los Alamos took some action, Livermore was setting itself up to be a leader in small-warhead designs. Bradbury did not respond, and there the matter was set to rest, at least for the next couple of years.[6] Foster supplemented the GMX-6 Division hydrotests with an effort he called Operation Tealeaf, a diagnostic campaign set in Nevada.

He received more help from Stanford Research Institute, which performed tests at its facility at Calaveras Reservoir in Fremont, California, about twenty miles southwest of the Laboratory.

York had to get past the Koon debacle, so he took stock of the Laboratory's past performances. He determined that too many mistakes had been made because his design teams were working under the stress of tight schedules, tempting them to take shortcuts. Mark Mills, the new T Division leader, had a suggestion: conduct internal reviews through "pre-mortems." The choice of this term came about because York had expressed frustration over all the postmortem studies conducted after the failure of the Koon device. Mills suggested they could avoid such postmortems only by identifying problems before they occurred, thus *pre*-mortems.

Thereafter, any new initiative for a nuclear warhead from the Megaton and Hectoton Groups warranted the creation of a pre-mortem committee run by scientists who were not directly involved with the initiative. The way a pre-mortem worked was for the review committee to investigate the warhead and present arguments as to why the device would fail; it was up to the designers to convince the committee members their device would work.[7] Pre-mortems were a significant expenditure of time and effort—review sessions were painful exercises for Brown and Foster to go through. But they worked, and neither Brown nor Foster eliminated them when they were later promoted to be associate directors and had the authority to do so.

In October 1954 Mills organized a pre-mortem committee for the Cleo, with Ted Merkle, a former associate professor of physics at the University of California, assigned to lead it. The committee combed through the design, argued why the device would fail, and allowed Foster to defend design decisions made by the Hectoton Group. The committee noted the multidimensionality of the Cleo made it difficult to model on a computer; its design pushed into areas of physics not well understood. All that being the case, after weeks of study, the committee accepted the Cleo design except for one part. Some recent measurements done at Los Alamos suggested Foster should add plutonium to the device, which is what he did.

Cleo was an ambitious undertaking, yet it was a conservative design. Conservatism, in this context, was the practice; if there was a doubt about the proper amount of nuclear fuel to use, more nuclear fuel was added.

The culture of conservatism led to placing generous amounts of plutonium into the Cleo until there was a concern its pit (center) could prematurely become a critical mass.

At the heart of the issue was whether the Cleo became critical when a technician assembled it in Nevada. The concern was over the technician's hands, which would be close enough to the device to reflect neutrons back into it and possibly cause the plutonium in the Cleo's pit to go critical. If it did, it would release a flash of radiation harmful to anyone nearby. A Laboratory engineer, Myron Knapp, was responsible for building the device and decided to conduct a criticality test to make sure its assembly on the test tower would be safe.

Inside a Laboratory blockhouse, the Cleo was constructed into two parts that were placed on two conveyor belts. To model the hands of a technician, Knapp used petty cash to purchase ten pounds of short ribs from Kelly's Butcher Shop in downtown Livermore, across First Street from the Donut Wheel bakery. Knapp wrapped the ribs around each of the two parts of the device. The conveyor belts were activated, and the two sections moved closer and closer until the Cleo was joined together. To everyone's relief, the device remained subcritical. The jerry-rigged experiment was not exactly high-end science, but it got the answer they needed— and that night, Knapp's pet dog got to enjoy a large meal of short ribs. The Laboratory's first atomic device since the debacles of the previous two years was ready for Nevada.[8]

*⁄⁄ ⁄⁄ ⁄⁄*

Harold Brown grew up in a comfortable household in a bustling Jewish neighborhood in New York City. At an early age, it became obvious he was exceptionally intelligent. Brown attended one of the city's "magnet high schools," the Bronx High School of Science, where he excelled in mathematics and science. (These are extremely competitive public high schools that require an entrance exam for the thousands of eligible New York City students.) By his twenty-second birthday, he had earned his PhD in experimental physics from Columbia University. Afterward, the chance to participate in physics discoveries at the Rad Lab and the opportunity to work for Lawrence drew him to Berkeley. Years later, Brown would serve as President Carter's secretary of defense.[9]

Like Foster, Brown also had an excellent team of physicists to support him. His computer-code support came from May's Radiative Transport Group in T Division, which concentrated on writing "burn codes," which modeled thermonuclear reactions. The physicists of the Megaton Group were all in their middle to late twenties, fresh from university. York's trust in Brown by making him leader of the Megaton Group had not been misplaced. He was one of the most competent physicists available to address the challenges facing the Laboratory. Brown took stock of his situation following the failure of the Koon event and realized the monumental challenge ahead of him.

Showing a never-ending enthusiasm for previous ideas, Teller wanted to keep on the course set since Operation Castle. He felt once the diagnostics from the Koon event were analyzed, adjustments could be made, and a revised thermonuclear design could be tested anew. There was a serious problem with this scenario, of course: it assumed the fundamental principle guiding the Koon design was sound. Worse, at the time the Koon device detonated, there was a rainstorm that disabled the diagnostics measuring the device's performance. How does one make corrections when there are no measurements on which to base the changes?

Teller introduced the Sirius, envisioned as being a larger version of the Koon device. Brown reviewed it and judged pushing up the size was simply not a good idea. Teller also introduced a smaller version of the Koon device, dubbed the Companion. It did not arouse much support, either, sharing too many attributes with its ill-fated predecessor. Brown wrote a review of the Companion program and concluded that its design offered challenges making it difficult to match the performance of even the smaller Los Alamos devices tested in Castle. With that being the case, he judged the Companion could not be competitive. So, he inferred, why should they pursue it?

Brown decided to take a new path to designing a thermonuclear device, and once again, it is to Teller's everlasting credit that he did not use his veto power to force Brown to follow his lead. That was not his nature. For Teller, the challenge was to convince a listener his ideas were correct, not to push an idea by fiat. Another of his beneficial traits was, once a decision was made, he did not sulk but gave enthusiastic support to new ideas.

So how did Teller fit in at the new laboratory? He assumed the role of a mentor. Practically every physicist who worked at the Laboratory, whether they personally liked him or not, admitted Teller was a constant inspiration. He had a remarkably charming personality capable of making young physicists receptive to his ideas, combined with an ability to explain his ideas in ways that could be readily understood. There would be no more "Teller designs" from the Laboratory, but his fingerprints were everywhere. Wherever he got involved, innovative things seemed to happen, and they happened often enough it could not be a coincidence. Teller had become a better associate to Lawrence than Oppenheimer had been.

Brown, too, needed to set a strategy for his group to follow, to focus on a device that succeeded when it was tested, yet different than anything to date. He was going to pursue a small thermonuclear device since Los Alamos had amply shown in Operation Castle a proficiency to make large ones. In a monthly progress report written to the AEC, Brown declared his strategy: it appeared to him there was a need for a warhead weighing 2,500 pounds or less, having a yield of one to three megatons, and small enough to be carried by several different types of missiles and/or fighter-bomber aircraft.[10] To solidify his strategy into an actual design, Brown collaborated with York, who had studied the Los Alamos tests in Castle and noted most of the weight in those thermonuclear devices was in their massive cases. Get rid of the case, and the warhead would be small indeed. But how does one do that when the Teller-Ulam paper suggested one needed a massive case?

On June 12, 1953, York had presented a novel concept for a hydrogen bomb to Laboratory leaders at a biweekly technical meeting. It radically altered the way radiative transport was used to ignite a secondary—and his concept did not require a weighty case. After the Koon event, he and Brown cloistered themselves to work on the concept. After a month of brainstorming, the two physicists announced a design for a new type of thermonuclear device. Their scheme made it look like they had taken the Teller-Ulam concept and turned it on its head. Brown led a small team to convert the new idea into a real device, and in August 1954 his team wrote a document describing to the nuclear-weapons complex of the United States a revolutionary concept for designing a thermonuclear device.[11]

Because of the added importance of properly understanding radiative transport for any design using a new and untested concept, Matterhorn-B veteran Louis Henyey, still a T Division consultant, tackled the new idea with his own set of calculations. As an astrophysicist, Henyey was a master at solving such a challenge. Loaded with feedback from thermonuclear tests, May worked in parallel with Henyey. Both physicists benefited from each other's special insights: Henyey's expertise with the physics of radiation flow in stars, and May's growing proficiency in applying radiative transport into the form of a code. Their early calculations looked encouraging, showing the collapse time for the new device—that is, the amount of time it took for an atomic blast to compress the secondary—was favorable compared to older ones tested in Castle.

Brown, following the Laboratory's protocol, gave a female name to the new device, calling it the Linda. On July 16, 1954, he gave an eloquent description of York's concept and formally announced the Megaton Group was planning to test the Linda the following year in Operation Teapot. Various materials to serve as the device's case were explored, tested, and retested. The device went through a sequence of revisions, each usually reflecting some advancement in a calculation. By August 1954, a Los Alamos atomic device of proven ability was selected to be the primary for the Linda.

T Division leader Mills led the pre-mortem committee for the Linda; his team included Bill Grasberger. After a month of study, the committee made some modest recommendations for improving the device, all of which were accepted. Mills was still not satisfied, however, and ordered some additional studies. These calculations further validated the basic design as being sound. York got involved with the detailed design work, reinforcing a recommendation made by Grasberger for making an improvement in the radiation channel.[12]

By the beginning of 1955, the design of the Linda was set, and an engineer team began its manufacture. This was a difficult time for the designers, as doubts about various decisions crept into their thoughts: Was there an appropriate amount of nuclear fuel? Was the distance between the primary and the secondary correct? (If the distance was too short, the primary would destroy the secondary before it had a chance to implode; if it was too great, there would not be enough energy reaching the secondary to make it properly implode.) But doubts or no doubts, it was time to see if a bold concept for a thermonuclear warhead would work.

*// // //*

Operation Teapot began in the spring of 1955 at the Nevada Test Site. Base Camp Mercury was located at the range's southern end, where the headquarters and administrative buildings were located as well as the living quarters for the scientists and engineers conducting the test. The regular workers at the site were contractors belonging to companies such as the Reynolds Electrical & Engineering Company (Reeco) or Edgerton, Germeshausen, and Grier, Incorporated (EG&G) and lived predominantly in Las Vegas, about sixty miles south of Mercury.

About thirty miles north of Mercury, past Frenchman Flat and along the sole two-lane road in the area, was Control Point 1, or as it was universally called, CP-1. This was the nerve center for executing nuclear tests at NTS. Dug into the side of a mesa, with its roof about flush with the mesa's top, it had several levels that extended deep into the ground; it *looked* like it was built to withstand the blast of a nearby nuclear explosion. Inside was a cafeteria known as Sully's Armpit, which served cold sandwiches, hamburgers, and chili. Down two stories from the entrance was the control center, where a test director could execute or postpone a test. Nearby was a conference room, with a projector, where physicists gathered after a test to examine the initial data coming from ground zero. CP-1 came to life as the time came to test the Cleo.

This was Livermore's first atomic test since the Rae event. The upstarts had little precedent for delivering a warhead for testing, so the Teapot experience was a classic example of improvisation. For its transport to NTS, the Cleo was split into two parts, each placed into a reinforced Samsonite suitcase. Walt Arnold, a mechanical engineer responsible for putting the device together in Nevada, was assisted by a young man named Tommy, an electrical-engineering student from San Jose State University hired as a summer intern.[13] Arnold ordered Tommy to manhandle two hefty suitcases out of the Laboratory's assembly building and put them into the back of a "woody" station wagon. Then he gave the intern an Army-issue .45-caliber pistol and told him to guard the suitcases.

Tommy, Arnold, and a naval officer named Art Werner departed in the station wagon and headed out for Nevada. The intern sat in the back of the vehicle with the Cleo; a priceless photograph shows Tommy eating a sandwich while using one of the suitcases as a lunch table. Once at the test site, the suitcases were moved from the station wagon to a government sedan, which traveled in the middle of a small convoy. After this drive, Arnold's crew began the preassembly of the Cleo in Building 10.[14]

A few days later the Cleo was hoisted through a floor panel and into a cab atop a tower by a team of engineers from Sandia Laboratory called bomb hoisters. The assembly team then mounted the device to the floor. This took place adjacent to an area called Yucca Flat. The assembly crew had set aside hours to do their work, since the process was slow and careful. The phone in the tower rang about once an hour; test-site officials wanting to know if everything was staying on schedule. The assembly crew finished after midnight, then the arming crew left CP-1, climbed up the tower, and armed the Cleo.

The military wanted servicemen to experience atomic warfare, part of a training operation called Desert Rock. Bob Pursley, an Air Force captain stationed at Connally Air Force Base north of Waco, Texas, was ordered to arrive at NTS a few days before the test of the Cleo. He was joined by a group of Army soldiers and Marines also ordered to observe and participate in an atomic test. Pursley had graduated from West Point six years earlier at a time when the Military Academy commissioned one-third of its graduates into the Air Force, since the U.S. Air Force Academy did not yet exist. Pursley was commissioned in the Air Force, went to pilot training, and was afterward sent to Korea, where he flew more than fifty combat missions and was awarded the Distinguished Flying Cross.

In the cold dawn in Nevada, Pursley stood in a ditch in Yucca Flat staring across the desert at a tower clearly visible about a mile away, an atomic device on top of it. A loudspeaker came on and started a countdown. Pursley lay down prone in the ditch per instructions. He heard the countdown go to zero and then felt heat in the air above him. A few seconds later the shockwave from the atomic blast arrived, and the ground trembled, caving in the front of his ditch. The captain took out a shovel and dug himself out of the soft earth that had piled on top of him, then stood up. A large mushroom cloud rose from where the tower had been. He thought that warfare in an atomic environment was nothing like conventional combat, regardless of what strategists at the Pentagon thought.

Pursley began walking to where the detonation had occurred as he had been instructed. When he arrived at the site, he received a broom and teamed with another man to sweep the dust off each other's uniform. After that they marched back to their encampment and returned to their home stations. They wore no dosimeters—personal radiation detectors—so they had no idea how much radiation they had been exposed to.[15]

The Cleo had worked, the first Laboratory warhead to do so. Regardless of whatever feelings the exposed soldiers and airmen had out in the desert, the scientists who had designed and built the device were thrilled. Charlie Blue, the Laboratory's administrative officer, ran down the length of the CP-1 corridor yelling, "We're still in business, we're still in business." But there was one small glitch: the device's yield was greater than predicted, which Foster forever after blamed on the pre-mortem committee for having him add plutonium to the Cleo's pit. Nevertheless, the Laboratory had a successful test. Someone had leaked to the press how the device had been delivered to the tower, and *Time* magazine ran a story about a new type of nuclear weapon that could fit inside a suitcase.[16]

Foster could not contain his happiness, bursting to spread news of the results. He was pacing back and forth inside CP-1 when he abruptly decided to let Lawrence know the good news. It was not typical of Lawrence to be absent from a Laboratory experiment, but he was still recovering from the bout of colitis that had flared up during the Oppenheimer hearing. Foster telephoned him with the news. Doctor's orders or not, Lawrence said he was coming out to the test site immediately. After hanging up the phone, Foster realized he had committed a gaffe in protocol by calling up the boss directly rather than going through channels. He found York on the roof of CP-1 and told him what he had done, apologizing for his impertinence. York simply smiled.[17]

To fly to NTS from Berkeley, one had to catch a flight from Oakland through Los Angeles and then to Burbank. There one boarded a flight to Las Vegas, where a government car would pick up the traveler and drive the sixty miles to the site. This itinerary consumed an entire day, so it was already too late for Lawrence to make the trip same day. Instead, he went to the Laboratory that afternoon, planning to leave for Nevada the next morning.

An administrative assistant to the Laboratory director, Dale Nielsen, was sitting at his desk when Lawrence stepped in and wanted to know exactly what had happened. Once filled in on the details, he cried, "Isn't that great! Isn't that great!" He wanted to tell somebody how happy he was. Lawrence paced back and forth, continuing to call out, "Isn't that great!"[18]

Lawrence arrived at CP-1 the next day. He met with York, Foster, Brown, Teller, and Sewell, who all escorted him down to the conference room to provide a recap of the Cleo results. Then they all took a walk around the large parking lot outside. Lawrence opened a discussion by asking, "Why do we need small nuclear weapons?" Teller responded that they were required for nuclear artillery, which had been identified as a need for the Army. Then Lawrence asked, "Where do we go from here?"[19]

That question started up a lively discourse. When Lawrence had started the conversation, he knew perfectly well where the Laboratory was headed. He wanted everyone present, the leaders of his Laboratory, to reaffirm they were all on the same page about what they had accomplished and what it meant. His questioning cemented decisions already being made: their goal, their overriding focus, would be to make weapons smaller.

Next up for testing was the Linda, which sat atop a five-hundred-foot tower. Yield restrictions held, so much of the thermonuclear fuel in the device was inert. Jim Frank, a prominent member of the Linda design team, went to Nevada a week early to prepare the device for testing. The day before the test, Frank returned to Livermore. He rose early the next morning to go outside to see if he could catch a glimpse of the event. He witnessed the eastern sky light up "like an extremely rapid dawn." Other members of the Laboratory staff, who knew the event was going to occur, drove their cars into the Altamont Hills for a better view; some reported there was a red glow in the sky for several seconds following the initial brightness. It was an impressive sight for them to be able to see the effects of their work from five hundred miles away.[20]

The measured yield of the Linda was within a few percent of the calculated yield. Brown had written one year before, "If the new idea is

practicable, it may have an impact in the design of all multistage thermonuclear weapons."[21] His statement was more prescient than he could
have imagined. It took a year or two for the realization to sink in, but with
the successful test of the Linda, previous thermonuclear designs became
obsolete. York's concept on how to make a thermonuclear device was
that radical.

This was a landmark achievement for the young Laboratory and an
auspicious start for subsequent designs. The Navy requested the AEC
license the Laboratory to develop a thermonuclear warhead for warships.
Likewise, the Air Force requested it design a thermonuclear device for its
fighter-bombers. The Pentagon's Military Liaison Committee united these
requests into a single weapons requirement.[22] A smaller version of the Cleo
was tested a few weeks later; it, too, was a success. The second device was
the smallest-diameter fission bomb to be detonated up to that time, and its
performance caught the attention of Army officials. The Cleo was small,
but its design was complicated, and it used more fission fuel than other
atomic devices with a similar yield—there was still work to do. This was a
good start, but the team would have to do better.

*# # #*

Avid baseball fans remember 1955 as the year the Brooklyn Dodgers
beat the New York Yankees in the World Series. For the young upstarts
in Livermore, it was a year to be remembered for reasons that were just as
momentous. The dual successes of its atomic and thermonuclear programs
gave the Laboratory some badly needed respite from incessant criticism.
The Teapot events had demonstrated the abilities of the Livermore physicists and ended talk of shutting down the Laboratory, or even of making
it a subsidiary to Los Alamos. Livermore's scientists and engineers could
finally concentrate without the vociferous ridicule of critics on what they
had originally set out to do: develop new ideas.

York set the tone when he said his working philosophy was to push
at technological extremes. He did not wait for government or military
authorities to say what they wanted and only then seek to supply it.
Instead, he set out to construct nuclear devices that had the smallest
diameter, the lightest weight, the least investment in rare materials, the
highest yield-to-weight ratio, or that otherwise carried the state of the

art beyond the currently explored frontiers. He was confident the military would find a use for a technological breakthrough, and that usually turned out to be true.[23]

# 12

//////////////////

# Hydrotests, Hydrocodes, and a National Strategy

The successful tests of the Cleo and the Linda brought signs of recognition from the AEC and Los Alamos that Livermore had become a viable nuclear-weapons laboratory. Those who looked closely at the results of Operation Teapot noted the new laboratory had set records for achieving atomic and thermonuclear yields from small devices. One sign of its maturing appeared in a letter from Lawrence addressed to the San Francisco office of the AEC, dated on the second anniversary of the Laboratory's opening. The communication announced Herb York as having the formal title of director of the University of California Radiation Laboratory at Livermore.[1] Before that, Lawrence had been considered director by the AEC.

Another sign of recognition came with the establishment of the Livermore branch of Sandia Laboratory. Sandia was created at Kirtland Army Air Station in Albuquerque, New Mexico, as an outgrowth of LASL's Z Division, which had been responsible for weaponizing atomic devices. It was managed by the University of California as part of its original Manhattan Project contract until 1949, when management of Sandia switched to American Telephone and Telegraph (AT&T). Six months after the Laboratory's Teapot shots, seven Sandia employees, led by Bill Marsh, arrived at Livermore and took up residence in Building 217, an old naval barracks.

In the jargon of nuclear-weapons designers, Sandia continues to be responsible for components outside the "physics package" of a nuclear weapon—its engineers develop and perfect components that make an atomic or thermonuclear device a weapon, such as firing sets, electrical wiring, and other nonnuclear components. Once the "Sandians" arrived, they set to work to help the Laboratory prepare its first warhead to enter the country's nuclear stockpile. To complement the Sandia crew, York created W Division, which had the responsibility of ensuring a nuclear device met military specifications: the device had to work within a prescribed range of temperatures, function after going through a vibration test, and meet other such parameters.

The Sandia group soon moved into a permanent site south of the Laboratory across East Avenue. In March 1956 the AEC announced Sandia Livermore as a permanent branch of the main Sandia campus. As a sign of the Laboratory's growing success, the staff of Sandia Livermore expanded to almost one thousand engineers and technicians by 1958. The leader of the Sandia Device Systems Group was Bob Burton, who became as much a presence at warhead assemblies as any Livermore engineer.

With a crop of new weapons designs coming up on the horizon, Foster wanted components made smaller and lighter and the way they were made improved. The Sandia engineers could have easily taken the attitude, "It's good enough for Los Alamos; what's wrong with you?" But they did not, instead viewing Foster's demands as a challenge they should meet. The achievements of the Sandia team and the degree of cooperation they gained with Livermore engineers proved the wisdom of creating the Sandia branch across the street from the Laboratory.[2]

The AEC finally released funds to build a badly needed high-explosives test facility for weapons designers. This complex was located on land purchased about twenty miles east of Livermore in the Altamont Hills. Its entrance was off the north side of a rural country lane, Corral Hollow Road. Contractor blueprints identified Berkeley's Rad Lab as Site 100 and the Livermore Laboratory as Site 200; keeping with the same scheme, they designated the new facility Site 300. Altamont was an ideal spot for Site 300, a rustic area inhabited by cougars, deer, rattlesnakes, roadrunners, and occasional ranchers. (The nearby Altamont Speedway was the site of a Rolling Stones concert in December 1969, during which a member of the Hells Angels, hired as a bodyguard, stabbed a spectator.)

*// // //*

In order to conduct a hydrotest of a prototype device at a facility like Site 300, a designer made a model of the device dictated by hydrodynamic calculations. (Hydrodynamics is a branch of physics that treats energized materials as though they are liquid.) Computer codes utilizing hydrodynamics are called hydrocodes and come in two varieties, Lagrangian and Eulerian, named after two eighteenth-century mathematicians, the Italian French Count of Lagrange and the Swiss Leonhard Euler.

A typical hydrocode problem involves calculating how an object responds when energy strikes it—how does the object move, or bend, or compress, or expand? A problem is defined by creating a coordinate system of small zones that enclose the object, with each zone containing a small segment of it. In the Eulerian formulation, the coordinate system remains fixed as the object reacts to pressure. The code has to account for all material moving into a zone as well as material leaving it.

In a Lagrangian formulation, material that starts in a particular zone stays in that zone. When pressure from a high-energy explosion causes the object to contort into odd shapes, the Lagrangian coordinate system takes on the shape of the bending object. This approach has the advantage of providing higher-order accuracy with the least cost in computer time, so most hydrocodes in those early days were Lagrangian. All too often, however, the motion became violent, causing boundaries of a zone to "bowtie"—that is, a rectangular zone folded over on itself into the shape of a figure eight. When a bowtie formed in those run-throughs, it caused a discontinuity at the crossover point, and the code "crashed," or stopped running—an annoying outcome, especially since most calculations were run at night

When a problem crashed, often at an inconvenient hour like 3 a.m., the technician running the computer, who had little knowledge of the problem, had no choice but to contact the physicist—usually at home asleep—who submitted the problem and report the situation. If the calculation was important, which was always the case, the designer had to go to the computer center and fix the problem by "untying" bowties. That process involved rezoning meshes by using corrective computer cards put into the computer deck. The following morning it was easy to spot those who had come in overnight as they dragged themselves into their offices to look over the results of the night's calculations, then generated another computer problem for that evening.

Bowties were not the only annoyances faced by weapons designers. Sometimes the computer itself was the problem. The IBM 701, NASA's new wonder computer at the time (and shown at the end of the 2016 movie *Hidden Figures*), used Williams tubes to store memory. A Williams tube, which looked like an old-fashioned CRT television, stored data on pixels arrayed on the screen and had issues, as Dan Patterson, a weapons designer, remembered. On one occasion late in the year, a problem had been run seven times on an IBM 701, and each time it gave a different answer because the Williams tubes dropped bits. Finally, someone stumbled onto the idea that the computer glitched whenever a door opened, exposing the Williams tubes to direct sunlight, which upset the memory. So, they hung up a black curtain in front of the computer, and it performed consistently again.[3]

Physicists needed to print out solutions to their calculations and did so as much as practical, often pushing printers to the limits of their capabilities. Printer speeds of about 150 lines per minute were available, with each line being 120 characters in length. For each "snapshot" in time selected during the run of a problem, pages were printed with the time and a summary shown at the top of a page, followed by lines of numbers, each line representing a zone in the problem. These numbers might refer to temperature, velocity, position, or pressure. The printers could barely keep up with the calculations being generated. The arrival of the IBM 704 computer, with its larger memory storage and faster calculational speed, simply overwhelmed the printers on hand.[4]

*// // //*

The Teapot successes reinforced a spirit of cooperation between the Laboratory's physicists and RAND's analysts. Walking among the offices of the Laboratory, it did not take long to spot an analyst. Prominent intellectuals like Dick and Al Latter, David Griggs, and Herman Kahn, to name a few, kept regular offices in the same building that housed the Laboratory's weapons designers. Other RAND analysts, including William Kaufmann and Bernard Brodie, made frequent visits and occupied temporary offices.

This was 1956, and the world watched anxiously as Russian tanks crushed a revolt of the Hungarian people against Soviet repression. Watching the ruthlessness of the Red Army on television made many

Americans question their own security, and national debates surfaced about whether the country's nuclear-deterrent posture was adequate to stave off a Soviet nuclear attack. RAND analysts offered answers, arguing to deter an aggressor, the size of a nuclear arsenal is not nearly as important as its quality. What in retrospect is astounding is how this philosophy arose out of a collaboration of those RAND analysts working with the physicists at Livermore. The products of this association would emerge as effective warhead designs that met the needs of a well-thought-out strategic-deterrent policy.

Proof this collaboration occurred was amply illustrated years later in a series of essays written by Mike May.[5] In one, "Some Advantages of a Counterforce Deterrence," May exhibited how well he understood the nuances of deterrent strategies coming from RAND and how particular types of weapons (i.e., highly survivable) best served the national-security needs of the country.

The ideas that emerged from this Livermore-RAND collaboration directly challenged the Eisenhower administration's defense doctrine. When Dulles gave his Massive Retaliation speech, members of the foreign-policy establishment understood his portrayal of actions they thought were great achievements, like the Marshall Plan, the Berlin Airlift, and the creation of NATO, as being merely reactions to Soviet-engineered emergencies. To Paul Nitze, who had served in Truman's State Department, Massive Retaliation made no sense. Dulles said the Korean War was the kind of limited military response to be avoided. To Nitze, the Korean War had demonstrated U.S. nuclear weapons had not deterred China from intervening in the conflict.[6] Nitze felt Dulles also had not grasped how powerful hydrogen bombs were. If America used a nuclear weapon in a regional conflict, and it then provoked nuclear retaliation by the Soviet Union, the damage to the United States would be catastrophic.

Serious criticism of Eisenhower's defense strategy came ten months after Dulles' speech from a short man with a slightly high-pitched voice, a professor of political science named William W. Kaufmann. In an essay entitled "The Requirements of Deterrence" for the Center of International Studies at Princeton, Kaufmann, who was an active participant in the Livermore-RAND collaboration of the 1950s and would later educate a generation of political science students at MIT, provided the intellectual logic that challenged Massive Retaliation as a Cold War strategy.[7]

A policy of Massive Retaliation, Kaufmann recognized, carried a potentially costly risk that the antagonist will challenge the United States to make good on its threat. If that happened, the country must accept the consequences of executing its threatened action. If it backs down and lets the challenge go unheeded, the United States would suffer loss of prestige, decrease its capacity for instituting effective deterrence policies in the future, and encourage the opponent to take further actions of a detrimental character. If America is challenged to fulfill the threat of Massive Retaliation, it would likely suffer costs as great as it inflicts. That, he declared, was unacceptable.[8]

Kaufmann noted further that a history of America's foreign policy showed it was out of character to retaliate massively against anyone except in the face of provocation as extreme as Pearl Harbor. There must be some relationship between the value of the objective sought and the costs involved in its attainment. A policy of deterrence that does not fulfill this requirement is likely to result only in deterring the deterrer. In other words, aggressive countries would be unlikely to treat America's threat to use strategic nuclear weapons in response to regional crises as credible. Indeed, Kaufmann argued, as had General Ridgway, a policy of Massive Retaliation encouraged the Soviets to engage in piecemeal aggression. A proper deterrent was one that fit the punishment to the crime, that prevented aggression or, if that failed, defeated it at all levels of intensity.

Eventually, a more flexible strategy emerged to replace Massive Retaliation. Much of the gist of Kaufmann's arguments could be seen in Kennedy's inaugural address in 1961, with the new president claiming the country would meet communism on every front, with whatever force was necessary.

In 1956, Kaufmann edited and published *Military Policy and National Security*, a book in which he stated the basic problem was not only for the United States to build the means for fighting limited wars but also to compel the Soviets to keep their own efforts confined to fighting a limited war—that is, to refrain from expanding any aggression into a nuclear war. A strategy of containment meant not only containing regional conflicts but also deterring the Soviets from seeking a global advantage with a nuclear attack on the United States itself. This last point brought Livermore's nuclear-weapons research to prominence. Just as much as the country's conventional military strength had to be a credible deterrent to keep regional aggression in check, so, too, the country had to have a highly credible strategic nuclear deterrent to keep Soviet global aggression in check.[9]

In February 1956, eight months after Livermore's Teapot successes and four months prior to its next series of tests, Kaufmann engaged in a series of RAND studies that became part of a doctrine its analysts called "Counterforce Strategy." The RAND participants included iconic members like Andy Marshall, Charles Hitch, and Victor Hunt. They devised Counterforce Strategy to be at once both less destructive than Massive Retaliation and more congruent with rational war objectives: If the United States were forced to use nuclear weapons, to say thwart an invasion of Western Europe, it could focus only on military targets within the Soviet Union instead of a broader range that would initiate a massive response. In that way there was an implicit threat that, unless the Soviets quit their aggression, America could ratchet up its nuclear response by attacking Soviet industry and cities.[10]

Brodie supplemented Kaufmann's points in an internal RAND working paper titled "Must We Shoot from the Hip?," which called for a decreased vulnerability of the nation's deterrent force. For a Counterforce Strategy to be credible, survivability was the key: it was not as important to prevent a surprise attack by the Soviets as it was to ensure that enough nuclear weapons survive the strike to allow for retaliation. That is, America had to retain a surviving retaliatory force as a bargaining lever without having to worry the Soviets might knock out this reserve force in a first strike.[11] That posed a problem for the nuclear forces of the United States at the time, which were vulnerable to surprise attacks. RAND studies showed there was no adequate objective basis for deterrence unless U.S. defense programs and plans were drastically altered.[12]

The country's liquid-fueled rockets and strategic bombers needed time to launch and take off, and the locations of ICBM launch sites and SAC bases were known. That threatened the logic behind Counterforce

Strategy. What worried strategists most was it could tempt the Soviet Union to think about a surprise attack to remove the United States as a threat to its national security and an obstacle to the progression of communism worldwide. The vulnerability problem gave General LeMay one more argument why the country should produce more bombers and thermonuclear warheads. Eisenhower opposed LeMay vigorously, preferring to limit the size of the nuclear stockpile, not build thousands more bombs.[13] That the deterrent force needed to be invulnerable to a Soviet surprise attack meant taking a position that emphasized the importance of making strategic warheads small enough to be survivable. As it happened, the innovations needed to accomplish that feat would demonstrably come from Livermore. The upstarts were about to make much of LeMay's arguments moot by allowing the construction of strategic nuclear systems that were invulnerable to attack.

This would happen with the next major series of nuclear tests, Operation Redwing, scheduled to take place at the Pacific Proving Grounds in the spring and summer of 1956. With success in his pocket, Harold Brown prepared to test three thermonuclear warheads that were congruent with a Counterforce Strategy by exploiting the design features of the Linda. As the Laboratory prepared itself for this next round of testing, the Megaton Group adopted a protocol of naming each thermonuclear design after a musical instrument. The program for 1956 included the Bassoon, a second device to serve as a warhead for a tactical missile, and the Flute.[14]

*♯ ♯ ♯*

Following the debacle of the radiation fallout from the Castle Bravo event, the government requested a design for a thermonuclear weapon that reduced radioactive contamination—a clean weapon. In December 1954 York reported that Livermore was working on a promising approach for a clean bomb, and the Defense Department awarded its program an urgent status. This program was called Bassoon, based on an idea of Mike May's.

On June 10, 1953, May was at a biweekly meeting of the Megaton Group when von Neumann challenged designers with a new concept for a thermonuclear device. He thought about von Neumann's points and came up with a scheme for a warhead as revolutionary to the Linda as it had been to all previous devices. May's experience with code development gave him an enviable ability to create a design that, in von Neumann's words, achieved a very successful compression.

To qualify as a clean weapon, there had to be a far-greater reliance on fusion reactions than fission reactions. The latter generated so-called fission fragments, the main source of radioactive contamination emanating from a nuclear blast. What May did was to generate incredibly high temperatures long enough to allow a substantial amount of the warhead's energy to come from thermonuclear reactions. It was a masterful accomplishment that exemplified his talents and von Neumann's computer culture.

The second device in Brown's program was a warhead for a tactical missile or bomb. Although the Linda served as the basis for it, the new device needed to be initiated by more energy, which required a larger-yield primary from Los Alamos. Also, to withstand anticipated accelerations that a missile warhead experienced upon launch, the device needed to be mechanically strengthened. Engineers at the Bendix Aviation site in Kansas City, Missouri, provided an internal structural frame integrated with the rest of the warhead.[15] In a sense, this device could be described as being a weaponized Linda.

Brown's third warhead, the Flute, brought the Linda concept down to a smaller size. The Linda had done away with a lot of material in a standard thermonuclear warhead. Now the Flute tested how well designers could take the Linda's conceptual design to substantially reduce not only the weight but also the size of a thermonuclear warhead. This was the most ambitious part of Brown's program, its biggest challenge.

Up to this time the Megaton Group had used Los Alamos primaries to drive their secondaries because the LASL devices had already been tested and were therefore considered reliable. But the Hectoton Group had progressed enough to offer alternatives, and their atomic devices were smaller. The temptation to make a thermonuclear device as small as possible was too great; Brown decided to use an untested primary designed by the Hectoton Group to drive the Flute. This would be the first Livermore thermonuclear event to use both a Laboratory primary and secondary.

The Flute's small size—it was the smallest thermonuclear device yet tested—became an incentive to improve codes. Characteristics marginally important in a larger device were now crucially important. For instance, the reduced size of the Flute's radiation channel could cause it to close early, which would prematurely shut off radiation flow. The code had to accurately predict if such a disaster would occur before the device was even tested in a nuclear event. Designers for the Flute must have been opera buffs, for they named each series of calculations for the device after a character in Mozart's opera *The Magic Flute*. One series was called Papageno, another series was called Sarastro, and then Pamino. The extra work paid off, for the calculations showed changes had to be made from the Linda's design for the Flute to perform correctly. As always, the verification of their calculations had to wait for the results of a nuclear test.

♯ ♯ ♯

Foster's Hectoton Group also had three devices to test in Operation Redwing. The new devices were hardly recognizable as coming from the same team that produced the Cleo. Just as the Megaton Group named their devices after musical instruments, the Hectoton Group adopted a new protocol of naming their devices after birds. Their three atomic devices were dubbed Swan, Swallow, and Swift.

Because there were no precedents for the Redwing atomic devices (they were that radical), Foster had to explain to the AEC the theory behind their designs. He wrote two elegant papers describing the physical concepts used by his physicists. He said the goal was to achieve a more efficient warhead for a given amount of fissionable material. This occurred by using the energy of a high explosive to dynamically fashion a fissionable fuel into a critical mass—an extraordinary challenge, and yet another example of the fruits of Livermore's computer culture. In line with the adopted strategy of the Laboratory, the warheads were small.[16]

The first device was the Swan. Morris Scharff, a physicist from T Division, introduced the design during a seminar on June 9, 1955, and Foster adopted it. The Swan used a high-explosive configuration called an air lens—a concept developed by Dr. Sigmund Jacobs of the Naval Ordnance Laboratory. A prototype was constructed for hydrotesting that used depleted uranium as a surrogate for plutonium or enriched uranium. Depleted uranium, called D38, was uranium bereft of uranium-235. Since it had a low fission cross section—that is, a low probability of nuclear fission—it would not give off a nuclear yield. Nevertheless, its hydrodynamic properties were like plutonium or enriched uranium, so it served as an excellent substitute for use in hydrotests.

A D38 Swan prototype was transported to Site 300 and hydrotested. The results showed its imploding inner surface formed spikes, meaning a new shape and mass distribution was needed. A modified prototype was built and the process was repeated. If a fix was not obvious, the design team, led by Walter Birnbaum, relied on intuition to tweak design parameters further, and progress continued. Eventually, a Swan emerged that imploded correctly and was ready to undergo a full nuclear test.

Foster's second device, the Swallow, was smaller than the Swan—it could qualify as a nuclear artillery shell for the Army's 8-inch gun. The Swallow's small size brought problems, however, so major changes were made; these appeared in a new design called the Swallow II. The team became understandably frustrated: getting the Swallow to implode into a critical mass was a vexing problem, almost to the end.

In a testament to Foster's integrity, six months before the Swallow's nuclear test, he candidly reported to the AEC the device was not performing as expected. He gave a stark description of the situation but said he could arrive at an acceptable design in time for the nuclear test. York, who as Laboratory director was the first recipient of this report, passed it up the chain of command unaltered. Like Foster, he chose to relate the situation as accurately to his sponsors as he could. Another exceptional aspect of this episode is, once the report was received by Major General Alfred Starbird, the AEC's deputy director for military affairs, he did not interfere with the program. Starbird took no steps to cancel the test but trusted Foster's judgment and his team's ability to fix the problem. The degree of integrity, trust, and professionalism among the various layers of management was extraordinary.

A hydrotest in January 1956 led to abandoning the Swallow II design. A major modification, Swallow III, was introduced and looked promising at first. Finally, some of the more complicated aspects of its design were removed, and a simpler Swallow IV emerged. That latest modification looked like it would perform well.

The smallest of the Hectoton devices was the Swift. The design-team leader was Captain Jasper Welch, an Air Force officer temporarily assigned to the Hectoton Group. (Welch would later rise to the rank of major general and become director of Air Force research and development.) The goal for the Swift team was to explore the lower limits of the concepts introduced by Foster. If the challenges facing the Swallow team were daunting, Swift's were even more so. Achieving a critical mass inside such a small device was difficult, and like the Swallow, the Swift went through major renovations. Changes were still occurring ninety days before shot time. Materials were switched, and other materials were added. It is not hard to imagine the last three months before the test were filled with late nights, early mornings, and a lot of stress. Somehow, Welch and his team managed it.

*# # #*

The physicists, engineers, and technicians who diagnosed the performance of a nuclear device faced difficult challenges; regardless, their success was essential to a nuclear-weapons program. Electromagnetic surges and shockwaves threatened to interfere with measurements and to destroy instruments. If a diagnostic meter was close to the nuclear device, which was often the case, there was less than a thousandth of a second to record and transmit data to a safe receiving station. It took a special talent to perform such work.

Bill Grasberger thought of a way to measure the speed of a shockwave traveling down a radiation channel, the space that runs between the primary and the secondary of a thermonuclear device. His idea was to place a small plug of material with a relatively low melting point into the sleeve of the channel. As a shockwave reached the plug it melted it, causing a bright light to shine through the small hole where the plug had been. Recording when each hole lit up told the diagnostic physicist the amount of time it took the shockwave to reach it (and thus gave the wave's speed). Grasberger could then compare his measured time with the time predicted by a code. The Bassoon device, for example, had three diagnostic plugs implanted in it.

This diagnostic is an exquisite example of extracting data in a harsh environment. Grasberger had to calculate the temperatures his plugs would experience and design them to function properly. He had to record only the signals coming from the plugs and not those from the extraneous emissions of an atomic blast. Lastly, he had to interpret the recorded signals. Even the best experiments will not behave exactly as planned, requiring patience to unscramble the results. Fortunately, Grasberger was an excellent physicist.

Another branch of diagnostics involves radiochemistry. This is a field of study whose origins began with chemists studying the radioactive elements discovered by Marie Curie. Radiochemists analyze radioactive debris to measure the performance of a device, and it is hard to match their data in any other way. It requires a lot of education and training and an overabounding sense of devotion to be a good radiochemist. Gary Higgins was someone who fit that bill.

While still at the Rad Lab late in the fall of 1951, Higgins received some radioactive debris from a nuclear test. It came from a filter the size of a large handkerchief mounted on an aircraft that had flown through a mushroom cloud. In the course of dissolving and analyzing the filter, Higgins, working with a small group of radiochemists, discovered two elements that had never been seen before, referring to them as elements 99 and 100. Once the discovery had been confirmed, the two new elements were given the names einsteinium and fermium, named after Albert Einstein and Enrico Fermi. Soon after, Higgins was awarded his doctorate in chemistry.

In the spring of 1953, the head of the Chemistry Division, Ken Street, made Higgins the leader of the Heavy Element Group; at first it had only one member—Higgins himself. His first task was to determine whether the elements americium and curium were useful as bomb-fraction tracers. (A tracer is an element placed inside a nuclear device and used to "trace" its performance by, for instance, measuring how much of it has absorbed neutrons.)

By the time of Operation Redwing in 1956, Higgins' Heavy Element Group had grown to eight members. They were an eclectic and effective investigative team capable of diagnosing a nuclear explosion to exquisite detail. They were perfecting the art of radiochemical investigation as they worked, and the discoveries they made along the way were like receiving shots of adrenalin. Their morale was high, even as they often worked well into many nights.

When samples of nuclear debris arrived, the radiochemists went into action. They dissolved samples in acid, which took from four to eight hours, and separated out tracers and other radioisotopes. In the process, they added original science to their profession. They learned 14MeV neutrons released by deuterium-tritium interactions caused different nuclear reactions than neutrons released by fission. They also learned certain nuclear reactions were prevalent at only limited ranges of temperatures. The group proved some tracer elements worked, and others did not. All in all, they were good at figuring out how well a warhead performed.

The Heavy Element Group had to be careful, though. Much of the radiation emitted by nuclear debris comes from beta rays, high-speed electrons usually stopped by the skin. Unless a radioisotope was breathed in or ingested, overexposure to beta radiation often resulted in skin burns. When a filter was removed from an aircraft and placed in a radiochemical laboratory, a radiochemist first checked the radioactivity of the room with a Geiger counter to provide a baseline. Geiger counters primarily measure gamma rays (high-energy photons); beta rays do not necessarily register. If the radiochemist misunderstands how his instruments work, he could get a false sense of radiation levels in the room. Much of how safety rules evolved over the years is owed to lessons learned from mistakes, and misinterpreting a Geiger counter reading is a big mistake. One Los Alamos radiochemist, put off-guard by low readings, picked up a filter with his bare hand and later needed skin grafts to repair his burnt skin.

The AEC limited the amount of radiation a radiochemist could receive in a specified period. One standard established the upper limit of body exposure to be one rad per week. As a comparison, normal exposure to background radiation is about one-half rad per year. Higgins' attitude was that the safety rules were overly restrictive. As he became inundated with work, he built an igloo-shaped structure near the entrance of his laboratory by piling up lead bricks. As he entered his laboratory room, he dropped his dosimeter inside the lead igloo. The sensor, normally worn on his outer clothing, thus was not exposed to the radiation in the room. In that way he was able to work longer without running afoul of regulations. Despite the antics, he was not reckless—Higgins lived for another sixty years.[17]

In later years Higgins' group grew to be the Radiochemistry Division, and it continued to build a legacy. Just as Higgins had contributed to the discovery of einsteinium and fermium, Livermore radiochemists joined with Russian colleagues fifty years later to discover two other new elements, berkelium and livermorium, named after the sites of Lawrence's two laboratories.

Some radioisotopes are very short-lived, so analyses of those elements had to be done as quickly as possible before they decayed away. During test operations in the Pacific, half of the Heavy Element Group did immediate analyses in Quonset huts transformed into chemistry laboratories out at Eniwetok, Bikini, and Johnston Island. Doing sophisticated radiochemical analyses far from the Laboratory required an ability to improvise. One who possessed this essential talent was Arne Kirkewoog.

Assigned as an electronic technician with Street's Chemistry Division, Kirkewoog was introduced to a new instrument used for measuring radioactivity and learned how to put it together. In 1956 he flew to Johnston Island to join a team conducting a radiochemistry experiment for one of the Redwing tests. He prepared a Quonset hut for the experiment.

It was about a week before the test and a chemist came up to Kirkewoog and asked if he had shipped in an induction heater. He had not, which jeopardized the experiment since one could not be flown in on time. But Kirkewoog understood the apparatus enough that he thought he could build one. Unfortunately, he had no parts. So, he went to the head of the EG&G contractors and asked to go into their storage shed to pick out some materials. He found copper, capacitors, and transmitting tubes, and with these he built a high-voltage power supply and an oscillator.

Kirkewoog used his newly built oscillator to recreate the missing induction heater. He assembled the experiment, calibrated it, tested it— and it worked. On the day of the nuclear test, the refrigeration unit in the Quonset hut broke down. If the interior got too hot, the experimental apparatus would not function correctly. Kirkewoog remembered seeing a tank of liquid nitrogen near the EG&G shed, so he procured a jeep and two large Dewar flasks, drove over, and filled the flasks with liquid nitrogen. At the Quonset hut he poured the liquid nitrogen on the floor. Hearing the floor crackle and with the temperature beginning to fall, he recalibrated all of his instrumentation.

His timing was good; radioactive samples arrived as he got the equipment ready for use. The radiochemistry team conducted their analyses, and the equipment functioned well. The experiment that had been headed for disaster was instead a success. There was a lot of backslapping and hoo-raying afterward, and the team went to the beach to party.

When the excitement died down, Kirkewoog went back to the hut to celebrate with a smoke. He put a cigarette in his mouth and flicked his lighter, but it failed to put out a spark. He thought that was strange at first, but an instant later he ran as fast as he could for the door and bolted out. He had forgotten the liquid nitrogen on the floor had evaporated, filling the hut with nitrogen gas and displacing the regular air. With no oxygen inside, Kirkewoog would have collapsed within a minute if he had stayed.[18]

# # #

It was time for the Hectoton Group to test its nuclear devices, beginning with the Swift. It was tested atop a two-hundred-foot tower on Aomon Island in Eniwetok Atoll. This smallest of the three devices gave a low yield, smaller than what had been expected. This was not an encouraging start. The Swift's exceedingly small physical size had caused unforeseen compli-cations to dominate its performance. The physicists hoped this was not a bad omen.

They found out two weeks later with the test of the Swallow. This was the same device Foster said was having implosion problems six months ear-lier. The physicists knew its design was as much a result of intuition as it was of hard science; now the mediocre performance of the Swift added to the tension. At midmorning a detonation switch in the control bunker was activated, and the tower holding the device became bathed in light and con-sumed in an explosion. There had been no need for fretting, for the Swallow performed well, rendering a yield slightly greater than had been predicted.

The final Hectoton device to be tested was the Swan. It went through its final assembly atop a two-hundred-foot tower on Rujoru Island. When test day arrived, the same controls that had detonated the Swallow now triggered the Swan. The South Pacific sky lit up, and the Swan gave a yield in the upper part of its predicted range of values, which was gratifying. This was the mother ship of the Redwing atomic devices, the main hope for the Hectoton Group, and it had performed well.

Next was the Megaton Group's turn, beginning with May's Bassoon device. It performed just the way he had predicted it would. It gave a high yield and was four times cleaner than any device that had been tested in Castle two years earlier. May's conceptual design became a progenitor to one of the most successful nuclear weapons in U.S. history. It was an astounding achievement for a young physicist with no previous experience.

The second Megaton Group test was the warhead for a tactical missile. When it was detonated, diagnostics measured a yield a quarter less than expected; later, this was blamed on the metallic struts inserted to strengthen the warhead. Despite the lower-than-expected yield, it still performed well enough for the Navy to want it as the warhead for its Regulus cruise missile. It became the first Laboratory warhead to be contracted by the Defense Department, entering the country's nuclear stockpile in 1957 as the W-27.

The tail end of the Megaton Group's device tests was the Flute, the design that shrank the Linda concept to a smaller size. Assembled atop a three-hundred-foot tower, the Flute, driven by a Livermore primary, performed almost precisely as predicted, another gratifying outcome. It meant the United States had successfully tested a thermonuclear weapon weighing about one thousand pounds, roughly three times lighter than many of its contemporaries. The test proved it was plausible to place a thermonuclear device on a small missile or on a fighter-bomber, a warplane much smaller than a strategic bomber. As had happened after the test of the Linda the previous year, it took a little time to fully appreciate the influence the Flute would have on national defense.[19]

All in all, the six Redwing devices showed an impressive degree of sophistication, especially from an institution that was less than three years old and had run close to being shuttered. For Brown's Megaton Group, it was a validation of the Linda concept from the previous year. They had taken that fundamental design and expanded it both ways, with a larger Bassoon and a smaller Flute. For Foster's Hectoton Group, its three devices were an excursion in design well beyond the previous year's Cleo device. Both groups saw singular successes, a few disappointing results, but no catastrophes. Sophisticated codes and experience were molding design physicists into exceptional professionals. The Livermore designs also lived up to the Laboratory's unwritten charter to be creative: all of the Redwing devices were innovations.

# 13

////////////////

## *First the Flute and Then the Robin*

P rogressive Air Force officers like Colonel Bernard Schriever, director of strategic planning, strove to adopt intercontinental ballistic
missiles (ICBMs) into the fabric of the country's defensive structure. Schriever's strategic vision for an ICBM force won favor with Trevor
Gardner, assistant secretary of the Air Force for research and development. Gardner created a prestigious committee with a charter to advise
the Air Force on missiles, and he asked von Neumann to lead it. The great
Hungarian-born mathematician foresaw an ominous threat emerging
from the Soviet Union, and he feared the United States needed to act with
haste to meet it. On February 10, 1954, three years before Sputnik, his committee issued a report stating an ICBM was technologically feasible and the
Soviets were most likely developing one. They suggested an American missile program needed to be developed as early as 1960.

Gardner arranged to have a presentation on the ICBM issue placed on
President Eisenhower's schedule for July 28, 1955. He did not squander his
time before the president and the National Security Council as he carefully
laid out a briefing in three parts: an introduction by himself, a warhead
discussion by von Neumann, and a missile presentation by Schriever. The
briefing brought together an assemblage of the most powerful men in the
government: President Eisenhower, Vice President Nixon, Secretary of
State John Dulles, CIA Director Allen Dulles (John's brother), Secretary of
Defense Erwin Wilson, other cabinet members, and the members of the
Joint Chiefs of Staff.

Gardner started the briefing by saying the Soviet Union was aggressively developing a missile that could strike the United States within thirty
minutes after launch. The country had no defenses against it; there would

hardly be warning of an imminent attack. Next, von Neumann warned that America needed to have a credible nuclear deterrent to thwart this threat from becoming an actual attack. He spoke about advances in thermonuclear warheads, recalling the success of the Linda device tested three months earlier. As he faced the president, he may have smiled while thinking about the work being done by physicists like Mike May, who also served liverwurst sandwiches to houseguests. Von Neumann understood the implications of the Linda: the behemoth bombs of 1954 were a thing of the past—nuclear warheads were getting small enough to fit inside an ICBM. He knew Foster planned to develop a small atomic device based on the Geode concept to complement Brown's revolutionary thermonuclear secondary. Schriever wrapped up the briefing by describing steps needed to quickly develop an ICBM force.

Afterward, Eisenhower smiled, stood up, and thanked the three speakers.[1] Within a year, the Defense Department had four long-range nuclear-tipped missile programs. Three of these were under Air Force auspices (Atlas, Titan, and Thor), while the other was a combined Army-Navy development (Jupiter). Despite his early enthusiasm, Eisenhower was wary of a proliferation of missile programs—he remained adamant about keeping control of his defense budget and limiting further growth.

In the spring of 1955, von Neumann learned he had pancreatic cancer. The first time members of his missile committee were aware of his sickness was when he arrived at a meeting in a wheelchair attended by a military aide. A year and a half later, he was hospitalized at Walter Reed Army Hospital in Washington, D.C. Von Neumann had converted to Roman Catholicism with his mother in 1930, prior to his first marriage and his departure for America. Although he lived pretty much as an agnostic in the ensuing years, the approach of death awakened a spiritual need within him, and he called for a priest to receive the Church's last rites. Throughout his ordeal, his mind remained clear, and he entertained his brother while on his deathbed by reciting from memory the first lines from each page of Goethe's *Faust*.

Von Neumann died on February 8, 1957, and was buried in a cemetery in Princeton, New Jersey, near the Institute for Advanced Study, his workplace for a quarter century. He left quite a legacy. In the 1920s, he developed the first rigorous mathematical theory for the new field of quantum mechanics, and his textbook on the subject became a classic. He invented "game theory" and helped develop computational mathematics; the "von Neumann architecture" underlies practically all modern computers. In addition to these stunning achievements, he was an extraordinarily strong force in helping start the Livermore Laboratory.[2]

*// // //*

As has been noted, strategic bombers and liquid-fueled missiles shared a key characteristic: both weapon systems required an appreciable amount of time to deploy, thus making them vulnerable to surprise attacks. As Kaufmann and Brodie had pointed out in RAND analyses, that exposure undermined the credibility of America's nuclear deterrent. Admiral Arleigh Burke, Chief of Naval Operations since 1955, picked up on the nuances of RAND's vulnerability studies quickly and acted on them. He stepped into policy discussions with a radical solution. As a deterrent, deploy submerged submarines capable of launching solid-propellant fleet ballistic missiles with nuclear warheads against any adversary. Powered by a nuclear reactor, a submarine could remain submerged for months at a time—it would be invulnerable to a surprise attack.

Burke's notion was a direct challenge to the supremacy of SAC bombers as America's nuclear deterrent force. General LeMay aggressively argued against the Navy initiative, but it was difficult for any levelheaded intellectual to avoid Burke's logic. Air Force officers like Schriever separated themselves from LeMay's arguments and offered an alternative to the Navy's initiative. Solid-propellant missiles do not need lengthy preparation periods before launch, making them less vulnerable to surprise attacks. Further, by placing such missiles in silos buried below ground, it would require a direct hit, even from a nuclear weapon, to destroy the missile. Russian missiles of the time did not have that kind of accuracy. Underground silos added a lot of survivability to an ICBM force.

Those Navy and Air Force solutions made a strategic deterrent more credible, helping make Counterforce Strategy a viable policy, although missile technology still needed improvement to be accurate enough to strike military targets. There was, however, one underlying problem. Missiles, unlike bombers, could not carry heavy payloads. Thermonuclear warheads of the time were large and heavy, some weighing several tons. Skeptics openly wondered whether such a weapon could be made small enough to fit within the cone of a missile. In 1956, Nobel laureate Patrick Blackett wrote in his book *Atomic Weapons and East-West Relations* that this seemed unlikely.

In fact, a warhead for the liquid-fueled Atlas ICBM was being developed, but it weighed over three thousand pounds, heavier than desirable for a solid-propellant rocket of the day. That being the case for land-based ICBMs, how could a thermonuclear warhead possibly be produced small enough to fit within a quick-response ballistic missile launched from a submarine? That challenge set the stage for Admiral Burke to strike a deal with the Laboratory.

Burke had contracted the National Academy of Sciences to conduct a conference in the summer of 1956 to study the "growing Russian submarine menace." The academy extended the charter of the conference to study the feasibility of Burke's concept of a fleet ballistic missile. Called the Nobska Conference, it took its name from the Nobsque Lighthouse that marked the Massachusetts coast at Woods Hole, where Burke's conference was held.[3]

With a broader charter, the academy expanded its list of participants to include scientists with nuclear-weapons experience. Invited to the conference were Edward Teller and Johnny Foster from Livermore, Carson Mark and Harold Agnew from Los Alamos, and Isidor Rabi from the AEC's GAC.[4] They were members of the Weapons Effects and Limitations Subcommittee, chaired by David Griggs, who was now a professor of geophysics at the University of California, Los Angeles.[5]

The conference went through its courses, concentrating on submarine and antisubmarine warfare. In response to a challenge from a naval officer, Teller asserted a nuclear weapon with a significant yield could fit within the warhead compartment of a torpedo. Practically everyone sitting in the room thought this statement incredible.[6]

When the discussion switched to ballistic missiles, the payload limitations of a fleet ballistic missile, necessarily a less energetic solid-propellant missile, were brought out. No thermonuclear warhead was small and light enough to fit within a submarine-launched missile. Teller stood up and said the Livermore Laboratory could design just such a thermonuclear warhead by 1961. When Admiral Burke asked Mark if Los Alamos could also produce such a warhead, he responded no such warhead currently existed, it would be costly to produce, and it would take more than five years to design and develop.[7]

A debate started whether a fleet ballistic missile could deter the Soviet Union, with skeptics insisting it was not a useful concept. One participant, Rear Admiral Sinclair, left the conference room and went upstairs to where there was a library with naval volumes. He found a copy of Alfred Mahan's *Influence of Sea Power upon History, 1660–1805*, and brought it downstairs. Opening the book, he read a passage in which Mahan claimed changes of tactics take place usually after changes in weapons and only after an unduly long time, while changes in tactics have to overcome the inertia of a conservative class. History shows that it is vain to hope that military men generally will be at the pains to change—a lesson in itself of no mean value. Sinclair placed the book down, and the mood of the conference changed. There was no longer dissent about the need for the Navy to develop the missile.[8]

Admiral Burke sat at the conference table and listened intently to the exchange; he did not pursue the matter further. He had a distinguished physicist declare the Laboratory could provide a warhead for his fleet ballistic missile, and that was all he needed to make his case for the program.

Foster went back to Livermore and told Harold Brown about Teller's promise to the Navy, to which, understandably, Brown replied, "He said what?" But, in fact, he was prepared to meet the challenge. With the recent success of the test of the Flute in Operation Redwing, Brown felt confident enough to map out a development plan to accomplish the Navy's goals.[9] The Navy gave a name to its fleet ballistic missile program, calling it Polaris.

*※ ※ ※*

By 1957, there were rumblings coming from Washington, D.C., about a nuclear-test ban looming on the horizon. This was the backdrop when the AEC's director of military applications, Major General Starbird, felt the United States had to come to grips with a more assertive Soviet Union—to meet that looming threat, the country needed a highly effective nuclear force. If the rumors were true, Starbird was adamant that before nuclear testing stopped, warheads under development had to be thoroughly tested and deployed. He had two upcoming operations in which to accomplish this: Plumbbob, already underway in 1957 at NTS, and Hardtack, to be held at the Pacific Proving Grounds in 1958. The general sent a letter to his laboratory directors and asked what they thought the long-term effects of a test moratorium would be.

Bradbury replied that LASL would benefit from a halt. Reading his response to Starbird, one gets the feeling Bradbury was tired, perhaps from the stressful pace of meeting warhead demands from the Defense Department coupled with the growing pressure of having to compete with Livermore: "It is my own impression that LASL has let itself get too bogged down in mass production of weapon designs, and that we should try to take that aspect of our life a little easier and work a little harder in general research—which is thought to be good for the country too!"[10]

The response from Livermore was quite different. Teller told the general there were new ideas for nuclear weapons that needed exploring. He said there was far more useful work to be done than UCRL could possibly do in the immediate future.[11] The competitive spirit at the Laboratory, born out of the necessity of making itself relevant, affected U.S. posture in the Cold War. Bradbury felt the military situation with nuclear weapons was mature; that was proven in Operation Castle, when Los Alamos tested multiple hydrogen bombs to give the military whatever yields it wanted. On the other hand, Livermore's physicists challenged the way nuclear weapons were designed. The consequences of these disparate views were inevitable. After Los Alamos tested the first successful thermonuclear device in the Mike event, many of the major innovations to America's nuclear stockpile that emerged in the 1950s and 1960s would instead be invented in Livermore, instigated by its small warheads.

Regardless of his desire to take a respite from nuclear-weapons work, Bradbury led LASL through Operation Plumbbob. He was a cautious man, conservative in his outlook, and in his demeanor. If he were to choose a measure of merit to gauge how well LASL performed, no doubt he would choose to count how many of his laboratory's warheads were in the nation's nuclear stockpile at the time. Until 1956, Los Alamos had had a monopoly on providing the country's nuclear weapons, but that monopoly no longer existed. Bradbury had fought against the creation of a second laboratory, but with the establishment of that facility, he found himself in an uncomfortable competitive situation.

To deal with this, Bradbury offered a proposal in a letter he wrote to Herb York in July 1956, sending a copy also to General Starbird. In it he stated, since both laboratories possessed the ability to provide satisfactory designs, it would seem to be more efficient if each concentrated its future tests only in separate specific areas.[12] York disagreed. He responded each laboratory should remain competent in all fields of nuclear-weapons research, and the weapons workload should be equitably distributed.

Starbird reacted to Bradbury's letter separately. He was an aggressive officer and also yet another one of those West Pointers originally commissioned as an engineer. Starbird had graduated fourth in his class and had competed in the pentathlon at the 1936 Olympics in Berlin. In World War II he led a combat-engineer battalion during the Allied landings at Normandy on D-Day. Now, Starbird saw Bradbury's suggestion as a way for him to get more involved in managing the country's nuclear-testing program. The general called for representatives from the weapons laboratories to meet with his staff and hold two conferences to decide how to break up nuclear responsibilities. A preliminary meeting would be held at Los Alamos, followed by a formal meeting at San Francisco.

The Los Alamos meeting took place at about the same time as the end of the Nobska Conference, on August 13 and 14, 1956. The LASL representatives opted to develop warheads for ICBMs and other weapons systems about to be deployed. The Livermore delegation chose to develop small warheads for longer-term projects, including tactical missiles, tactical bombs, and artillery shells. (The UCRL physicists at the meeting were unaware of the Laboratory's commitment to the Navy made by Teller at Nobska.) By the time of the next meeting in San Francisco, Los Alamos took responsibility for developing as many as eight warheads, while Livermore took responsibility for two programs.[13]

There were unintended consequences to Bradbury's initiative, as taking responsibility for a defense contract brought with it obligations. For instance, a designer had to make sure the device worked as a real-world weapon: it must function after being shocked with sharp accelerations or after being dropped from a bomber at altitudes where the ambient temperature may be minus 60° Celsius. As a result, several tests are usually required before a warhead can be certified to enter the nuclear stockpile. With eight programs to support, LASL had a lot of development tests to conduct. Livermore had fewer obligations and, therefore, a freer hand to pursue new ideas.

The way nuclear tests were conducted over the following two years bears this out. The atomic device (the primary) developed in Operation Redwing by Los Alamos performed yeoman's service in development tests for the defense programs LASL had been assigned. Livermore's legacy primary, the Swan, saw only half as much use. Livermore designed three new primaries, weaponizing two of them, and developed two revolutionary new secondaries as well. Chairman Rabi had skeptically asked the GAC in 1954, "Where were the 'good ideas' coming from the new laboratory?"[14] He could not have avoided noticing the plethora of new inventions emanating out of Livermore after 1956.

The way that things turned out was an important development for the United States. Los Alamos, nine years older than Livermore, saw itself as the senior representative of the partnership. It was proud of that distinction and wanted to continue as the main source of weapons for the country. Livermore had little history and, at that time, no weapons that it could point to in the country's nuclear arsenal. Instead of trying to outdo Los Alamos in producing warheads, Livermore designers were more enamored with new ideas for the long-term future. They assumed their "good ideas" would eventually be used. In this way, the two laboratories complemented one another, spurring each other to do better and checking each other from straying off with ideas that were not good. At least in the late 1950s, Livermore led the new-concepts bandwagon.

*※ ※ ※*

Amid the AEC deciding which laboratory would do what, the everyday activities of physicists, mathematicians, chemists, and engineers had to go on. Hydrotests were essential to design an atomic device, but the procedure to conduct them was slow and cumbersome. Miscommunications among physicists and engineers led to heated arguments. York's solution to the problem was to integrate elements supporting the Hectoton Group into a single organization, which he called B Division, appointing Foster to lead it.

Being in B Division with Foster was an invigorating experience. The newly formed unit held a weekly meeting in the auditorium, which was hot and stuffy. An air-conditioning unit was installed in one corner, but it was noisy and so was seldom used. At each meeting Foster appointed a chairman and a so-called S.O.B.—sort of a devil's advocate. It was difficult to stay awake at these meetings. In particular, one man named Ray Brandey was always falling asleep. He was cured of this practice rather abruptly when Foster lit a firecracker from his cigar and threw it under Brandey's chair.

Appropriate engineers and shop management attended a separate meeting every Friday afternoon in Foster's office, where the status of experiments were discussed. The engineers were expected to design, and the shops expected to build, all kinds of odd parts to unheard of tolerances in almost zero time. It is no wonder the engineers and shop people called this meeting the "Inquisition" or "Foster's Friday Frolics."[15]

Bob LeLevier's team of code developers was called the Hydrodynamics Group, which appropriately enough concentrated on producing hydro-codes. Their work was as essential to B Division as it had been to the Hectoton Group. To recall, hydrodynamics treat materials as fluids acting under stress created by an influx of energy—for example, from a high explosive that produces shockwaves through the material. The assumption of treating matter driven by an explosion as a fluid works very well except for that portion of the material the moment it undergoes the shock.

When modeled mathematically, a shockwave introduces a discontinuity in the hydrodynamic equations. That mathematical discontinuity will disrupt a computer code. A fix to the problem came from von Neumann and a LASL physicist named Robert Richtmyer, who coauthored a paper in March 1950 in the *Journal of Applied Physics*.[16] To get rid of the mathematical discontinuity, they introduced what they called an artificial viscosity into the matter experiencing the shockwave.

Viscosity is a measure of how difficult it is for a fluid to move; for instance, fluids like water have low viscosities, while molasses has a relatively high viscosity. By giving a material an artificial viscosity, which they labeled as Q, von Neumann and Richtmyer artificially slowed down the movement of the material as the shockwave ran through it, thereby getting rid of the sudden discontinuous lurch the substance otherwise went through. This artificial viscosity caused the material to slightly smear out the shockwave over a small amount of time, adding just enough of a time differential to avoid a discontinuity without seriously jeopardizing the calculation. The mathematical trick worked.

The mathematician Mark Wilkins was a member of LeLevier's group, and he took a special interest in the von Neumann–Richtmyer paper. He found if he used von Neumann's formula for Q, there was a minor rippling effect after the shockwave. Keeping with the same concept, he thought he could improve the formula for Q so the rippling stopped. He succeeded.[17]

Collaborating with Jim Wilson, Wilkins used his viscosity model to write one of the most successful hydrocodes to come out of the 1950s. This dynamic duo would have appeared bizarre to an outsider. Wilson, who was enthralled with Buddhist culture, including its Zen Koan, wrote his technical papers with a distinctly Eastern flair. He was a colorful contrast to the staid, laid-back Wilkins, who later became the chief mathematician at Freddie de Hoffman's General Atomics Corporation in San Diego. (De Hoffman had been Teller's assistant at Los Alamos and, in April 1951, wrote the follow-on paper to the Teller-Ulam article.)

*# # #*

With a new round of nuclear tests to plan, it might have appeared that Foster's task was straightforward: weaponize his Redwing devices. But following an unchallenging path was not a characteristic Foster trait. He still harbored a desire to design a nuclear artillery shell for the Army, the driving force behind developing the Cleo and then the Swallow. As it happened, Los Alamos had developed a nuclear artillery shell for the Army's 8-inch gun in 1953, but its use required a significant amount of specialized training by the artillery crews who fired it. Foster wanted to take things a step further by designing a shell for the Army's 155-millimeter howitzer, which had a diameter of roughly six inches, that did not require a lot of special training.

To design a new and "easier to use" nuclear artillery shell, B Division designers started with the Swallow's design and improved it. After six months of fiddling with ideas and performing calculations and hydrotests, they came up with an elegant design for a nuclear artillery shell. When it was tested, it gave a smaller yield than expected, but it was large enough to meet the Army's requirements. The new warhead provided the Army with a nuclear artillery shell for its ubiquitous 155-millimeter howitzer, which should make enemy armies more cautious when facing American combat units.[18] The warhead was simple to deploy and required little specialized training. It went into production in 1963 and has remained in the Army arsenal for decades.[19]

Foster had other things to think about—most importantly, designing an atomic device to drive a thermonuclear warhead for Polaris. To do that, he reached back to a concept that had emerged when his Hectoton Group was engaged in the Redwing tests on Eniwetok. His physicists had spent time thinking about the future in a Quonset hut with a blackboard on one wall (an essential item to have whenever there are physicists in a room). They sat together in their shorts and shirtless, a tropical breeze moving through two doors on either side of the hut. There were no distractions.

Wilson threw out an idea and sketched it on the blackboard. It was an updated version of the Geode, which had been introduced in 1953. Wally Birnbaum looked at the sketch and offered a novel way to use a detonation shockwave for implosion, then others in the group chimed in with ideas. They were all experts in hydrodynamics, having each participated in scores of hydrotests for the Redwing devices. (The Swan alone went through over one hundred hydrotests at Site 300.) These men had reached a stage of expertise where they did not need a computer code to tell them how the model on the blackboard would react to a high-explosive shockwave. As they went through their discussions, day after day, Wilson's original idea took on the form of a fission bomb smaller and lighter than any other device developed to that time.[20]

At a meeting of B Division designers held in August 1956, Foster announced: "A study named Robin has been started on a different method of implosion. It aims to achieve a device characterized by light weight, ruggedness, and moderate efficiency."[21] At first there were two variations of Robin, the Robin A and the Robin B. The Robin A accentuated using uranium as its major fuel component. It was weighty and went through several difficult tests, then was forgotten after the alternative Robin B design worked out much better.

Using plutonium as a nuclear fuel, the Robin B was a true descendent of the original Geode concept. It was light and rugged, and it gave a significant yield. The physicists of B Division knew they were designing a revolutionary atomic warhead for America's nuclear arsenal. When they were done, the device weighed less than sixty pounds—light enough to be carried in a person's hands. They calculated it would have a higher yield than the Fat Man device, tested in the Trinity event, which was five feet in diameter and weighed several tons. The Robin was tested in Operation Plumbbob, and it worked just as predicted.

The Robin, however, never showed up in America's nuclear stockpile. Its legacy was much more important than that, for the Robin became the foundation upon which to build warheads for the future. It was the ultimate fission weapon, the prototype used to build the country's modern stockpile. Part of its revolutionary concept was the way it melded with a secondary (fusion bomb), which not only saved energy but also made it simpler to slim down thermonuclear warheads further than had been possible up to that time.[22]

*# # #*

In 1958 Herb York left the Laboratory to become the founding director of the Advanced Research Projects Agency, tapped by the secretary of defense to bring more scientific expertise into the Pentagon. York had discussed leaving the Laboratory a year earlier, but Lawrence had dissuaded him from departing. Now he relented and appointed Teller to be the interim director of the Laboratory, with T Division leader Mark Mills appointed deputy director. The plan was for Mills to become permanent director once the regents of the University of California and the commissioners of the AEC approved his appointment.

Before departing for Washington, York had organized a consolidation of Brown's Megaton Group, which became A Division. In A Division, physicists dealt with high temperatures generated by atomic explosions. Their mandate of designing a fusion device—a secondary—did not entail conducting a hydrotest, so there was much less of a hands-on experimental climate than existed in B Division. The major focus for Brown was to coordinate the needs of secondary designers with the work of code developers. The emphasis was on radiative transport codes, as it had to be, but hydrodynamics and neutron reactions (neutronics) were also important.

May's Radiative Transport Group provided A Division with "burn codes," that is, codes that performed the radiative transport, hydrodynamics, and neutronics calculations needed to make a secondary work. This group had some illustrious members, including Roland Herbst, William Schulz, John Nuckolls, and Bill Lokke.

Herbst was a character. He joined the group in October 1954 after completing his PhD dissertation in general relativity the year before at Saint Louis University. Herbst had no experience writing codes, but that was soon to change. One of his first, written for the IBM 701, was GHOTI. He later revealed that the pronunciation of the name came from George Bernard Shaw's play *Pygmalion*. A lead character in the play, Professor Higgins, might explain that "gh" was pronounced like an "f" as in "enough"; "o" was pronounced as a short "i" as in "women"; and "ti" was pronounced as "s" as in "attention." Putting the three phonetic sounds together, GHOTI was pronounced as "fish." Once they got over Herbst's eccentricities with literature, designers found GHOTI to be a powerful code, and it became a favorite within A Division, an accolade coveted by a code developer. It remained a popular code for years until surpassed by yet another Herbst code.[23]

May wanted a code that had an improved physics package and was convenient to use. He assembled Herbst, Schulz, and Norman Hardy into a code-writing team, with Herbst as its leader. They were joined by a computer scientist, Bob Kuhn, who was a specialist in translating mathematical equations into computer instructions that did not waste time or space. Herbst held meetings in his office, where the code was written, first on a blackboard, then transcribed into a computer. Herbst found it hard to speak in a low voice when he became excited. Physicists down the hallway could hardly work as they heard him bellowing verbal shots of abuse to his teammates, "Well, that's stupid!" The team bore these tirades, and after months of toil, they created one of the most powerful codes used throughout the country's nuclear-weapons complex. They called their creation Coronet.[24]

In early 1957, Brown laid out his plans for A Division. Devices tested in Plumbbob would be precursors for the Hardtack tests one year later.

Brown wanted to develop a large, medium, and small thermonuclear warhead, the same strategy he had used in Operation Redwing. The large warhead would serve as a bomb dropped from a strategic bomber. The medium warhead was meant to be a backup for an ICBM. The small one, a successor of Redwing's Flute device, was meant to fulfill the Laboratory's recently accepted commitment to develop a warhead for Polaris.

The first challenge was to design a strategic bomb. Using his Bassoon device as a basis, May and his design group were given one test in Plumbbob to assess some revisions they had made to the original concept. The new design worked well. A second device was tested a year later in Hardtack, and it broke records for a weapon its size for its efficiency and its ratio of fusion to fission power.

The thermonuclear bombs deployed by the Air Force at the time were the B17 and the B21, which weighed 42,500 pounds and 17,500 pounds respectively. May's device, which became the B41, was a quarter the size and weighed 10,500 pounds, yet it delivered a much higher yield. The B41 offered significant advantages to the Air Force since it could be carried by multiple aircraft, not just the largest bombers. It was placed into the nuclear stockpile and served the country for almost two decades.

The second A Division challenge was a medium-sized warhead for delivery by an ICBM and also was developed through two phases: a proto-type design tested in Plumbbob, and then a fully loaded design tested the following year. Mills, the physicist designated to be the next Laboratory director, went to observe phase two at Eniwetok. He wanted to make sure the diagnostics were correctly aligned, so he asked to go to the island where they had been set up. A helicopter was brought in to take him there. He was joined by Harry Keller, the head of the Livermore element for Hardtack, and Air Force colonel Ernest Pinson, Mills' military escort.

Mills was seated with his back to the pilot on the port (left) side of the helicopter next to a door that was kept open during the flight, a standard procedure for interisland flights. Keller was seated next to Mills on the starboard side of the helicopter, where he was enjoying an aerial view of Eniwetok. Passing over Riunit Island, the aircraft flew into a rainsquall, which buffeted it with severe turbulence. Within two minutes of flying into the squall, the pilot lost his sense of equilibrium. The helicopter tilted and struck the water, then settled onto a reef and rolled over on its side in ten feet of water.

Colonel Pinson, who had been sitting opposite Mills, unbuckled his own seat belt but could not get out of the aircraft because the starboard door, now facing upward, had shut. He floated to the top of the passenger compartment, reached a small pocket of air, took a deep breath, and kicked out the door. Pulling himself through the opening, he cleared the wreckage and rose to the surface.

Once at the surface, Pinson dove back to the wreckage and worked his way into the passenger compartment. He groped in near-complete darkness and felt Keller, who was unconscious but still alive; the colonel released him from his harness and brought him up to the surface, where he passed him on to the helicopter pilot, who had also freed himself and was treading water nearby. Pinson then dove again into the wreckage, but he could not find Mills, who was belted in at the side of the helicopter that was now on the bottom, and the growing darkness made it difficult for Pinson to see him. Mills did not survive. An autopsy revealed that he had struck his head severely during the accident and was most likely unconscious when the helicopter submerged into the water.[25] The Laboratory would not get to experience his leadership as director; Teller remained director instead.

The nuclear test went on the day after the Mills tragedy. Its performance exceeded expectations, giving a significant yield. Its performance made the device an ideal backup for the Atlas and Titan systems undergoing development for the Air Force. It would be needed.

A Division's third challenge was a small thermonuclear warhead for Polaris. The starting point was the Flute, that revolutionary secondary that had performed so well the previous year. Its successor was called the Piccolo. For Plumbbob, the design team tested three variations of the Piccolo as a parameter test. One of the variants outperformed the others, albeit by a small amount, which set the stage for the Hardtack tests. Three additional variations for the Piccolo—labeled A, B, and C—were tested then, and again an optimum candidate was selected. That established a basis to take the next step beyond Piccolo toward building a deployable warhead for the Navy. Brown asked his deputy Carl Haussmann to take charge of the effort.

Haussmann organized a design team for Polaris before a test ban could set in, and they benefited by having a multidimensional burn code available—yet another tribute to the computer culture that was von Neumann's legacy. Human intuition as well as computer calculations played crucial roles in achieving a workable design under trying circumstances. Finally, a revolutionary device was completed and tested in the final days of Hardtack. Its measured yield was precisely as predicted, and its yield-to-weight ratio made it the most efficient warhead of its time.

It appeared the Navy now had a viable warhead for its Polaris missile. From the time Brown gave Haussmann the assignment to develop this secondary until the time they tested the device in the Pacific, only ninety days had passed. As a parallel to the Robin atomic device, this secondary for Polaris laid the foundation for modern thermonuclear weapons in the United States.

//////////////////

# The Navy Gets a Warhead for a Missile

How the Navy established the key segment of America's Counterforce Strategy is a study in sheer grit. Admiral Burke graduated from the Naval Academy in 1923 and served in the surface Navy on battleships and destroyers. In World War II he commanded Destroyer Division 23, the "Little Beavers," which was credited with sinking a cruiser, nine destroyers, and one submarine. He was a hard-driving officer and a strategic thinker with a vision for a fleet ballistic missile. When he became chief of naval operations (CNO) in 1955, there was no such thing as a nuclear-tipped, solid-fueled ballistic missile launched from a submarine.

Once placed in charge of the Navy, Burke harnessed the wherewithal of the country's scientific community and used it to achieve his goals in much the same way Hap Arnold recruited the aerospace industry to service the Air Force at the end of World War II. Three months after becoming CNO, Burke established the Special Project Office (SPO) to consolidate the Navy's ballistic-missile programs, placing Rear Admiral William Raborn in command of it. Burke's selection of Raborn, a naval aviator, was shrewd. Having a respected aviator promote missile technology made the program more credible. The SPO broke with Navy tradition by running its own budget; in other Navy programs, procurement was the responsibility of established bureaus.[1]

To overcome President Eisenhower's determination to limit missile programs, Burke planned to quietly achieve technical breakthroughs and, once there was a viable system, show it off to the secretary of defense as a fait accompli. To meet that goal, the program needed a technician who was also a good program manager. Raborn provided that leadership when he appointed Captain Levering Smith to manage the solid-fuel missile project for Polaris. Smith approached the Aerojet-General Corporation and the Lockheed Missile and Space Division for technical assistance, and the result was the development of the Jupiter-S, a solid-fueled missile propelled by a cluster of six first-stage rockets and a single second-stage rocket. This was a start, but the Jupiter-S was too large for a submarine, standing forty-four feet high, with a ten-foot diameter, and weighing eighty tons.[2]

What the Navy needed was a missile small enough to fit vertically within the pressure hull of a submarine, which meant reducing the height to around thirty feet. Captain Smith employed his former staff at the Navy's China Lake research facility to get the weight and size of a solid-fuel missile reduced. After months of hard work, they produced plans for a fifteen-ton missile with a height of twenty-eight feet, five inches that had essentially the same performance characteristics as the Jupiter-S. When tested, it carried a one-thousand-pound payload fifteen hundred miles—enough range to reach Moscow from a launch point in the ocean.

With that accomplishment and with the successful test of the Flute by Livermore, Burke had his technological breakthrough. He then arranged for Raborn to brief Secretary of Defense Wilson on Polaris, emphasizing how much it would save in funding. In the budget-strapped atmosphere of the 1950s Pentagon, that was an influential argument; the briefing went well. As Wilson said to Raborn, "You've shown me a lot of sexy slides, young man. But that's the sexiest, that half-billion-dollar saving."[3] On December 8, 1956, Wilson issued a directive to start a Polaris program for a fleet ballistic missile.

Captain Smith procured the hull of an attack submarine, the *Scorpion*, then under construction at Electric Boat's shipyard in Groton, Connecticut. He had the vessel cut in half to insert a missile section in the middle. At that time, discussions commenced about how many missiles to insert into the submarine. Economy of costs argued for more, around thirty, while naval officers argued for fewer missiles, from eight to twelve, in order to gain survivability and maneuverability for the submarine. As a compromise solution, but deferring significantly to the submariners, Raborn intervened and chose a sixteen-missile complement.

Polaris needed to be compatible with RAND's Counterforce Strategy. Analysts like Brodie and Kaufmann had been preaching the merits of striking military targets as an alternative to Eisenhower's Massive Retaliation strategy, which meant Polaris needed to be accurate enough to put relatively small targets, rather than entire Soviet cities, at risk. Two technologies were needed to at least put Polaris in the ballpark of being acceptable: a guidance system to steer the missile to its target, and a navigation system to pinpoint the location of its launch point.

A Navy team went to MIT and engaged Charles Stark Draper, the director of the Instrumentation Laboratory, to develop a missile-guidance system. Draper had been doing pioneer work on inertial guidance since 1945, when he refined a gyroscope for gun-control systems. Two of Draper's mathematicians, Richard Battin and J. Halcombe Laning Jr., had developed a mathematical-guidance formulation called Q-guidance that was well suited for Polaris, partly because it relied on a digital computer rather than a bulkier analog machine. Also, Draper's floating gyroscope was easier to adapt to the higher accelerations of a solid-fuel missile. Working on a very tight schedule, his laboratory designed and developed the Mark 1 guidance system for Polaris. This combined inertial components and electronics into one module weighing 225 pounds.

A navigation system that precisely pinpoints a submarine's location at the time of launch came from the Autonetics Division of North American Aviation. It had developed the XN6 Autonavigator for the Army's Navaho missile program, but it was cancelled in July 1957—a devastating blow for the division, which now faced laying off ten thousand employees. In desperation, the company sent a physicist to sell five instruments to the Navy Department. The Navy invested in one of them and was immediately rewarded. In August 1958 that instrument navigated the nuclear-powered submarine USS *Nautilus* on its famous voyage from the Pacific Ocean to the Atlantic by crossing under the polar ice of the Arctic Ocean.[4] The XN6 became the navigation system for Polaris.

SPO still needed to design a capsule to house Livermore's warhead atop the Polaris missile. That responsibility fell on the shoulders of Bob Wertheim, a 1945 graduate of the Naval Academy. In the final months of World War II, Wertheim was stationed on a destroyer cruising off the western shores of

Japan to protect the flank of the fleet assembling for the invasion of Japan. Two atomic bombs ended the war and the need for an invasion fleet. After two years, Wertheim received orders to join SPO and report to Levering Smith. He was about to start a career in the nuclear Navy.

Wertheim was the only one at SPO who had a nuclear background, thanks to his earlier associations and education. He was the chairman of what was called the Reentry Body Coordinating Committee. Its member organizations were Livermore (represented by Haussmann from Brown's A Division) for the warhead, Sandia for the nonnuclear parts of the warhead, and the Naval Ordnance Laboratory at White Oak, Maryland, for the arming and fusing system, which the Navy provided. Lockheed was the contractor on missile-related parts of the workload.

Wertheim was passionate to get the job done in the best manner for the country. To make his reentry body the tight, coherent system required, he integrated the warhead body with the heat shield, something that was unprecedented. He ruffled feathers by taking lucrative contracts away from usual Pentagon contractors and having the reentry body assembled at an AEC facility, Pantex, in Amarillo, Texas, where the country's nuclear arsenal was produced. His innovative approaches to the problem put the program three years ahead of schedule.

Against all odds and the expectations of military and government onlookers, in three years Wertheim succeeded in creating a reentry capsule light enough for a Polaris missile. The weight of the entire reentry body—warhead, heat shields, arming and fusing system, everything—was 850 pounds; by comparison, the Atlas warhead weighed over 3,000 pounds. In January 1960 the USS *George Washington*, America's first Polaris submarine, was launched for sea trials. The warhead reentry capsules for its sixteen missiles were provided by Wertheim's innovative team.

Wertheim had every reason to be proud of his achievement: "It was the most satisfying, time consuming, and challenging job I could possibly have imagined. . . . I interacted with all these great folks in industry and government and the Laboratories: Harold Brown, Johnny Foster, Carl Haussmann, and folks at Sandia, and the great designer and engineer at Lockheed, Lloyd Wilson. Admiral Raborn said we had a government-industrial team and he managed it that way."[5]

Bernard Schriever, now a general and still with the Air Staff, saw the innovations going on with Polaris. The Navy program alerted him to the progress Livermore had made in reducing the size of a thermonuclear warhead; the devices were getting smaller at a rate that even surpassed von Neumann's predictions. Schriever sought to create a solid-propellant ICBM to provide all the advantages such a system had over its liquid-fueled predecessors. The missile would be smaller and simpler in construction, making it more reliable and affordable to produce. It could be stored in full readiness inside an underground silo for lengthy periods of time, which made it invulnerable to a preemptive nuclear strike barring a direct hit. And most important, it could be launched into space in a minute or less. By January 1958, Schriever planned to build what became known as the Minuteman missile by leveraging the warhead developed for Polaris at Livermore.

*# # #*

As Laboratory physicists labored to design a nuclear warhead for Polaris, a perceptible threat emanated from the Soviet Union. The foreboding was strong enough for Eisenhower, on April 4, 1957, to direct the National Security Council to form a panel to take stock of Soviet nuclear forces. Its formal title was the Security Resources Panel, but it was better known by the name of its first chairman, Rowan Gaither, a San Francisco attorney who had a longtime interest in nuclear matters. Its charter was to study how best to protect the civil population of the country from a nuclear attack.

The panel issued a report in November, one month after the launch of Sputnik. The Russian satellite induced Americans to assemble outside in the evenings to watch an artificial moon from the Soviet Union fly over them. Perhaps goaded by the shock of that event, the Gaither Panel's report urged an aggressive approach to passive and active defenses and to increase the country's retaliatory forces: "The USSR will achieve a significant ICBM delivery capability with megaton warheads by 1959. The next two years seem to us critical. If we fail to act at once, the risk, in our opinion, will be unacceptable."[6]

Eisenhower disagreed with the alarmist tone of the report and withheld it from publication, but several members of the Senate Armed Services Committee had seen it, and Lyndon Johnson, the senate majority leader, demanded its contents be made public. He partially got his wish, as sections of the report were covertly leaked to news media. Their effect on the American public, fueled by sensationalism in the press, was immediate—schools held air-raid drills, with school children participating by crawling under their desks, while a program for the city of Livermore built fallout shelters to house hundreds of families.[7]

*Washington Post* reporter Chalmers Roberts wrote on December 20, 1957, that the top-secret Gaither Report portrayed a United States in the gravest danger in its history. America faced an immediate threat from a "missile-bristling" Soviet Union. The nation's long-term prospects were in cataclysmic peril in the face of rocketing Soviet military might and a growing Soviet economy. The article said the report stripped away the complacency and laid bare the highly unpleasant realities of the relative postures of the United States and the free world on one side, and the Soviet Union and the communist orbit on the other.[8]

Although Roberts' "missile-bristling Soviet Union" was an overheated version of the report's "significant ICBM delivery capability," the tone of the article did reflect the tone of the Gaither Report. Eisenhower felt betrayed when the contents were leaked to the press, but undoubtedly Gaither's panel felt obligated to express its concerns the administration was undervaluing the threat. As Herman Kahn suggested during this period in his book *On Thermonuclear War*, military power concentrated in the hands of a few unpredictable countries, accompanied by the expansionist doctrine of communist nations, had brought Americans face to face with the sobering thought that their triumph of material progress and human security following World War II could be reversed.[9]

A new phrase soon appeared in newspapers and political speeches: the missile gap. The public was being told there was a widening gap in nuclear strength between the Soviet Union and America, with Soviet nuclear-tipped missiles in the works that would be able to overwhelm U.S. defenses as early as 1961.

Part of the problem was Eisenhower had been inarticulate in handling the news of Sputnik. He felt Americans should unquestioningly trust his judgment on how to protect them. He and his administration dismissed the Soviet satellite launch as a feat of simple and well-understood mechanics and rocket science. They did not seem to understand that Americans saw Sputnik not in scientific terms, but in military ones: if the Soviets could launch a satellite into orbit, then they could launch a nuclear weapon that could strike the United States. There would be no warning, and if the Soviets attacked the country's SAC airbases first, the United States would be defenseless, its bombers and its strategic nuclear deterrent destroyed in an instant.[10]

While the public digested the news of the Gaither Report, at the same time the United States was starting Operation Hardtack, the Soviets announced on March 31, 1958, they were unilaterally discontinuing nuclear testing and called on other nations to follow their lead. Eisenhower held a news conference on April 2 and called the Russian move a "gimmick" that should not be taken seriously.[11] Khrushchev, who was now Soviet premier, two days later wrote a personal letter to the president reiterating the appeal.

Eisenhower had little interest in a test ban except as part of a broader agreement covering other areas of disarmament as well. His reliance on Massive Retaliation had allowed him to reduce the size of U.S. conventional forces significantly; the 750,000-man Army, especially, was substantially smaller than its Russian counterpart, having 2.5 million soldiers. The president wanted a Soviet commitment to reduce its conventional forces before there was any discussion of a test ban. Nevertheless, public fears ignited by the Gaither Report and Sputnik pressured him to move toward nuclear disarmament as an issue separate from other forms of disarmament.

Eisenhower opted to follow the Soviet lead to stop testing, although he harbored concerns over the Russians cheating. He asked Harold Stassen, governor of Minnesota, to chair a panel of experts that included Lawrence, Teller, York, and Griggs that could meet with Soviet counterparts to discuss and agree upon verification technologies to detect covert nuclear tests.

Then Eisenhower, without consulting the AEC, wrote to Khrushchev on April 28 that U.S. policy was changing—America would cease nuclear testing by November 1—but he still wanted experts to meet and discuss verification issues. Khrushchev agreed to such a meeting of experts provided there were two sets of specialists, one coming from the United States, Great Britain, France, and Canada, and the second coming from the Soviet Union, Czechoslovakia, Poland, and Romania. With this stipulation,

Khrushchev achieved parity of representation, which he felt he could not get in the United Nations.[12]

Soviet leaders pushed for a test ban in part because their country had developed a hydrogen bomb, which meant the Soviet Union had achieved a rough parity of nuclear capability with the United States. They realized the United States had a commanding lead in developing nuclear weapons (the Americans had conducted sixty-six nuclear tests compared to the Soviets' fourteen), which could expand with time. The Soviets may have believed the best way to avoid nuclear inferiority was to get the Americans to stop testing.

In accordance with the president's order, the AEC set a deadline to end testing on October 30, which created a scramble to complete tests for warhead programs, especially Polaris, before the deadline set in. At the same time, new safety standards were instituted, which caught weapons designers off guard. The most important new safety measure involved atomic devices, the one-point safety rule.

The idea behind this rule was to prevent an inadvertent atomic explosion if the device was struck at a single point. For instance, if a nuclear warhead fell from a loading crane onto a hard surface, the safety rule required that, should the impact cause the high-explosive inside the device to detonate, this would not cause a release of nuclear energy exceeding four pounds of TNT; likewise, if a terrorist fired a gun into a warhead and the bullet struck the high explosive and caused it to detonate, then the resulting explosion could not have a nuclear yield exceeding four pounds of TNT. The four pounds of TNT criterion apparently came from a Navy study that established it as the safe radiation level for a crew serving on a vessel with a nuclear weapon stored on board.[13]

Since this safety rule was relatively late in coming, little consideration had been given to it by designers. The AEC instituted Operation Millrace in the fall of 1958 to conduct seven one-point safety tests of Livermore devices at NTS. These took place in tunnels and featured starting a warhead detonation at a single point and measuring the resulting nuclear yield to see if the device met the new safety requirements. Some of the warheads did, but some did not. Those that failed went through rapid modifications and were shoved back into a tunnel to be retested.

A dramatic scene occurred on the afternoon of October 30. A Livermore device had been tested for safety and had failed, so a redesigned device needed testing. On the day of the test, winds were blowing toward Las Vegas, so the safety officer, who was a Laboratory physicist, would not allow the event to proceed. The test crew waited at their stations, ready to respond the moment they received permission to execute. The hours passed, the wind remained unchanged, and by midnight the time for testing had expired. The untested warhead was put into the stockpile after it was fitted with a mechanical device that let it meet the new safety standards.

Amid this flurry of activity, Johnny Foster met a man who would later play an important role in his life. Foster refers to this meeting as the time "he got me." The Senate Armed Services Committee requested the Laboratory send an expert to testify about the nuclear-test ban, and Foster was chosen to be that witness. Bill McMillan, a RAND analyst and a consultant to the Laboratory, joined him for the flight to Washington, and they discussed the upcoming testimony. McMillan wrote a draft statement and presented it to Foster to use in his presentation the next morning.

Foster had no experience addressing a committee of Congress; he nervously fidgeted with McMillan's draft in the committee room as he prepared to give his statement. Among the members entering the committee room was Massachusetts senator John Fitzgerald Kennedy, known for his ability to concentrate on a speaker—he seldom interrupted until the witness had made all his or her points. His rapt attention and unblinking gaze could be unnerving.

Foster stood to give his briefing, first stating the views he was about to present were technical and not political. He emphasized the importance of nuclear tests to guarantee the reliability of the nation's nuclear stockpile. With a cessation of testing, further refinement of the nation's atomic weapons would stop since it was too dangerous to rely on weapons whose performance was predicted on the results of calculations alone.

At the end of the presentation, Senator Kennedy asked a question: he understood that Foster was giving a technical briefing, but he wondered whether Foster had made a few political judgments. Foster responded that no, he had limited himself to technical advice only. Kennedy picked up the paper McMillan had written and read aloud a sentence dealing with the need for continued testing, then said, "Doesn't that sound political to you?" Foster thought about it and said, "Yes sir, it does." With that, Foster's mind went blank; he sat down and kept quiet for the rest of the meeting.[14]

*// // //*

The Cold War made Laboratory physicists like Nicholas C. Christofilos feel anxious about the security of the nation. Christofilos had joined Livermore in a most unorthodox way. Born in Boston, Massachusetts, in 1916, at the age of six he moved with his parents to their native Greece. He was a good student and earned degrees in mechanical and electrical engineering at the National Technical University. Thereafter, he stayed in Athens to work at a factory that installed and repaired elevators.

World War II descended on Greece with the German invasion of that country, and Christofilos occupied himself during those years by reading German-language physics texts and journals. In 1948 he wrote a letter to the Rad Lab purporting to describe a new type of accelerator. When a physicist deciphered the letter, it was found to describe the synchrocyclotron, an accelerator invented several years before by Edwin McMillan. Physics journals had described that invention the year before Christofilos' letter, so it was set aside and forgotten. About a year later he sent another letter describing a more complicated design for an accelerator. This second invention was revolutionary; it was later adopted by Brookhaven Laboratory.

Fortune then intervened when York, who had heard about Christofilos, invited him to join the Laboratory's Sherwood Project to study nuclear fusion. Christofilos arrived in 1956 and developed ideas for thermonuclear reactors that produced energy. He might have been content doing that indefinitely had it not been for the launch of Sputnik. That event strongly affected him, leading him to believe the Russians were about to gain a decisive military advantage over the United States.

He developed an idea to protect America against a Soviet missile attack by building a defensive shield surrounding the earth made up of high-energy electrons. Christofilos believed the electrons would damage anything crossing through them, including Russian missiles carrying thermonuclear warheads (something of a prelude to President Reagan's Strategic Defense Initiative of the 1980s). Christofilos proposed exploding nuclear weapons into the earth's magnetosphere, which is above the atmosphere.

These would release electron-emitting radioisotopes that would become trapped by the planet's magnetic field for perhaps months or even years. Presidential Science Advisor James Killian held a conference with physicists in Livermore February 10–21, 1958, and concluded the idea had merit.[15]

Christofilos proposed a series of experiments called Project Argus to measure electrons released by nuclear warheads exploded high above the atmosphere. While planning his experiment, he concluded there must already be a natural belt of electrons circling the earth. Another experiment in this regard was already underway by a team from the University of Iowa led by physicist James Van Allen. Launching Explorer satellites in early 1958, they discovered what came to be known as the Van Allen Belt, which contained the trapped electrons Christofilos had predicted three months earlier.

By then, York was at the Pentagon leading ARPA. He had a limited amount of Defense Department funding available to conduct final nuclear tests before the test ban set in, so he thought he would give Christofilos' idea a try. York's fourth order as ARPA director was to execute Project Argus over uninhabited Gough Island, claimed by the British, in the South Atlantic.

Since Explorer 4 was still in orbit, experimenters could use its instruments to detect an influx of electrons into the magnetosphere. Project Argus comprised three experiments, each one using a low-yield nuclear warhead, between one and two kilotons, detonated at an altitude of about three hundred miles. The experiments occurred over a period of two weeks, from the first event on August 27, to a second event on August 30, and then a final event on September 6. The Explorer 4 measurements found the earth's magnetic field was too weak to hold the emitted beta electrons for an extended period. Christofilos' idea was sound—it just would not work here.[16]

On November 26, 1958, Queen Frederika of Greece visited Livermore. When her upcoming trip was announced in Livermore schools, the schoolchildren became confused, wondering why there was a "Queen of Grease." Their teachers soon straightened out the confusion, and the kids learned Greece was a country. The queen rode in a motorcade through the city and was greeted by the city's grammar-school students, who poured out on sidewalks to wave at the smiling royalty. The Associated Press captured the event with a photo of Stirling Colgate, Christofilos, and Teller greeting the queen at the entrance to the Laboratory. She was in Livermore to honor the Laboratory's son of Greece, Christofilos, for his contributions to the defense of western democracies. It was another extraordinary episode in the life of an extraordinary Greek physicist.[17]

⫻ ⫻ ⫻

Meanwhile, the Conference of Experts was held in Geneva to see whether it was possible to verify a test ban. Lawrence, a pro-testing advocate, was there and convinced Harold Brown to serve with him. Brown, although an aggressive weapons designer, was an advocate for a test ban, so the two complemented each other. As it turned out, once committed to the president's agenda, Lawrence turned his energies to seeing the negotiations succeed. The meetings focused on the question of how cheating could be detected.

Initially, it appeared cheating was feasible. Albert Latter, a RAND physicist who worked extensively at Livermore, proffered a nuclear-decoupling theory, his "Big-Hole Theory," which suggested a country wishing to cheat could reduce the seismic signal of an underground nuclear explosion by placing the device inside a large cavity. This was the kind of activity the Americans were wary about since the Soviets would be reluctant to accept inspection teams freely roaming about their country checking for subterranean cavities. While the delegates debated Latter's idea, Lawrence and Brown concentrated on the detection of high-altitude nuclear tests by an orbiting satellite.[18]

Brown asked Colgate to make a series of presentations to convince delegates the detection of a high-altitude or outer-space nuclear blast was feasible. With a Laboratory mathematician named Dick White, Colgate wrote a computer code to predict signals coming from such a nuclear test. He had to convince listeners he could distinguish weapons signals from naturally occurring signals, as, for instance, from a supernova. To accomplish that, Colgate and White calculated signals expected to come from supernovae and were utterly surprised. They wrote a paper explaining that a supernova occurs when subatomic particles called neutrinos are created when a star collapses. As the neutrinos escape, they collide with matter, pushing out the star's outer layers in a flash.[19] Their paper was historic.[20]

Colgate also stated nuclear tests on the earth's surface could be detected from outer space. His presentation helped lead to the creation of the Vela Program, which culminated with the launch of Vela satellites, each equipped with sensors trained at the earth to detect atmospheric nuclear tests. *Vela* is a Spanish word meaning "she watches over."[21]

In the third week of July, Lawrence began to feel ill. His wife, Molly, was with him, and she could tell his symptoms indicated a relapse of colitis. Abruptly quitting the negotiations, the Lawrences flew back to San Francisco, and the next day, he was admitted to a hospital. Visitors found him pale and weak. President Eisenhower made inquiries and was told he seemed to be improving, but on August 22 he took a turn for the worse. His infected colon was removed, but there was little hope he could recover his health. Lawrence died a few hours later, on August 27, 1958, less than a month after his fifty-seventh birthday.[22]

Ernest Lawrence left a huge legacy. He was a natural leader: a Nobel laureate himself, five physicists who worked for him also won the Nobel Prize. He took an experimental apparatus he invented and made it a tool that opened our knowledge of the atom and its nucleus. The mix of his intellectual abilities and his managerial skills made him a formidable individual. Lawrence, often alone, most consistently kept the American atomic-bomb project alive during World War II. When the Soviet Union appeared to be developing the means to overcome the United States in military prowess during the early Cold War, he became a formidable advocate for developing the hydrogen bomb. His influence on events around him was remarkable. West Point recognized Lawrence's contributions to the nation several months before he died by making him the first recipient of the Sylvanus Thayer Award.

The loss of Lawrence was profoundly felt in Berkeley and Livermore. For all his commitments in Washington, he was still a continuous presence in the running of his Laboratory. Soon after his death, the regents of the University of California remembered Lawrence by renaming the Berkeley and Livermore sites of the University of California Radiation Laboratory as the Lawrence Radiation Laboratory.

# 15

//////////////////

# *From Berlin Back to Berkeley*

O nce Harold Brown left the Conference of Experts in Geneva, he returned to Livermore to become deputy director. Teller, a theoretical physicist, did not thrive in the world of management, and after eighteen months as Laboratory director, he stepped down. In 1960 Brown took over the Laboratory, but he would not have much time to make his mark as director. Within another nine months, York called and asked him to come to the Pentagon to replace him as director of defense research and engineering; Brown accepted and departed for Washington. Duane Sewell filled in on an interim basis until the University of California regents selected Johnny Foster to be the next director.

In January 1961 John F. Kennedy became the thirty-fifth president of the United States. Early on in his administration, he turned his interest to the country's nuclear forces. On May 19 he called for a meeting of his top national security advisors to discuss the nuclear test ban. Those invited to the meeting included Secretary of Defense Robert McNamara, who brought along his new director for defense research and development, Harold Brown. Other invitees were Secretary of State Dean Rusk, National Security Advisor McGeorge Bundy, AEC chairman Glenn Seaborg, CIA director Allen W. Dulles, and General Curtis LeMay, chief of staff of the Air Force. Kennedy set the tone for the meeting by asking if the country's security would be weakened by continuing the test moratorium.

LeMay assured the president of the readiness of SAC to keep the nation secure, after which Brown gave the principal briefing of the meeting. He reviewed advances made in the development of thermonuclear weapons during Operation Hardtack. Kennedy asked whether the Soviets could use testing to improve their nuclear systems, to which Brown answered yes, it worked both ways. Kennedy continued with adjunct questions: Could the Soviets benefit by testing in secret? Was the country better or worse off if both superpowers tested? Brown felt the president was expecting him to express an opinion like "we ought to resume testing," but he kept his opinions to himself. If asked, he would have said he did not believe testing was needed. That fit well, for Kennedy's inclination was not to continue testing as long as the Soviets did likewise.[1]

To get an independent perspective, Kennedy appointed the Disarmament Study Group, led by Dr. James Fisk of Bell Laboratories, which reported to John J. McCloy, the president's disarmament advisor.[2] The group included members of academia, the military, and the AEC. They found critical warheads had not been tested for weaponization. For instance, the warhead for Polaris had been tested in the final days of Operation Hardtack, but there had been no follow-up tests to ensure it performed as a weapon in a real-world environment. *Time* magazine highlighted this in a cover article devoted to Livermore's latest nuclear weapons. It said the nation was gambling its whole deterrent posture and billions of dollars on its Polaris, Minuteman, and advanced Titan missiles. Although the AEC claimed their nuclear warheads would work, the complete systems had never been tried.[3]

Those who had experience designing nuclear weapons knew a device that performed well in an experimental test could perform differently when tried out in its weapon configuration, like being enshrouded in the warhead compartment of a missile. In a realistic situation material surrounding a device could bounce neutrons back into the pit, the device could be abnormally reshaped after high explosives detonated, or other physics effects could occur that had the potential to affect performance. Nuclear devices were complex and fickle; several tests were needed to understand them adequately. Those untested devices had become the backbone of America's strategic nuclear forces, and although the AEC stated they would perform, the level of assurance was not as high as was desirable. Such a lack of confidence, it turned out, was warranted. It was later found after testing resumed in the 1960s that a good percentage of the warheads placed into the stockpile during the test ban had fatal defects.[4]

Weighing against uncertainty was the satisfaction of knowing the Soviets were equally constrained by their inability to test. The Disarmament Study Group concluded the situation favored the Americans, and Fisk recommended the United States refrain from testing unilaterally.[5] But there was a problem: intelligence reports indicated the Soviets were surreptitiously preparing to resume testing, which made the Fisk report a moot point. The daily routine that had developed at the Laboratory during the test moratorium was about to end.

*⫻ ⫻ ⫻*

Brigadier General Austin Betts, another Corps of Engineers officer, had replaced Major General Starbird as deputy for military applications at the AEC. As Betts settled into his job, his boss, Chairman Seaborg, ordered him to be ready to resume nuclear testing. Preparing the Pacific Proving Grounds for renewed testing was not an option for Betts. Two years earlier, representatives from the Marshall Islands had asked the United Nations to prevent testing at the Eniwetok and Bikini Atolls, and Secretary of State Dulles had told the AEC it would be impolitic to test nuclear weapons there again. By the end of 1959, there were twenty AEC contractors remaining at Eniwetok, down from over one thousand employees twelve months earlier. The only option now left for Betts was the Nevada Test Site (NTS).

On August 11, 1961, Betts sent a warning order to the directors of his weapons laboratories and to the managers of his field offices in San Francisco and Albuquerque: be prepared to resume testing.[6] He planned to segment nuclear testing into three parts—short, medium, and long term. The short-term program, consisting of thirteen underground tests, would be executed immediately at NTS upon a presidential order. Tunnels had been dug in Rainier Mesa during the test ban as a precautionary measure, and they could be used quickly. To prepare for additional testing, Betts ordered holes dug in the Nevada bedrock to supplement the tunnels. The medium-term program consisted of developmental tests. These would be conducted underground as well after completion of the short-term program. The long-term program, to be called Operation Dominic, would be full-yield nuclear tests based mostly on results of the earlier tests. These would include atmospheric tests of thermonuclear devices in the Pacific, which would require coordination with the Defense Department.[7]

On August 28 Betts met with his test directors in Albuquerque and told them to be ready to conduct a test by September 15. The Livermore test director, Dale Nielsen, replied he needed six weeks' warning, or at least four weeks in an emergency. Betts reiterated the president wanted to be ready with a meaningful test, and he expected to see it executed in less than three weeks. Los Alamos director Bradbury said his senior staff's opinion was unanimous that testing at that time appeared insane: for the country to be mousetrapped by the Soviets into testing would be a national blunder.[8] Betts was hardly in the mood for such dissension.

Foster, as the new Laboratory director, then said his laboratory would be ready. Those engineers diverted to other assignments during the test ban were called back to positions they had held during Operation Hardtack three years earlier. Some retirees, feeling a surge of patriotism, also volunteered to return to their old positions at the Laboratory.[9]

The next day, August 29, the AEC ordered the initiation of Operation Nougat, Betts' short-term program. On September 1 Nielsen received a Teletype message from Betts: "President Kennedy orders you to shoot the [warhead] in the E-03 tunnel on September 15 at 10 o'clock in the morning." Nielsen responded he could not guarantee containment of a nuclear explosion with a two-week deadline and no substantial test data would be collected. Betts told him to do the best he could.

Nielsen had his teams working day and night and cut corners whenever he could to make the expected date. On the day of the first test, called the Antler event, Betts was at NTS speaking on a telephone connected to Chairman Seaborg, who had President Kennedy on another line. Nielsen fired the shot on time with no apparent problems. A few minutes afterward, he heard Kennedy announce on public radio the United States had resumed testing with a shot at NTS and no radiation was released.

Nielsen sent an initial radiation survey team to the portal of the tunnel. Twelve minutes after the shot, he received a radio message saying a large cloud of steam was coming out of the adit. Nielsen could see it himself and asked what the radiation reading was there. When told it was 500 Roentgens per hour—450 Roentgens per hour is the mean lethal dose—he ordered the survey team to evacuate immediately.[10]

It was later determined that when the cavity created by the detonation collapsed, perched water above ground zero had dropped into the vacated space, lashed to steam, and the resulting pressure had peeled sandbags off a plug. The pressure was so high it not only destroyed the alcove with the diagnostics, including thirty brand-new Tektronix scopes and cameras, but also contaminated the entire E-03 tunnel and a portion of E main tunnel. Nevertheless, the Antler event answered the administration's need to make a quick response to the Soviets. The warhead performed as it should have, which, despite the loss of data and the radiation leaks, was reassuring.

The following days were marked with hectic and chaotic events. Nielsen reentered a test tunnel after a shot to manually collect samples for radiochemical analysis. The device had been detonated about 225 feet from the portal, equipped with two blast doors. It also had two sand-bag plugs: one, about twenty feet long, and the other, about ten feet long. Nielsen entered the tunnel dressed in radiation safety clothing and wore an air pack for breathing. He opened the first blast door without any difficulty, but the second one had been distorted by the blast and took longer than expected to open. After checking the air pressure in his tank, he continued to go deeper into the tunnel.

Using the light from his flashlight, Nielsen soon came to the first sand-bag plug, where he found the top row had been peeled off by the blast, although only enough so he could barely squeeze through. As he did, the air tank on his back scraped against the top of the tunnel. When he reached the second plug, he had to drop down into the shot chamber. After a short while, he grabbed a bag of samples, scrambled up to the second sandbag plug, and started out. About halfway through the second plug, he realized he had no air. The rest of the return journey seemed like holding his breath without really trying, and he made it out. A check at the Laboratory showed his gauge actually had been stuck, giving him a false reading to the amount of air left in the pack.[11]

A decontamination team scrubbed the walls of E-03 at a rate of one hundred feet per day, and Betts ordered excavation operations started for other tunnels. He hoped by deepening them he could resume testing. To make matters worse, his program to drill holes into the Nevada bedrock abruptly stopped when pipe fitters, specialists who attached pipe sections continuously onto the drill rig while operating, went on strike. They established a picket line that members of other unions refused to cross. Operations at NTS slowed down rapidly.

Seaborg received this news with aplomb. On October 7 he wrote a letter to the president saying the underground test program had to be supplemented with atmospheric tests; key weapons in the stockpile needed to be tested. Kennedy had an aversion to atmospheric tests, but Seaborg reminded him the Soviets had already detonated twenty-four devices that way. The president said he would reconsider his options.[12]

Amid political tensions tightening the atmosphere in Washington, D.C., Betts' medium-term program started with a charter to partially explore new nuclear-weapons concepts. In line with this, Foster offered to test an experimental device directed at addressing the enormous military might of the Soviet Union in Eastern Europe. The warhead would increase the relative amount of radiation it released, especially neutrons, without increasing blast. It was called an enhanced-radiation weapon.

About this time, Sam Cohen, an analyst at RAND Corporation, visited Livermore and asked Foster about current projects. The director told him about the enhanced-radiation weapon he had offered to test. Foster said the idea was to use a weapon system like nuclear artillery to detonate a relatively low-yield warhead high above the ground so it would emit radiation, especially neutrons, that could penetrate the top of Soviet tanks without destroying the surrounding countryside. This meant NATO forces could have viable weapons to defeat a Soviet invasion of West Germany, which would be led by hordes of tanks. Cohen responded, "That's a neutron bomb!" To the everlasting chagrin of Foster, Cohen then wrote a RAND analysis paper in which he described how an enhanced-radiation weapon would be an effective deterrent if deployed in Europe, claiming he himself had invented the weapon.[13]

In the years to come, the enhanced-radiation device described by Foster was fully developed. Cohen's nickname for it, "neutron bomb," had stuck, which gave the weapon a sinister connotation in a society that increasingly disliked references to radiation. It became the focus of heated debates in Congress, and during his presidency, Jimmy Carter ultimately cancelled it. Foster's passion to give soldiers the means to protect themselves from overwhelming enemy forces was put on hold.

⫻ ⫻ ⫻

After tensions in Washington, D.C., had risen to a feverish pitch, one might wonder if the invention of a thermonuclear warhead that could be launched from a submarine really made a difference in the Berlin Crisis of 1961. Did it add backbone to the Kennedy administration to stand up to Khrushchev's threats? National Security Advisor Bundy certainly thought so. As he stated in a memoir he wrote about this period, "American superiority [in ballistic-missile technology] may in some degree have stiffened American determination. I believe that it did."[14] He went on to say this strategic superiority was decisive during the Berlin Crisis.

Would a small warhead have been developed for Polaris by 1961 if there had been no Livermore Laboratory? Could LASL have developed the innovations needed for a fleet ballistic missile within a two-year span? The professional staff at LASL was of the highest quality, so it is possible, but hardly likely, that would have happened. The new concepts coming out of Livermore were a legacy to Lawrence's leadership, his management style, and to that unique computer culture started by von Neumann. Up until Livermore's creation, there had been precious little incentive for Los Alamos to have a crash program in innovative designs, and consequently, those types of projects did not occur often. Harold Agnew, director of Los Alamos in the 1970s, grudgingly admitted as much years later. Hans Bethe, who was against creating the Livermore facility, admitted thirty years after it opened the Laboratory played a crucial role in changing the course of the Cold War.[15]

Khrushchev's erratic behavior in 1961 backfired. The Berlin Crisis created a reaction among those living in the German Democratic Republic. Their exodus from East Germany increased until the flow of migrants reached fifty thousand during the first twelve days of August 1961. They reacted to what they called the panic of the closing of the gate. The hemorrhaging of Germans into West Berlin had been one of the major causes for Khrushchev's demands for a change in the city's status; now the migration had reached epic proportions.

Representatives from the Warsaw Pact nations met in Moscow and accused NATO of using West Berlin as an espionage center. That led the East German government to close sixty-eight of eighty crossing points along the intracity border and move in tanks to enforce the closures. Later, East German work gangs emplaced barriers between East and West Berlin—the beginnings of the Berlin Wall. The Berlin Crisis had passed.

Almost one year later, a significant event occurred on the other side of the world. On May 5, 1962, the USS *Ethan Allen*, a Polaris submarine, participated in a nuclear event called Frigate Bird, part of Operation Dominic. The submarine launched a Polaris missile that flew over one thousand miles across the Pacific Ocean, carrying a Livermore warhead that successfully detonated at a high altitude. It was a historic moment—the Polaris system worked perfectly. Admiral Burke's dream of a fleet ballistic missile had become reality. From the time Burke became CNO until the commissioning of a Polaris submarine was about five years, an astounding achievement. The country had needed it.

// // //

Harold Brown's office was in the E Ring of the Pentagon, the outermost ring of offices—with views to the outside, these are where senior officials of the Defense Department reside. Brown was responsible for funding military research and procuring weapons systems. He enjoyed a close relationship with Secretary of Defense McNamara. This was apparent when eyeing his desktop telephone, which had a push button that directly linked him to the secretary. In February 1962, about six months after the height of the Berlin Crisis, Brown's phone rang, but it was not the secretary's line. When he answered, Brown heard a familiar voice at the other end: "Hello, Dr. Brown? This is the President."

Kennedy asked what was the best way for him to visit the scientists in Livermore, and, since he had been the director there, could Brown join him for a visit. Kennedy wanted to meet and thank the scientists who had given the country the warheads for Polaris and to acknowledge their part in helping keep the nation out of a nuclear war. Brown assured the president he would join him on the visit. Brown contacted McNamara, and together they arranged for the presidential visit.

Kennedy saw the Livermore physicists by taking advantage of a scheduled visit to California to see the launch of an Atlas missile at Vandenberg Air Force Base. The president's schedule was tight, so Brown decided not to motor him out to Livermore. Rather, he arranged for briefings to be given in a secure facility at the Lawrence Radiation Laboratory in Berkeley. McNamara and Brown flew to California the day before Kennedy's arrival and drove to Livermore to get advance briefings. It was an opportunity to educate McNamara about how much the second weapons laboratory had grown and the significant contributions it had made during its first ten years.[16]

When Kennedy arrived in Berkeley the next morning, he posed for a picture in front of the Rad Lab. The photograph shows LASL director Norris Bradbury on the far left. Standing next to him is Johnny Foster, then Edwin McMillan, and then Glenn Seaborg. In the center of the picture is President Kennedy, with Edward Teller, Robert McNamara, and Harold Brown standing to the right. It is a symbolic image: The men face the president with broad smiles on their faces with the exception of Bradbury, who is standing with an expression of contemplation looking away from the scene. Los Alamos had provided the country what was needed during a world war. Now it was Livermore's turn to gain recognition for its achievements in a cold war. Standing around the president, beaming with delight, were the individuals who had helped transform the Laboratory from a place of dismal failure to one that had accomplished what would have been considered impossible a decade earlier.

It was a golden moment for the Laboratory, and the men facing Kennedy had good reason to feel proud. What a fitting legacy it would have been for Lawrence to have been there to see his Laboratory being honored. After the photograph was taken, the president went inside, where he met and shook hands with Mike May and other upstarts of Livermore. He personally thanked each of them for their contributions to the country.

Then the president stepped into a large display room, and Foster, who would give the main briefing, stood before Kennedy for the second time in his life. A full-scale model of the Polaris warhead was placed on a demonstration table, which allowed the president to see the revolutionary design that was becoming the backbone of the country's nuclear deterrent force. After showing him the strategic warhead, Foster planned to give a pitch for an idea he had conceived for securing tactical nuclear weapons.[17]

While touring nuclear installations in Europe, with General Andrew Goodpaster acting as his escort, Foster came away with an uneasy feeling that tactical nuclear weapons needed to be better protected against adversaries who would steal them and, once taken, use them against American forces. He had an idea about how to do this and, upon returning to Livermore, initiated a new development program. Laboratory engineers soon designed a sophisticated antitheft system that came to be called the Permissive Action Link (PAL).

When they were introduced to the PAL system, military leaders were at first skeptical about the concept. They considered a locking device for a nuclear weapon redundant to their existing security systems. They also suspected it could be a hindrance in an emergency. Foster persisted, and his idea reached the corridors of the AEC and eventually members of Congress. Secretary of Defense McNamara, when he first heard the idea, did not consider it an urgent matter, but a panel of investigation created by the JCAE put pressure on him to increase the security of nuclear weapons, especially those stored overseas. Now Foster wanted to brief the president on the idea.[18]

To demonstrate the PAL mechanism, Foster had to enter a proper sequence of numbers into the model on the table. Just before Kennedy had arrived, one of the technicians gave Foster the number sequence needed to activate the PAL, which he committed to memory. Foster explained the PAL concept, and Kennedy became animated with the demonstration. The president pulled up a chair, sat before the device, and leaned forward and rested his elbows on the demonstration table. Then the director came to the point where he had to enter the code. As he stood there, Foster realized he could not remember the PAL code—this was not a good time for such a faux pas. Somehow, he reached inside his mind and pressed a sequence of numbers on the PAL device. It worked.[19]

The president liked the idea and agreed with Foster's approach to solving the problem. Kennedy asked his science advisor to look at the matter more deeply; Jerome Wiesner reported on May 29, 1962, that the

PAL system seemed to be a good idea and a timely solution to a national-security need. On June 6, one year after confronting Khrushchev in Vienna, Kennedy issued National Security Memorandum No. 160, directing the Department of Defense to install PAL systems into selected nuclear weapons, principally those in NATO countries overseas.[20]

Harold Agnew, who would become the director of Los Alamos in the 1970s, contributed his own refinements to the idea, and eventually the mission to execute the Defense Department directive and to maintain a PAL program was given to Sandia Laboratory. On July 6, 1962, President Kennedy asked Congress for $23,300,000 to install electronic locks on nuclear weapons in this country and abroad as a safeguard against accidental or unauthorized firings.[21]

*※ ※ ※*

On the afternoon of March 23, 1962, an hour or so after he had met the Livermore scientists and received the briefing from Foster, Kennedy stepped onto a platform at the football stadium on the campus of the University of California to receive an honorary degree. Secretary of Defense McNamara, an alumnus of the university, also received an honorary degree. Joining the president were seven Nobel laureates, including AEC chairman Seaborg and Lawrence Radiation Laboratory director McMillan. Kennedy received his honorary degree and, in front of a crowd of 85,000 spectators, declared the democratic world could look forward to the future with a new confidence.

Kennedy had come to California because he wanted to see the Livermore scientists who had given the country the strategic deterrence it needed. He had received briefings from those same scientists in the morning, and, perhaps thinking back to the Berlin Crisis of the previous year, that afternoon, he remarked, "I am forced to confront an uncomfortable truth. The New Frontier [his administration's nickname] may well owe more to Berkeley than to Harvard."[22]

/////////////////////

# *Epilogue*

The tensions over Berlin that peaked in the late summer of 1961 simmered during the next year. Fear of a thermonuclear war remained in the psyche of many Americans: five months before making his speech in Berkeley, on October 6, 1961, Kennedy set a civil-defense goal of fallout protection for every American as rapidly as possible.[1] Soviet officials were softening their aggressive rhetoric from the previous June. On the same day the president set his civil-defense goal, Premier Khrushchev's wife, Nina Petrovna, reassured members of the Western press that the Soviet Union would not build fallout shelters; she insisted Russians were not getting ready for war. Regardless, Khrushchev had to shed an impression given to the Politburo that he had suffered a setback over Berlin.

Khrushchev tested Kennedy once again in October 1962 over Cuba, but this was not the Berlin Crisis all over again. Unlike the confrontation over Berlin, McGeorge Bundy thought the Cuban crisis would not lead to a general war with the Soviet Union. But he thought the president did believe that things could have gotten out of control: the Russian commander in Cuba and Soviet submarine commanders in the Caribbean had the ability to commit to military actions on their own authority. The chances of that happening, Bundy believed, were less than the chances of something catastrophic happening the year before. After going through the Berlin Crisis, Kennedy and his staff felt the United States was simply too strong for Khrushchev to want to risk that level of confrontation.[2]

There was no purpose to threaten the United States with a nuclear attack, for the adversary was aware America would retaliate. Khrushchev knew an erratic act would be self-destructive—so he would not do that. Said one State Department aide, "Now in the light of hindsight it is fairly clear that the Soviets could not afford, in terms of their own rational evaluation of the situation, to put us under heavy pressure in other sensitive areas such as Berlin."[3]

In an ironic twist, Kennedy's call for strengthening the armed forces in 1961 worked out well for him in 1962, when he decided to use a military show-of-force against this Soviet Cuban adventure. The Navy's quarantine of the Caribbean Sea, the Air Force's mobilizing squadrons for air combat over Cuba, and the Army's mobilization of a large invasion force in Florida had all benefited from increased personnel and materiel numbers engendered by the bipartisan actions of Congress the previous year. Bill Kaufmann's belief that a deterrent needed to be backed up with a sufficient conventional military force was being tested.

The president pursued the same strategy in the Cuban Missile Crisis that saw him through the Berlin Crisis, and it worked. This time, Minuteman missiles supplemented the formidable Polaris missiles still on station off the coast of the Soviet Union. Once again, America's nuclear counterforce convinced Premier Khrushchev not to push the situation beyond the breaking point. On June 26, 1963, Kennedy went to Berlin and gave a stirring address to 400,000 residents, declaring, "*Ich bin ein Berliner*"—I am a Berliner. The president, along with 2.5 million Berliners, celebrated having turned back a despot intent on expanding communism.

*# # #*

Herb York eventually left the politics of Washington, D.C., behind and became the first chancellor of the University of California, San Diego, his dream to settle down and pursue an academic career finally coming true. Yet he did not totally shake off his lust to be involved with national-security issues. From time to time, he could be seen back at the Pentagon, offering advice to one official or another. On one occasion, he arranged for a Livermore physicist to brief dignitaries at the White House about an idea for a powerful laser capable of disabling a nuclear-tipped Soviet missile in outer space. It would later become the forerunner of a system of weapons called the Strategic Defense Initiative by President Ronald Reagan. York continued to come back to the Laboratory, where he occasionally gave lectures and advice to a younger generation of weapons designers—happily including me. He died in San Diego in 2009.

Edward Teller remained in Livermore for the rest of his career. He continued to be a principal advisor for the Laboratory's weapons program in the same capacity he had since 1952, focusing his indomitable spirit to safeguard the country against communism. In the 1980s he became an avid enthusiast for the Laboratory's X-ray Laser Program, which he used as a springboard to persuade President Reagan about the advantages of the Strategic Defense Initiative. Teller died in September 2003.

In 1965, during the Johnson administration, Harold Brown served as secretary of the Air Force, and in the late 1970s he was President Carter's secretary of defense. While holding the latter position, Brown played a major role in getting the SALT accords with the Soviet Union passed by Congress. He remained active in arms-control-related politics while in retirement until he died at his home in San Diego in April 2019.

Johnny Foster left his position as director of the Livermore Laboratory three years after he briefed President Kennedy about his ideas for the PAL system. He went to the Pentagon and served three successive secretaries of defense—Robert McNamara, Cyrus Vance, and Melvin Laird—as director for research. After leaving the Pentagon in the 1970s, he became the chief scientist for innovation at TRW Corporation, a position he held until he retired in the 1990s. Foster remains active in national politics, having been cochairman of the President's Strategic Posture Commission. Even in his mid-nineties, he travels across the nation on his own and can often be found back at the Laboratory as a member of the Director's Laboratory Review Committee. Foster lives out his retirement years in Santa Barbara, California.

Mike May remained the epitome of a Laboratory physicist, working closely with political scientists from RAND Corporation in the 1950s to formulate a national strategy that carried the nation through the Cold War. He followed in Foster's footsteps by replacing him as B Division leader and later as the Laboratory's director. His fascination with national strategies and arms-control negotiations never stopped. In the 1980s May joined the Center for International Security and Arms Control at Stanford University. He created a fellowship program that attracted outstanding political scientists to the Laboratory to conduct research and write papers concerning arms control and deterrent strategy. One of his fellows, Sybil Francis, wrote a seminal PhD dissertation (quoted in this book). May has been a regular witness at congressional hearings concerning arms control. He presently lives in San Francisco, California.

Physicist John Wheeler settled down in Princeton and devoted the rest of his life to research and teaching. He turned his attention from nuclear and particle physics to the theory of general relativity, and after joining the faculty of the University of Texas, he wrote a textbook on the subject that became an instant bestseller. Wheeler died at his home in New Jersey in 2008. His assistant, Ken Ford, also devoted himself to academia. Ford became an accomplished writer, and in 2006 he was awarded the Oersted Award by the American Association of Physics Teachers. Now in his nineties, Ford remains very active and lives comfortably with his wife in the Philadelphia area.

*// // //*

A distinguished political scientist recently gave a lecture at the Laboratory; his topic was the Cold War. In the course of his presentation, he mentioned there were four major perturbations during the period that caused the Soviets to react. All served a function: they kept Soviet planners off balance and prevented them from feeling overly confident. As he was speaking, someone asked, "Are you aware that each of those perturbations you mentioned were started here in Livermore?" The speaker, a historian and Cold War "subject matter expert," said he had not realized that.

The Laboratory has survived the Cold War and the arms race, adapting to the world it finds itself in by redefining its mission. In the 1990s it pursued a program called Stockpile Stewardship, a national strategy to maintain the reliability of America's nuclear deterrent in the context of a long-term nuclear-test moratorium.

Its mission has also expanded to address a number of new challenges in a changing political climate that includes nonproliferation, arms-control implementation, counterterrorism, homeland security, cybersecurity, and space warfare. The Laboratory's primary mission remains nuclear deterrence, as it continues to attract some of the nation's leading minds with its spirit of innovation and scientific leadership. And it still serves as a catalyst for broader thinking about the changing requirements of deterrence, assurance, and strategic stability.

Today, Livermore and Los Alamos remain the only nuclear-weapons design laboratories in the United States. The early antagonism that marked the creation of Livermore subsided, eventually transforming into a quiet, more-or-less friendly competitiveness between the two weapons laboratories. They complement each other, and the competitiveness adds a sharp crystallization to the innovative spirit that brings out the best in America's nuclear deterrent. That is a good thing: they serve America well.

///////////////

# BIOGRAPHICAL GLOSSARY

**Luis Alvarez** was an early recruit to the Rad Lab and became a valuable asset to Ernest Lawrence's endeavors, including the MIT Rad Lab, the Manhattan Project, and the MTA Project in Livermore. In 1968 he won the Nobel Prize in Physics.

**Hap Arnold** was a general in the U.S. Army Air Forces during World War II. After the war he ordered the creation of an analysis center to serve the U.S. Air Force's technological needs. The result was the creation of the RAND Corporation.

**Hans Bethe** was a German American physicist and Nobel laureate. He led the Theoretical Division at Los Alamos during the Manhattan Project and was an outspoken critic of thermonuclear research and the creation of the Laboratory.

**Austin Betts** was a brigadier general in 1961 when appointed deputy for military affairs in the Atomic Energy Commission. He orchestrated the nation's nuclear-weapons testing program after a three-year moratorium.

**Art Biehl** was a Lab physicist and ran the Small Fission Weapons Group for the Ruth and Rae events. He helped originate ideas for the Geode concept used by Johnny Foster and the Linda device used by Harold Brown. He then left the Lab and joined a technical firm in Los Angeles.

**Niels Bohr** was a Danish physicist and Nobel laureate who created a model of the atom and helped create quantum physics. With American physicist John Wheeler, he published a theory for nuclear fission only nine months after it was discovered.

**Harold Brown** joined the Rad Lab in 1950 and assisted Herb York on the MTA Project. With the creation of the Laboratory, he took over the Livermore Megaton Group, which designed thermonuclear weapons. In 1960 he became the director of the Laboratory, then the director for defense research and engineering, secretary of the Air Force, and finally the secretary of defense in the Carter administration.

**McGeorge Bundy** was President Kennedy's national security advisor during the Berlin Crisis.

**Arleigh Burke** was an American admiral. Becoming chief of naval operations in 1955, he initiated a program to develop a fleet ballistic missile, which led to the Polaris system.

**Vannevar Bush** was an American engineer who served in a position that would now be called the president's science advisor. Bush worked with General George C. Marshall to create the Manhattan Project during World War II.

**Nicholas C. Christofilos** was a Greek American physicist who conceived Project Argus, a program to insert electrons into the magnetosphere as a defense against Soviet missile attacks.

**Stirling Colgate** was an American physicist who designed and built diagnostic instruments used in the Laboratory's earliest nuclear tests. With mathematician Dick White, he developed a model for a supernova. Colgate was instrumental in starting the Vela satellite program to detect nuclear tests in outer space.

**Frank Collbohm** was an employee of Douglas Aircraft Corporation. He was tasked by General Arnold to create an analysis center to serve the Air Force, which resulted in creation of the RAND Corporation.

**Arthur Compton** was an American Nobel laureate appointed by Vannevar Bush to lead an atomic-bomb design effort. In the Manhattan Project, he ran the Metallurgical Laboratory in Chicago and supervised the program to produce plutonium.

**Wallace Decker** was a Laboratory engineer who pioneered many techniques engineers have used to blueprint and assemble atomic devices.

**Enrico Fermi** was one of the greatest physicists of the twentieth century. He immigrated to America after winning the Nobel Prize in 1938 and participated in the Manhattan Project. He was a close friend of Edward Teller and built the world's first critical nuclear pile.

**Johnny Foster** arrived at the Rad Lab in 1949 after being a consultant to the Army Air Force in Italy during World War II. Herb York appointed him the leader of the Livermore Hectoton Group after the failures of the Ruth and Rae tests, and he led the group to design the modern atomic bomb. Foster became Laboratory director in 1961 and four years later went to the Pentagon to become the director of defense research and engineering. Foster was later vice president of TRW Corporation.

**Otto Frisch** was an Austrian expatriate physicist and coauthor with his aunt, Lise Meitner, of a paper on the discovery of nuclear fission. He also worked with Rudolph Peierls to calculate the critical mass of uranium-235, which became the basis for the MAUD Report.

**George Gamow** was a Ukrainian physicist and icon of quantum physics. He befriended Edward Teller at the Bohr Institute and later brought him to America to take a position in the Physics Department of George Washington University. Gamow joined Teller at Los Alamos to develop the Super.

**Bill Grasberger** was an American physicist and member of John Wheeler's Matterhorn Project. He then joined the Laboratory to become one of its leading diagnostic and theoretical physicists.

**David Griggs** was an American geophysicist who succeeded Theodore von Kármán as chief scientist of the Air Force. He arranged for Teller to brief the secretary of defense about the need for a second weapons laboratory, a major event in the creation of the Laboratory.

**Leslie "Dick" Groves** was an Army officer appointed to direct the Matterhorn Project. He was handpicked for the assignment after he had supervised construction of the Pentagon.

**Werner Heisenberg** was a German physicist and Nobel laureate who was a major influence in creating quantum physics. He was John Stuart Foster's friend and Edward Teller's thesis advisor. Although Nazis suspected him of being a friend to Jews (Nazi officials referred to him as being a "White Jew"), they recruited Heisenberg to help develop an atomic bomb.

**Roland Herbst** was a physicist who was a code developer in Mike May's Radiative Transport Group. He created some of the Laboratory's most successful "burn" codes.

**Gary Higgins** was a radiochemist who led the Laboratory's Heavy Elements Group, which analyzed debris after a nuclear test to measure the performance of a warhead. In the 1960s he took over leadership of the Laboratory's Plowshare Program.

**Igor Kurchatov** was leader of the Soviet Union's atomic program in the 1940s and the early 1950s.

**Ernest O. Lawrence** was an American physicist and Nobel laureate who created the Rad Lab and invented the cyclotron. Following the Soviet detonation of an atomic bomb in August 1949, he created a laboratory in Livermore, California, to conduct thermonuclear research.

**Chuck Leith** was a mathematician and one of the nation's leading computer scientists. He wrote the first computer codes for the Laboratory and was a primary founder of the National Oceanic and Atmospheric Agency.

**Bob LeLevier** was a mathematician who led a group of code developers for the Hectoton Group's hydrocodes. He was Johnny Foster's lead computer programmer.

**Alfred Loomis** was a lawyer and financial tycoon who also dedicated himself to being an "amateur" physicist. He became a close friend of Ernest Lawrence, securing financing for Lawrence's technological schemes. Loomis was so closely connected to the Rad Lab and the Laboratory, Luis Alvarez and Johnny Foster treated him like a surrogate father.

**Mike May** was born in France; raised in Hanoi, Indochina; immigrated to the United States; and drafted into the Army, volunteering to be an Airborne trooper in a regiment slated to jump into Japan. At Livermore, he led the Radiative Transport Group that produced the computer codes needed to design thermonuclear warheads. May designed one of the largest-yield thermonuclear weapons to serve in the American nuclear stockpile.

**Edwin McMillan** was recruited in the early 1930s to the Rad Lab, where he became renowned for his invention of the synchrocyclotron. Soon after the discovery of nuclear fission, he discovered the first transuranic element, neptunium, which led to the discovery of plutonium one year later. He was awarded the Nobel Prize. McMillan was Ernest Lawrence's son-in-law and succeeded him as director of the Rad Lab in 1958.

**Nicholas Metropolis** was an American physicist who was a member of Edward Teller's group in Los Alamos that designed the Super.

**Mark Mills** was leader of T Division at the Laboratory. He was designated to be Laboratory director after Herb York in 1958 but was killed in a helicopter accident at Eniwetok Atoll during Operation Hardtack.

**Kenneth Nichols** was an Army lieutenant colonel responsible for establishing engineering specifications for building the atomic bomb in the Manhattan Project. He later became general manager of the Atomic Energy Commission.

**Mark Oliphant** was a British physicist, born in Australia, who rose to be the deputy director of the United Kingdom's Cavendish Laboratory. He led a team of British physicists to help Lawrence develop the calutron in the Manhattan Project.

**J. Robert Oppenheimer** was a physics theorist who collaborated with Ernest Lawrence at the Rad Lab on physics experiments. He directed Los Alamos during World War II. After the war he was chairman of the General Advisory Committee of the Atomic Energy Commission.

**Rudolph Peierls** was a German expatriate physicist who studied physics with Edward Teller under Werner Heisenberg. He joined with Otto Frisch to calculate the critical mass of uranium-235, which became the basis of the MAUD Report, and replaced Teller as a group leader in the Manhattan Project.

**Arthur Raymond** was chief engineer of the Douglas Aircraft Company. Raymond suggested that the new "think tank" ordered by General Arnold be called RAND, a takeoff from the phrase "research and development."

**Duane Sewell** was recruited from the Rad Lab in 1952 and was the deputy director for the first four Laboratory directors.

**Levering Smith** was a Navy captain who, after leading a missile-development team at the Navy's China Lake research facility, directed the development of the Polaris missile.

**Edward Teller** was a Hungarian American physicist who, almost alone, carried the idea of developing the Super through the Manhattan Project and into the 1950s. He was a profound influence on physicists during the earliest stages of the Laboratory's creation.

**Stanislaw Ulam** was a Polish mathematician brought to the Manhattan Project by John von Neumann. He joined Edward Teller's group to design the Super. In March 1951 he coauthored a paper with Teller that established the foundation for the hydrogen bomb.

**Theodor von Kármán** was a Hungarian American aeronautical physicist and creator of the Jet Propulsion Laboratory. He was General Arnold's chief scientist. Von Kármán led the group that developed the report "Towards New Horizons," which led to Arnold ordering the creation of the RAND Corporation.

**John von Neumann** was a Hungarian-born mathematician who immigrated to America in the 1930s and became an influential consultant to the military. He was an advisor to Alan Turing at Princeton and, along with Turing, helped create computer science. Von Neumann was also a prominent influence in starting the Laboratory by bringing a computer culture to it.

**John Wheeler** was an American physicist. He published a paper with Danish physicist Niels Bohr on a theory for nuclear fission. After the Soviets detonated an atomic device in August 1949, he created the Matterhorn Project to help Edward Teller design the hydrogen bomb. Wheeler was a major influence in starting the Laboratory by mentoring its earliest physicists.

**Eugene Wigner** was a Hungarian American physicist and Nobel laureate. He was a close friend of Edward Teller's and was responsible for running plutonium production in the Manhattan Project.

**Jim Wilson** provided theoretical support to Johnny Foster's Livermore Hectoton Group. He was the creator of several computer codes that were invaluable to the success of early designs for Laboratory atomic devices.

**Herb York** joined the Rad Lab during World War II and was one of the physicists selected by Ernest Lawrence to run the calutrons at the Y-12 Plant in Oak Ridge. York led the Measurements Group to design and build diagnostics to detect thermonuclear reactions in nuclear tests before Lawrence asked him to be the first leader of the Livermore laboratory in 1952.

///////////////

# NOTES

## Chapter 1. Clouds over Berlin

1. "History of the Marshall Plan," The George C. Marshall Foundation, https://www.marshallfoundation.org/marshall/the-marshall-plan/history-marshall-plan/ (accessed June 1, 2020).

2. McGeorge Bundy, *Danger and Survival: Choices about the Bomb in the First Fifty Years* (New York: Random House, 1988), 358–60.

3. Joseph Loftus, "Kennedy Pledges He Won't Retreat," *New York Times*, May 30, 1961, 1.

4. Robert C. Doty, "Kennedy and De Gaulle Agree to Defend Berlin," *New York Times*, June 1, 1961, 1.

5. Thomas P. Ronan, "British Warn Soviet of Risk of Atom War in a 'Limited' Clash," *New York Times*, June 2, 1961, 1.

6. Abram Chayes, interviewed by Eugene Gordon, July 9, 1964, John F. Kennedy Oral History Collection, John F. Kennedy Presidential Library, Boston (hereafter JFKOHC, Kennedy Library), 230, https://www.jfklibrary.org/asset-viewer/archives/JFKOH/Chayes%2C%20Abram%20J/JFKOH-ABJC-04/JFKOH-ABJC-04.

7. James Reston, "Kennedy and Khrushchev Stress Problem of Laos in 4-Hour Talk," *New York Times*, June 4, 1961, 1.

8. Charles E. Bohlen, interviewed by Arthur Schlesinger Jr., May 21, 1964, JFKOHC, Kennedy Library, https://www.jfklibrary.org/asset-viewer/archives/JFKOH/Bohlen%2C%20Charles%20E/JFKOH-CEB-01/JFKOH-CEB-01.

9. James Reston, "Vienna Talks End," *New York Times*, June 5, 1961, 1.

10. Bohlen, interviewed by Schlesinger, May 21, 1964.

11. Joseph W. Alsop, interviewed by Elspeth Rostow, June 18, 1964, JFKOHC, Kennedy Library, https://www.jfklibrary.org/asset-viewer/archives/JFKOH/Alsop%2C%20Joseph%20W/JFKOH-JWA-01/JFKOH-JWA-01.

12. Chayes, interviewed by Gordon, July 9, 1964, 239.

13. Martin J. Hillenbrand, interviewed by Paul R. Sweet, August 26, 1964, JFKOHC, Kennedy Library, 13, https://www.jfklibrary.org/asset-viewer /archives/JFKOH/Hillenbrand%2C%20Martin%20J/JFKOH-MJH-01 /JFKOH-MJH-01.

14. Dean Acheson, "Wishing Won't Hold Berlin," *Saturday Evening Post*, March 7, 1959.

15. Kennedy held numerous National Security Council meetings throughout July and August to address how the United States should respond to a Soviet siege of Berlin. See, for instance, National Security Action Memoranda (NSAM) 41, "Military Planning for a Possible Berlin Crisis," National Security Files, Presidential Papers, Papers of John F. Kennedy, Kennedy Library, https://www.jfklibrary.org/asset-viewer/archives/JFKNSF/329 /JFKNSF-329-016; NSAM 59, "Berlin," ibid., https://www.jfklibrary.org /asset-viewer/archives/JFKNSF/330/JFKNSF-330-009; NSAM 62, "Berlin," ibid., https://www.jfklibrary.org/asset-viewer/archives/JFKNSF/330/JFKNSF -330-012; and NSAM 78, "Berlin," ibid., https://www.jfklibrary.org/asset- viewer/archives/JFKNSF/331/JFKNSF-331-008.

16. Hillenbrand, interviewed by Sweet, August 26, 1964, 35–37; and Chayes, interviewed by Gordon, July 9, 1964. See also Bundy, *Danger and Survival*, 372–76.

17. Benjamin Welles, "U.S. Bombers in Spain Poised to Take to Air in 15 Minutes," *New York Times*, September 6, 1958, 2.

18. Albert Wohlstetter, "The Delicate Balance of Terror," *Foreign Affairs* 37, no. 2 (January 1959): 211–34.

19. Neil Sheehan, *A Fiery Peace in a Cold War: Bernard Schriever and the Ultimate Weapon* (New York: Random House, 2009), 150.

20. Vitaly I. Khalturin, Tatyana G. Rautian, Paul G. Richards, and William S. Leith, "A Review of Nuclear Testing by the Soviet Union at Novaya Zemlya, 1955–1990," *Science and Global Security* 13 (2005):1–42.

21. William Ogle was the director of nuclear testing for the AEC. He wrote a comprehensive and detailed account of how the Kennedy administration resumed testing in an AEC publication, *An Account of the Return to Nuclear Weapons Testing by the United States after the Test Moratorium, 1958–1961*, NVO-291 ([Las Vegas]: Department of Energy, 1985), 244.

22. Harold Brown, recorded interview, June 25, 1964, JFKOHC, Kennedy Library, 21, https://www.jfklibrary.org/asset-viewer/archives/JFKOH /Brown%2C%20Harold/JFKOH-HAB-05/JFKOH-HAB-05.

23. Wohlstetter made this assessment in a 1958 RAND paper he wrote, with contributions from William Kaufmann. See Wohlstetter, "Delicate Balance of Terror."

24. McGeorge Bundy, interviewed by Richard Neustadt, March 1964, JFKOHC, Kennedy Library, 41, https://www.jfklibrary.org/asset-viewer /archives/JFKOH/Bundy%2C%20McGeorge/JFKOH-MGB-01/JFKOH -MGB-01.

25. Sir Isaiah Berlin, interviewed by Arthur Schlesinger Jr., April 12, 1965, JFKOHC, Kennedy Library, https://www.jfklibrary.org/asset-viewer /archives/JFKOH/Berlin%2C%20Isaiah/JFKOH-IB-01/JFKOH-IB-01.

26. Jack Raymond, "World-Wide Threat by Soviet," *New York Times*, July 26, 1961, 1.

27. Letter, John F. Kennedy to Rear Admiral Ignatius J. Galantin, November 19, 1963. Courtesy of the U.S. Navy archives through the intercession of Commander Robert Vince, US Navy (Ret.). Galantin was the Navy's special project officer for the Polaris weapons system.

## Chapter 2. The Discovery That Started It All

1. Alden Whitman, "Robert G. Sproul, 84, Dies; Headed U. of California," *New York Times*, September 12, 1975, 36.

2. David A. Shirley, "Opening Remarks," in *Proceedings of the Celebrations of the 50th Anniversary of the Lawrence Berkeley Laboratory,* LBL-13613 (Springfield, VA: National Technical Information Service, 1982), v.

3. "Professor Enrico Fermi, Academician, Uses Neutrons Formed by Decomposition of Beryllium under the Action of Alpha Particles of Radium," *New York Times*, June 5, 1934, 25. This article reports on Fermi's experiments originally recorded in the Italian science journal *Ricerca Scientifica* (May 1934).

4. Lise Meitner and O. R. Frisch, "Disintegration of Uranium by Neutrons: A New Type of Nuclear Reaction," *Nature* 143, no. 3615 (February 1939): 239–40.

5. John Wheeler and Niels Bohr, "The Mechanism of Nuclear Fission," *Physical Review* 56, no. 5 (September 1939): 426–50.

6. The story of the creation of the MIT Radiation Laboratory is well documented in Luis W. Alvarez, *Alvarez: Adventures of a Physicist* (New York: Basic Books, 1987).

7. This correspondence of Oliphant to Lawrence is recorded in Herbert Childs, *An American Genius: The Life of Ernest Orlando Lawrence* (New York: E. P. Dutton, 1968), 271–72.

8. "The MAUD Report (1941)," *The Manhattan Project: An Interactive History*, U.S. Department of Energy, Office of History and Heritage Resources, https://www.osti.gov/opennet/manhattan-project-history/Events /1939-1942/maud.htm.

9. Richard C. Hewlett and Oscar E. Anderson Jr., *The New World: A History of the United States Atomic Energy Commission*, vol. 1, *1939–1946* (Berkeley: University of California Press, 1962), 43.

10. "Report of the National Defense Research Committee for the First Year of Operation, June 27, 1940 to June 28, 1941," taken from McGeorge Bundy, *Danger and Survival: Choices about the Bomb in the First Fifty Years* (New York: Random House, 1988), 44.

11. Hewlett and Anderson, *New World*, 33–46.

12. Bundy, *Danger and Survival*, 45–46.

## Chapter 3. The Super and the Onset of the Thermonuclear Age

1. K. D. Nichols, *The Road to Trinity* (New York: William Morrow, 1987), 25.

2. Leslie R. Groves, *Now It Can Be Told: The Story of the Manhattan Project* (New York: Harper, 1962), 19–32.

3. Nichols, *Road to Trinity*, chap. 5.

4. Laura Fermi, *Atoms in the Family: My Life with Enrico Fermi* (Chicago: University of Chicago Press, 1954), chap. 7.

5. Arthur Holly Compton, *Atomic Quest: A Personal Narrative* (New York: Oxford University Press, 1956), 110–36.

6. Eugene P. Wigner, *The Recollections of Eugene P. Wigner*, with Andrew Szanton (New York: Plenum, 1992), 239–40.

7. Compton, *Atomic Quest*, 136–44.

8. Edward Teller, *Memoirs: A Twentieth-Century Journey in Science and Politics*, with Judith Shoolery (Cambridge, MA: Perseus, 2001), 193.

9. Teller, 200–35.

10. Norris Bradbury's letter announcing the Super Conference in 1946, classified document vaults, Los Alamos National Laboratory Research Library, NM (hereafter LANLRL).

11. These excerpts are taken from the 1946 Super Conference report, classified document vaults, LANLRL.

12. Minutes of the classified LASL Coordinating Council meeting, October 1, 1945, LANLRL. Unclassified notes taken at the meeting can be found

in David Hawkins, Edith C. Truslow, and Ralph Carlisle Smith, *Project Y: The Los Alamos Story*, 40th anniv. ed. (Los Angeles: Tomash, 1983), app. A.

13. S. M. Ulam, *Adventures of a Mathematician* (New York: Charles Scribner's Sons, 1976), 151.

14. John Archibald Wheeler, *Geons, Black Holes, and Quantum Foam: A Life in Physics*, with Kenneth Ford (New York: W. W. Norton, 1998), 191.

15. Kenneth W. Ford, *Building the H-Bomb: A Personal History* (Hackensack, NJ: World Scientific, 2015), 3.

16. Fermi's calculations are in dozens of documents in classified document vaults at LANLRL and the Lawrence Livermore National Laboratory Archives, California.

17. This paper, which also includes contributions from physicist Harris Mayer, is kept within the classified document vaults, LANLRL.

18. William L. Laurence, "Bomb at Bikini Exploded Too Low, Reducing Effect, Experts Indicate," *New York Times*, July 5, 1946, 1.

## Chapter 4. Project RAND, the AEC, and the Russians

1. Theodore von Kármán Memorial, "Toward New Horizons," *Air Force Magazine* (June 1963).

2. Frank Collbohm, oral history interview by Martin Collins and Joseph Taterewicz, July 28, 1987, RAND History Project, National Air and Space Museum, Washington, DC.

3. Michael H. Gorn, *Harnessing the Genie: Science and Technology Forecasting for the Air Force, 1944–1986* (Washington: Office of Air Force History, 1988), 41–42.

4. Richard C. Hewlett and Oscar E. Anderson Jr., *The New World: A History of the United States Atomic Energy Commission*, vol. 1, *1939–1946* (Berkeley: University of California Press, 1962), 422.

5. Woman's College of the University of North Carolina newsletter, *W.C. Informer* 3 (1946), with thanks to Gina Bonanno, whose mother edited the newsletter.

6. Hewlett and Anderson, *New World*, chaps. 15–16.

7. David Holloway, *Stalin and the Bomb: The Soviet Union and Atomic Energy, 1939–1956* (New Haven, CT: Yale University Press, 1994), chap. 10.

8. Herbert F. York, *The Advisors: Oppenheimer, Teller, and the Superbomb* (San Francisco: W. H. Freeman, 1976), 33.

9. Thomas C. Reed, *At the Abyss: An Insider's History of the Cold War* (New York: Ballantine Books, 2004), 103.

10. Houston T. Hawkins, "History of the Russian Nuclear Weapon Program," November 11, 2013, Los Alamos document LA-UR-13-28910.

11. Doyle L. Northrup and Donald H. Rock, "The Detection of Joe 1," *Studies in Intelligence* 10, Center for Studies in Intelligence, CIA (Fall 1966).

12. News of Joe 1 appeared in newspapers the following day. See, for example, *New York Times*, September 24, 1949, 1.

13. William Henry Chamberlin, *Russia's Iron Age* (Boston: Little, Brown, 1934), 367–72.

14. Luis W. Alvarez, *Alvarez: Adventures of a Physicist* (New York: Basic Books, 1987), 153–69.

15. Lewis Strauss, *Men and Decisions* (New York: Doubleday, 1962), 216–18.

16. Kenneth W. Ford, *Building the H-Bomb: A Personal History* (Hackensack, NJ: World Scientific, 2015), 10. See also Reed, *At the Abyss*, 110. Tom Reed gained access to Soviet nuclear archives following the end of the Cold War.

17. David Lilienthal, *The Journals of David E. Lilienthal*, vol. 2, *The Atomic Energy Years 1945–1950* (New York: Harper & Row, 1964), 580.

18. K. D. Nichols, *The Road to Trinity* (New York: William Morrow, 1987), 272.

**Chapter 5. The GAC Rejects the Classic Super**

1. Robert C. Williams and Philip L. Cantelon, eds., *The American Atom: A Documentary History of Nuclear Policies from the Discovery of Fission to the Present, 1939–1984* (Philadelphia: University of Pennsylvania Press, 1984), 114–99.

2. "The General Advisory Committee Report of October 30, 1949, AEC Historical Document Number 349," in Herbert F. York, *The Advisors: Oppenheimer, Teller, and the Superbomb* (San Francisco: W. H. Freeman, 1976), app.

3. York, 10.

4. James Reston, "U.S. Hydrogen Bomb Delay Urged Pending Bid to Soviet," *New York Times* (January 17, 1950).

5. York, *Advisors*, 27.

6. John Archibald Wheeler, *Geons, Black Holes, and Quantum Foam: A Life in Physics*, with Kenneth Ford (New York: W. W. Norton, 1998), 189.

7. Wheeler, 206.

8. Oppenheimer to Conant, October 12, 1949, Headquarters Records of the AEC, Department of Energy Archives, Washington, D.C. See also Richard G. Hewlett and Francis Duncan, *Atomic Shield: A History of the United States Atomic Energy Commission*, vol. 2, *1947–1952* (University Park: Pennsylvania State University Press, 1962), 379.

9. Edward Teller, *Memoirs: A Twentieth-Century Journey in Science and Politics*, with Judith Shoolery (Cambridge, MA: Perseus, 2001), 284–85.

10. Wheeler, *Geons*, 214.

11. Ben Parnell, *Carpetbaggers: America's Secret War in Europe* (Austin, TX: Eakin, 1987), 99.

12. William Liscum Borden, *There Will Be No Time: The Revolution in Strategy* (New York: Macmillan, 1946), 209.

13. Hewlett and Duncan, *Atomic Shield*, vol. 2, *1947–1952*, 371–72.

14. Lewis Strauss, *Men and Decisions* (New York: Doubleday, 1962), 223–24.

15. York, *Advisors*, 66–67.

16. Dean Acheson, interviewed by Lucius D. Battle, April 27, 1964, John F. Kennedy Oral History Collection, John F. Kennedy Presidential Library, Boston (hereafter JFKOHC, Kennedy Library).

17. This appeared in major newspapers the next day. See, for example, *New York Times*, February 1, 1951.

18. Several physicists active in the 1950s have told me that during their college years, they had been approached by physics faculty to sign petitions opposing thermonuclear research.

19. Wheeler, *Geons*, 189.

20. Luis W. Alvarez, *Alvarez: Adventures of a Physicist* (New York: Basic Books, 1987), 172–74.

21. Harold Brown, recorded interview, June 25, 1964, JFKOHC, Kennedy Library.

22. These details about the MTA are taken from several interviews with Johnny Foster by the author, November 2015.

23. Alvarez, *Alvarez*, 173–75.

24. Laurie Powers, ed., *Fifty Years of Service: Lawrence Livermore National Laboratory* (Livermore: University of California, LLNL, 2002).

25. Foster, interviewed by the author, November 2015.

26. Alvarez, *Alvarez*, 174–78.

27. York, *Advisors*, 66, 67.

## Chapter 6. Computers and the New Super

1. George Dyson, *Turing's Cathedral: The Origins of the Digital Universe* (New York: Pantheon Books, 2012), 40–48, 181.

2. The *Entscheidungsproblem* ("decision problem") elucidated by the German mathematician David Hilbert early in the twentieth century asked whether provable statements can be distinguished from disprovable statements by strictly mechanical procedures in a finite amount of time.

3. A. M. Turing, "On Computable Numbers, with an Application to the Entscheidungsproblem," *Proceedings of the London Mathematical Society*, ser. 2, 42 (1937): 230–65.

4. Andrew Hodges, *Alan Turing: The Enigma* (New York: Simon & Schuster, 1983), 138. See also Dyson, *Turing's Cathedral*, 231.

5. Dyson, *Turing's Cathedral*, 72.

6. Stanislaw Ulam, "Stan Ulam, John von Neumann, and the Monte Carlo Method," special issue, ed. Roger Eckardt, *Los Alamos Science* 15 (1987): 125.

7. This paper, written by Ulam and Everett, provided the details for Ulam's calculation methodology in 1950 and is kept in a classified vault at Los Alamos National Laboratory Research Library, NM (hereafter LANLRL). Interpretations of the physics are by the author.

8. S. M. Ulam, *Adventures of a Mathematician* (New York: Charles Scribner's Sons, 1976), 214.

9. Ulam, 212–18.

10. Dyson, *Turing's Cathedral*, 207–9.

11. Françoise Ulam, *De Paris à Los Alamos: Une odyssée franco-américaine* [From Paris to Los Alamos: An odyssey] (Paris: L'Harmattan, 1998).

12. Ulam, *Adventures*, 220.

13. Edward Teller, *Memoirs: A Twentieth-Century Journey in Science and Politics*, with Judith Shoolery (Cambridge, MA: Perseus, 2001), 312.

14. Ulam-Teller paper, March 1951, classified document vaults, LANLRL. These interpretations of it are derived directly from the paper itself.

15. Edward Teller, "The Work of Many People," *Science*, February 25, 1955, 268.

16. De Hoffman's paper describing what a new Super would look like (and listing Teller as the author), April 1951, LANLRL.

17. These observations are based on personal correspondence with Dr. Kenneth Ford, 2017. Dr. Ford was a principal modeler of the Mike device.

18. John Archibald Wheeler, *Geons, Black Holes, and Quantum Foam: A Life in Physics*, with Kenneth Ford (New York: W. W. Norton, 1998), 218.

19. Von Neumann's MANIAC at Princeton was undergoing development at the time, so Ford used an IBM-CPC, a machine he was familiar with from his work at LASL. He supplemented this using the Standards Eastern Automatic Computer housed at the National Bureau of Standards in Washington, D.C.

20. Kenneth W. Ford, *Building the H-Bomb: A Personal History* (Hackensack, NJ: World Scientific, 2015), 144–51.

21. Gordon E. Dean, *Forging the Atomic Shield: Excerpts from the Office Diary of Gordon E. Dean*, ed. Roger M. Anders (Chapel Hill: University of North Carolina Press, 1987), 106–36 (January 26–June 17, 1951).

22. Dean, 146 (June 14, 1951).

23. Teller, *Memoirs*, 325.

24. Wheeler, *Geons*, 221–22.

25. Teller, *Memoirs*, 327–28.

26. US Atomic Energy Commission, *In the Matter of J. Robert Oppenheimer: Transcript of Hearing before Personnel Security Board and Texts of Principal Documents and Letters* (Cambridge, MA: MIT Press, 1971), 487.

27. Ulam, *Adventures*, 223.

28. Descriptions of these trips are taken from Bill Grasberger, interviewed by the author, 2015.

29. Gary Higgins, interviewed by Jim Carothers, 1978, classified document vaults, Lawrence Livermore National Laboratory Archives, CA.

30. David Holloway, *Stalin and the Bomb: The Soviet Union and Atomic Energy, 1939–1956* (New Haven, CT: Yale University Press, 1994), 305–8.

## Chapter 7. The Second Laboratory

1. Ivan A. Getting and John M. Christie, "David Tressel Griggs, 1911–1974: A Biographical Memoir," *Biographical Memoirs* (Washington: National Academy of Sciences, 1994), 113–34.

2. Bernard Brodie, *The Absolute Weapon: Atomic Power and World Order* (New York: Harcourt, Brace, 1946), 17. Brodie expresses the view that the atomic bomb has produced changes in the military affairs of nations and in their political relationships.

3. Albert Wohlstetter, "The Delicate Balance of Terror," *Foreign Affairs* 37, no. 2 (January 1959): 211–34.

4. Andrew F. Krepinevich Jr., "The Eroding Balance of Terror," *Foreign Affairs* 98, no. 1 (January/February 2019): 62–74.

5. U.P., "Gen. Collins Looks for Atomic Shells," *New York Times*, February 6, 1951, 3.

6. Sybil Francis, "Warhead Politics: Livermore and the Competitive System of Nuclear Weapon Design," UCRL-LR-124754 (PhD diss., MIT, 1995), 75–87.

7. David C. Elliot, "Project Vista and Nuclear Weapons in Europe," *International Security* 11, no. 1 (Summer 1986): 163–83.

8. Herbert F. York, *The Advisors: Oppenheimer, Teller, and the Superbomb* (San Francisco: W. H. Freeman, 1976), 119–20.

9. Francis, "Warhead Politics," 47. Francis quotes from John S. Walker, "Dr. Oppenheimer and the Vista Report," a report by that is kept in the Joint Committee on Atomic Energy Files.

10. Gordon E. Dean, *Forging the Atomic Shield: Excerpts from the Office Diary of Gordon E. Dean*, ed. Roger M. Anders (Chapel Hill: University of North Carolina Press, 1987), 175 (October 11, 1951), 212 (April 7, 1952).

11. Herbert F. York, *Making Weapons, Talking Peace: A Physicist's Odyssey from Hiroshima to Geneva* (New York: Basic Books, 1987), 63–68.

12. Teller's rationale for promoting a uranium-hydride device will be described in a following chapter. His talks with Bohr during their time together with the Manhattan Project were related to me by Teller's protégé Lowell Wood.

13. Edward Teller, *Memoirs: A Twentieth-Century Journey in Science and Politics*, with Judith Shoolery (Cambridge, MA: Perseus, 2001), 331–36.

14. Francis, "Warhead Politics," 48–50.

15. Dean, *Forging the Atomic Shield,* 206–9 (April 1, 1952).

16. Dean, 206 (April 1, 1952).

17. For York's description of this meeting with Lawrence, see *Making Weapons*, 62.

18. York, *Advisors*, 63–65.

19. Alvarez, *Alvarez,* chaps. 11, 15.

20. York, *Advisors*, 66–67.

21. Herb York, interviewed by Jim Carothers, 1983, classified document vaults, Lawrence Livermore National Laboratory Archives, CA.

22. Dean, *Forging the Atomic Shield*, 215 (June 5, 1952).

23. Francis, "Warhead Politics," chap. 3. Francis provides a highly descriptive narrative of how the chairman of the AEC finally came to grips with the formation of a second nuclear-weapons laboratory.

**Chapter 8. The Legacies of Lawrence, von Neumann, and Wheeler**

1. Harold Brown, conversation with the author, 2014.
2. Duane Sewell, "The Branch Laboratory at Livermore during the 1950s," in *Energy in Physics, War and Peace: A Festschrift Celebrating Edward Teller's 80th Birthday*, ed. Hans Mark and Lowell Wood (Boston: Kluwer Academic, 1988), 319.
3. These and the following descriptions of early life at the Laboratory are taken from minutes of biweekly meetings held by Herbert York, classified document vaults, Lawrence Livermore National Laboratory Archives, CA (hereafter LLNLA).
4. Mike May, interviewed by Jim Carothers, 1978, classified document vaults, LLNLA.
5. These excerpts of May's early life are drawn from several interviews by the author with Mike May, 2014 and 2016.
6. Herbert F. York, *The Advisors: Oppenheimer, Teller, and the Superbomb* (San Francisco: W. H. Freeman, 1976), 133.
7. Herbert F. York, *Making Weapons, Talking Peace: A Physicist's Odyssey from Hiroshima to Geneva* (New York: Basic Books, 1987), 15.
8. Art Hudgens, interviewed by Jim Carothers, 1978, classified document vaults, LLNLA.
9. Sewell never completed his doctoral work for the degree, but he had a successful career, eventually becoming an assistant secretary of defense.
10. Herb York, interviewed by Jim Carothers, 1983, LLNLA.
11. Sybil Francis, "Warhead Politics: Livermore and the Competitive System of Nuclear Weapon Design," UCRL-LR-124754 (PhD diss., MIT, 1995).
12. In 1983 Jim Carothers interviewed several scientists about their early experiences at the Laboratory, including the physicist quoted here. These are in classified document vaults, LLNLA.
13. Chuck Leith, interviewed by a senior Laboratory official in the computer directorate, 1976, classified document vaults, LLNLA.
14. Mike May, interviewed by the author, 2014.
15. William Lokke, *Early Computing and Its Impact on Lawrence Livermore National Laboratory* UCRL-TR-226840, (Livermore, CA: LLNL, 2007), eBook.

16. Leith, interviewed by a senior Laboratory official in the computer directorate, 1976, classified document vaults, LLNLA.

17. Lokke, *Early Computing.*

18. Cecelia Larsen, interviewed by a senior Laboratory official in the computer directorate, 1976, classified document vaults, LLNLA.

19. Lokke, *Early Computing.*

20. Bill Grasberger, interviewed by the author, 2016.

21. Carl Haussmann, interviewed by Jim Carothers, 1978, classified document vaults, LLNLA.

22. May, interviewed by Carothers, 1978.

**Chapter 9. An Inauspicious Start**

1. Feynman's Manhattan Project calculations of hydride fuels used for atomic bombs are in five documents in the classified document vaults, Los Alamos National Laboratory Research Library, NM (hereafter LAN-LRL). Physical interpretations of the calculations are by the author.

2. Stephen E. Ambrose, *Eisenhower,* vol. 2, *The President* (New York: Simon & Schuster, 1984), 47.

3. J. Foster Dulles, "Evolution of Foreign Policy: Text of Speech by John Foster Dulles, Secretary of State, before the Council on Foreign Relations, New York, N.Y., January 12, 1954" (Press Release 8, Dept. of State), Hathi Trust Digital Library, https://hdl.handle.net/2027/umn.31951d024881358. See also William S. White, "Dulles Says Goal of Defense Plan Is to Worry Soviet," *New York Times,* March 20, 1954, 1.

4. L. D. Attaway, J. R. Brom, Philip M. Dadant, V. S. Dudley, P. C. Keith E. J. Barlow, "Active Defense of the United States 1954–1960," January 1, 1954, RAND Corporation, R-250.

5. Special to the *New York Times,* "Ridgway Has Reservations on Slack in Army Strength," *New York Times,* March 16, 1954, 1.

6. David R. Mets, review of *From Pearl Harbor to Vietnam: The Memoirs of Admiral Arthur W. Radford,* ed. Stephen Jurika Jr., *Naval War College Review* 38, no. 4 (May–June 1985), https://digital-commons.usnwc.edu/nwc-review/vol38/iss4/15.

7. Albert Wohlstetter, "The Delicate Balance of Terror," *Foreign Affairs* 37, no. 2 (January 1959): 211–34.

8. Jim Carothers, *Caging the Dragon: The Containment of Underground Nuclear Explosives,* DOE/NV-388, DNA TR 95-74 (Oak Ridge, TN: OSTI, 1995), 11.

9. William Ogle, *An Account of the Return to Nuclear Weapons Testing by the United States after the Test Moratorium, 1958–1961*, NVO-291 ([Las Vegas]: Department of Energy, 1985), 43.

10. Gordon E. Dean, *Forging the Atomic Shield: Excerpts from the Office Diary of Gordon E. Dean*, ed. Roger M. Anders (Chapel Hill: University of North Carolina Press, 1987), 100 (January 11, 1951).

11. James E. Carothers, "An Interview with Wallace D. Decker," 2002, UCRL-MI-49361, University of California Library.

12. Art Hudgins, interviewed by Jim Carothers, 1977 (during a celebration of the Laboratory's twenty-fifth anniversary), classified document vaults, Lawrence Livermore National Laboratory Archive, CA (hereafter LLNLA).

13. Herbert York preoperational reports for the Ruth and Rae events, classified document vaults, LLNLA. Interpretations of the physics principles are by the author.

14. Carothers, "Interview with Wallace D. Decker," 15–21.

15. Duane Sewell, interviewed by C. Bruce Tarter, 2002, classified document vaults, LLNLA.

16. These observations are drawn from Carothers, "Interview with Wallace D. Decker."

17. Carothers, "Interview with Wallace D. Decker."

18. Edward Teller, *Memoirs: A Twentieth-Century Journey in Science and Politics*, with Judith Shoolery (Cambridge, MA: Perseus, 2001), 354.

19. Norris Bradbury to AEC headquarters, "Observations on the Livermore Laboratory Proposal," May 21, 1952, DIR-714, Los Alamos National Laboratory Archives, with thanks to Alan Carr.

20. Norris Bradbury to Carroll Tyler, "Future Full-Scale Weapons Tests," May 6, 1953, cited in Sybil Francis, "Warhead Politics: Livermore and the Competitive System of Nuclear Weapon Design," UCRL-LR-124754 (PhD diss., MIT, 1995), 72.

21. Herbert York, interviewed by Jim Carothers, 1983, classified document vaults, LLNLA.

**Chapter 10. Hitting Rock Bottom**

1. James E. Carothers, "An Interview with Wallace D. Decker," 2002, UCRL-MI-49361, University of California Library.

2. A major portion of the radioactivity came from beta decay, the emission of high-energy electrons. Beta rays are stopped readily by solid objects and usually do not penetrate the skin.

3. Samuel Glasstone and Philip Dolan, *The Effects of Nuclear Weapons*, 3rd ed. (Washington: Government Printing Office, 1977), chaps. 9–12.

4. Los Alamos National Laboratory Archives Department, "Stirling Colgate: 'Explosions I Have Known' from Testing to Treaties," videotaped interview, 2005, Los Alamos National Laboratory Research Library, NM.

5. Herbert F. York, *The Advisors: Oppenheimer, Teller, and the Superbomb* (San Francisco: W. H. Freeman, 1976), 134.

6. Minutes of Livermore Megaton and Livermore Hectoton Group meetings, 1953–54, classified document vaults, Lawrence Livermore National Laboratory Archives, CA (hereafter LLNLA).

7. This account of how the Echo event was canceled is different than how it is portrayed in several history books, but it accurately reflects the contents of classified reports written to the AEC at the time, and it generally agrees with York's version of events. Herbert York, interviewed by Jim Carothers, 1983, classified document vaults, LLNLA.

8. Bill Grasberger, interviewed by the author, 2015.

9. It took two years to come up with an explanation for the failure. These results of the Koon event are based on the author's interpretation of post-shot reports stored in the classified document vaults, LLNLA.

10. York, *Advisors*, 137–38.

11. Kai Bird and Martin J. Sherwin, *American Prometheus: The Triumph and Tragedy of J. Robert Oppenheimer* (New York: Alfred A. Knopf, 2005), 462–84.

12. Nichols recounts his role in the Oppenheimer hearing in *The Road to Trinity* (New York: William Morrow, 1987), 305–7.

13. Lewis Strauss, *Men and Decisions* (New York: Doubleday, 1962), app.

14. Nichols, *Road to Trinity*, 313.

15. U.S. Atomic Energy Commission, *In The Matter of J. Robert Oppenheimer: Transcript of Hearing before Personnel Security Board and Texts of Principal Documents and Letters* (Cambridge, MA: MIT Press, 1971).

16. Luis W. Alvarez, *Alvarez: Adventures of a Physicist* (New York: Basic Books, 1987), 178–80.

17. Edward Teller, *Memoirs: A Twentieth-Century Journey in Science and Politics*, with Judith Shoolery (Cambridge, MA: Perseus, 2001), 355–59.

18. Nichols, *Road to Trinity*, 320–24.

19. I have met and interviewed physicists who have told me the first time they heard of Livermore was when they were asked as graduate students to sign a petition condemning his testimony.

20. Emilio Segrè, *Enrico Fermi, Physicist* (Chicago: University of Chicago Press, 1970), 183–84.

21. Sybil Francis, "Warhead Politics: Livermore and the Competitive System of Nuclear Weapon Design," UCRL-LR-124754 (PhD diss., MIT, 1995), 94.

22. John Nuckolls, conversation with the author, 2018. Nuckolls, former director of the Laboratory, said he was one of the physicists who received the document.

**Chapter 11. The Upstarts Take Over**

1. These events in Foster's early life from Johnny Foster, interviewed by the author, 2015 (multiple occasions).

2. Allen Steck and Steve Roper, *Fifty Classic Climbs of North America* (San Francisco: Sierra Club Books, 1979), 322.

3. Laboratory physicists Douglas Miller and Jay Salmonson, two of Jim Wilson's graduate students, interviewed by the author, February 23–24, 2016.

4. Laboratory monthly progress reports to AEC headquarters, January–June 1955, classified document vaults, Lawrence Livermore National Laboratory Archives, CA (hereafter cited as LLNLA).

5. These paragraphs based on Foster, interviewed by the author, 2015 (multiple occasions).

6. Sybil Francis, "Warhead Politics: Livermore and the Competitive System of Nuclear Weapon Design," UCRL-LR-124754 (PhD diss., MIT, 1995), 96.

7. Duane Sewell, "The Branch Laboratory at Livermore during the 1950s," *Energy in Physics, War and Peace: A Festschrift Celebrating Edward Teller's 80th Birthday*, ed. Hans Mark and Lowell Wood (Boston: Kluwer Academic, 1988), 322.

8. These paragraphs describing how the Cleo was developed are based on various participating physicists, interviewed by Jim Carothers, 1978, classified document vaults, LLNLA.

9. Harold Brown, interviewed by the author, 2015.

10. Brown, Laboratory monthly progress report to AEC, June 1954, classified document vaults, LLNLA.

234 / Notes to Pages 137–148

11. This paper featured the work of five Laboratory physicists: Harold Brown, Art Biehl, Jim Frank, Mike May, and Ernie Martinelli. Biehl and Martinelli were also protagonists in the development of the Geode, which would lead to a revolutionary design for an atomic device.

12. Laboratory monthly progress reports to AEC, June–August 1956, classified document vaults, LLNLA.

13. Tommy, who has a Polish surname, told about his experiences as an intern to a Laboratory geophysicist, Brian Bonner, in the 1990s.

14. Ed LaFranchi, "History & Reflections of Engineering at Lawrence Livermore National Laboratory," Report UCRL-ID-147148 (Lawrence Livermore National Laboratory, 2002), 51.

15. Bob Pursley, interviewed by the author, 2015. Pursley had a distinguished Air Force career and eventually became commander of Fifteenth Air Force. He was recognized as a distinguished West Point graduate in 2014.

16. James E. Carothers, "An Interview with Wallace D. Decker," 2002, UCRL-MI-49361, University of California Library, 49; *Time*, March 7, 1955.

17. Johnny Foster, interviewed by the author, November 2015.

18. Dale Nielsen, interviewed by Jim Carothers, 1978, classified document vaults, LLNLA.

19. Foster, interviewed by the author, 2015.

20. Jim Frank, interviewed by Jim Carothers, 1978, classified document vaults, LLNLA.

21. Brown, monthly progress report to AEC, June 1954, classified document vaults, LLNLA.

22. Francis, "Warhead Politics," 108.

23. Herbert F. York, *Making Weapons, Talking Peace: A Physicist's Odyssey from Hiroshima to Geneva* (New York: Basic Books, 1987), 75.

## Chapter 12. Hydrotests, Hydrocodes, and a National Strategy

1. Ernest O. Lawrence to Dr. H. A. Fidler, September 2, 1954, Lawrence Livermore National Laboratory Archives, CA (hereafter cited as LLNLA).

2. Wallace D. Decker, interviewed by Jim Carothers, 1983, UCRL-IM-149361, transcript, 21.

3. Dan Patterson, interviewed by the author, 2015.

4. William Lokke, *Early Computing and Its Impact on Lawrence Livermore National Laboratory* UCRL-TR-226840 (Livermore, CA: LLNL, 2007), 30.

5. See, for instance, Michael May, "Some Advantages of a Counterforce Deterrence," July 1987, UCRL-97095, University of California Library.

6. Marilyn Berger, "Paul Nitze, Cold War Strategist, Dies at 97," *New York Times*, October 20, 2004.

7. Adam Bernstein, "Defense Expert William Kaufmann," Obituary, *Washington Post*, December 17, 2008.

8. William W. Kaufmann, *The Requirements of Deterrence*, Memorandum 7 (Princeton, NJ: Center of International Studies, Princeton University, 1954), 7.

9. William W. Kaufmann, ed., *Military Policy and National Security* (Princeton, NJ: Princeton University Press, 1956), 274.

10. Albert Wohlstetter collaborated with William Kaufmann and other RAND analysts in his work that led to Counterforce Strategy. See Wohlstetter, "The Delicate Balance of Terror," *Foreign Affairs* 37, no. 2 (January 1959): 211–34.

11. Bernard Brodie, "Must We Shoot from the Hip?," internal RAND working paper, September 4, 1951, quoted in Marc Trachtenberg, "Strategic Thought in America, 1956–1966," *Political Science Quarterly* 104, no. 2 (Summer 1989), https://www.jstor.org/stable/2151586?seq=1.

12. Albert Wohlstetter, F. S. Hoffman, and H. S. Rowen, *Protecting U.S. Power to Strike Back in the 1950s and 1960s*, Report R-290 (Santa Monica, CA: RAND, 1956).

13. Stephen E. Ambrose, *Eisenhower*, vol. 2, *The President* (New York: Simon & Schuster, 1984), 314.

14. Department of Energy classification rules prohibit revealing the nickname of the missile device.

15. Details of these designs are garnered from the author's interpretations of Laboratory monthly progress reports to AEC, 1956, classified document vaults, LLNLA.

16. These two Foster papers are found as B Division documents, 1956, classified document vaults, LLNLA.

17. Gary Higgins, interviewed by Jim Carothers, 1983, classified document vaults, LLNLA.

18. Arne Kirkewoog, interviewed by the author, June 2015.

19. Postoperational reports to the AEC, 1956, classified document vaults, LLNLA.

## Chapter 13. First the Flute and Then the Robin

1. Neil Sheehan, *A Fiery Peace in a Cold War: Bernard Schriever and the Ultimate Weapon* (New York: Random House, 2009), 211–99.

2. Herbert F. York, *Making Weapons, Talking Peace: A Physicist's Odyssey from Hiroshima to Geneva* (New York: Basic Books, 1987), 89.

3. Harvey M. Sapolsky, *The Polaris System Development: Bureaucratic and Programmatic Success in Government* (Cambridge, MA: Harvard University Press, 1972), 28.

4. Although Carson Mark is not listed as a principal participant in the conference program, both Teller, in his memoirs, and Foster, in a personal interview, state that he was there and represented Los Alamos. Edward Teller, *Memoirs: A Twentieth-Century Journey in Science and Politics*, with Judith Shoolery (Cambridge, MA: Perseus, 2001), 420; Johnny Foster, interviewed by the author, November 2015.

5. Taken from the 1956 Nobska Conference after-action report, classified document vaults, Lawrence Livermore National Laboratory Archives, CA (hereafter cited as LLNLA).

6. Sapolsky, *Polaris System*, 30.

7. Teller, *Memoirs*, 420. This account of Teller declaring the Laboratory could build a warhead for a fleet ballistic missile is backed up by Johnny Foster, who was present at the time and sat next to Teller. Foster, interviewed by the author, 2015.

8. Foster, interviewed by the author, November 2015.

9. One month earlier, Brown wrote a letter, signed by York, to Admiral Patrick O'Beirne, commander of the Navy's Special Weapons Project. It stated the Laboratory could deliver a thermonuclear warhead to the Navy small enough to be carried by a tactical fighter-bomber. York (and Brown) to Admiral O'Beirne, July 1956, classified document vaults, LLNLA.

10. Norris Bradbury to Major General Alfred Starbird, January 8, 1958, in William Ogle, *An Account of the Return to Nuclear Weapons Testing by the United States after the Test Moratorium, 1958–1961*, NVO-291 ([Las Vegas]: Department of Energy, 1985), chap. 1.

11. Ogle, 97.

12. Sybil Francis, "Warhead Politics: Livermore and the Competitive System of Nuclear Weapon Design," UCRL-LR-124754 (PhD diss., MIT, 1995), 116.

13. Francis, 117.

14. Francis, 99.

15. Gordon Repp, interviewed by Jim Carothers, 1983, classified document vaults, LLNLA.

16. John von Neumann and Robert D. Richtmyer, "A Method for the Numerical Calculation of Hydrodynamic Shocks," *Journal of Applied Physics* 21, no. 3 (March 1950): 232–37.

17. Mark L. Wilkins, "Hydrodynamics of Weapons," January 1967, UCIR-103, University of California Library, 3–5.

18. After Operation Desert Storm in 1992, interrogations of Iraqi officers revealed that a major reason armored and mechanized infantry divisions of the Iraqi army had not attacked the isolated 82nd Airborne Division was because they believed the U.S. troops had nuclear artillery and would use it against them.

19. These conclusions reached by the author's interpretation of several Hectoton Group reports written in 1956, found as B Division documents, classified document vaults, LLNLA.

20. B Division physicists, including Jim Wilson, Walt Birnbaum, Gordon Repp, and others (present in Eniwetok), interviewed by Jim Carothers, 1977, classified document vaults, LLNLA.

21. Johnny Foster, Laboratory monthly progress report to AEC, August 1956, classified document vaults, LLNLA.

22. Various post-shot reports of Operations Plumbbob and Hardtack, 1957–58, classified document vaults, LLNLA.

23. Roland Herbst, personal conversations with author, 1991.

24. A Division physicists William Schulz and Norman Hardy, interviewed by Jim Carothers, 1983, classified document vaults, LLNLA.

25. After-action report attached to report of Operation Hardtack, 1958, classified document vaults, LLNLA.

**Chapter 14. The Navy Gets a Warhead for a Missile**

1. Harvey M. Sapolsky, *The Polaris System Development: Bureaucratic and Programmatic Success in Government* (Cambridge, MA: Harvard University Press, 1972), 21.

2. Sapolsky, 24–28.

3. Graham Spinardi, *From Polaris to Trident: The Development of U.S. Fleet Ballistic Missile Technology* (New York: Cambridge University Press, 1994), 30–31.

4. Spinardi, 42–50.

5. Vice Admiral Wertheim, interviewed by the author, May 12, 2014.

6. Security Resources Panel of the Science Advisory Committee (Gaither Panel), "Deterrence & Survival in the Nuclear Age," Report NSC 5724 (Washington, November 7, 1957); Herbert F. York, *Making Weapons, Talking Peace: A Physicist's Odyssey from Hiroshima to Geneva* (New York: Basic Books, 1987), 97–99.

7. See, for example, "The Nuclear Option: Bay Areas Rich History of Bunkers, Shelters, and Other Cold War Relics," *Mercury News* (San Jose, CA), August 27, 2017, 1.

8. Chalmers M. Roberts, *First Rough Draft: A Journalist's Journal of Our Times* (New York: Praeger, 1973), 149–50.

9. Herman Kahn, preface to *On Thermonuclear War* (Princeton, NJ: Princeton University Press, 1960).

10. McGeorge Bundy, *Danger and Survival: Choices about the Bomb in the First Fifty Years* (New York: Random House, 1988), 334–40.

11. E. W. Kenworthy, "Eisenhower Calls Soviet Atom Halt 'a Gimmick,'" *New York Times*, April 3, 1958, 1.

12. William Ogle, *An Account of the Return to Nuclear Weapons Testing by the United States after the Test Moratorium, 1958–1961,* NVO-291 ([Las Vegas]: Department of Energy, 1985), 27.

13. Operation Hardtack safety regulations from AEC operational manuals, 1958, classified document vaults, Lawrence Livermore National Laboratory Archives, CA.

14. Johnny Foster, interviewed by the author, November 2015.

15. Ogle, *Return to Nuclear Weapons Testing,* 101.

16. York, *Making Weapons,* 128–49.

17. Jim Oliver, conversation with the author, 2018. Oliver participated in the queen's welcome as a Livermore schoolboy.

18. Ogle, *Return to Nuclear Weapons Testing,* 124–27.

19. What Colgate and White found was, when a proton in a star unites with an electron to create a neutron, a neutrino—a particle with no electric charge—is created. Neutrinos usually do not interact with matter, but a neutron star is so dense, even neutrinos will interact enough to blow off the outer surface of the star.

20. Dick White, interviewed by the author, November 5, 2014.

21. John C. Hopkins and Barbara Germain Killian, *Nuclear Weapons Testing at the Nevada Test Site: The First Decade,* 2nd ed. (N.p., 2010), 595–98.

22. Herbert Childs, *An American Genius: The Life of Ernest Orlando Lawrence* (New York: E. P. Dutton, 1968), 532–33.

## Chapter 15. From Berlin Back to Berkeley

1. Harold Brown, recorded interview, June 25, 1964, John F. Kennedy Library Oral History Program, John F. Kennedy Presidential Library, Boston, transcript, 8.

2. News Conference 1, held by President Kennedy, January 25, 1961, Kennedy Presidential Library, transcript.

3. "The Atom," *Time*, May 4, 1962, 21.

4. George Miller, Paul Brown, and Carol Alonso, *Report to Congress on Stockpile Reliability, Weapon Remanufacture, and the Role of Nuclear Testing*, UCRL-53822 (Livermore, CA: LLNL, 1987).

5. Arthur H. Dean, *Test Ban and Disarmament: The Path of Negotiation* (New York: Harper and Row, 1966), 87–88.

6. William Ogle was the director of nuclear testing during the transition from the Eisenhower to the Kennedy administrations. This specific account is from Ogle, *An Account of the Return to Nuclear Weapons Testing by the United States after the Test Moratorium, 1958–1961*, NVO-291 (Las Vegas: Department of Energy, 1985), 242–43.

7. Ogle, 251–57.

8. Ogle, 244.

9. For the Laboratory's response to the resumption of nuclear testing, see various documents and records, 1961, classified document vaults, Lawrence Livermore National Laboratory Archives, CA (hereafter cited as LLNLA).

10. The eyewitness account given here and following from Dale Nielsen, interviewed by Jim Carothers, 1983, classified document vaults, LLNLA.

11. Nielsen, interviewed by Carothers, 1983.

12. Ogle, *Return to Nuclear Weapons Testing*, 263–67.

13. Johnny Foster, interviewed by the author, November 2015. To be fair to Cohen, RAND did do calculations about this time on the radiative effects of weapons, but it is unclear how much discussion went on between the RAND analysts and the Livermore physicists.

14. McGeorge Bundy, *Danger and Survival: Choices about the Bomb in the First Fifty Years* (New York: Random House, 1988), 379–80.

15. Agnew, comments, ceremony celebrating Johnny Foster's ninetieth birthday, September 2012; Hans Bethe, interviewed by Lowell Wood, 1982, classified document vaults, LLNLA.

16. Harold Brown, recorded interview, April 25, 1964, JFK#1, John F. Kennedy Library Oral History Program, Kennedy Presidential Library, transcript, 13.

17. Johnny Foster, personal conversation with author, November 2015; Mike May, personal conversation with author, November 2016.

18. The Brookings Institution, "The JCAE and the Development of the Permissive Action Link" (September 24, 2015). Some ideas for controlling access to nuclear weapons emerged before Foster briefed the president. An amendment to the Atomic Energy Act of 1954 gave the JCAE the right to demand that the Defense Department secure nuclear weapons. A classified history of PAL devices was written for the Defense Nuclear Agency in February 1992.

19. Foster, interviewed by the author, November 2015.

20. National Security Action Memorandum 160, "Permissive Links for Nuclear Weapons in NATO," June 6, 1962, National Security Files, Presidential Papers, Papers of John F. Kennedy, Kennedy Library, https://www.jfklibrary.org/asset-viewer/archives/JFKNSF/336/JFKNSF-336-016.

21. Jack Raymond, "US to Install Locks on Atom Weapons as Extra Safeguard," *New York Times*, July 6, 1962, 1.

22. Tom Wicker, "President on Coast Tour; Watches Atlas Launching," *New York Times*, March 24, 1962, 1.

## Epilogue

1. "Kennedy Favors Shelters for All," *New York Times*, October 7, 1961, 1.

2. McGeorge Bundy, interviewed by Richard Neustadt, March 1964, John F. Kennedy Oral History Collection, John F. Kennedy Presidential Library, Boston, transcript, 31–34.

3. Martin J. Hillenbrand, interviewed by Paul R. Sweet, August 26, 1964, Kennedy Oral History Collection, Kennedy Library, transcript, 29.

# INDEX

## *ABOUT THE AUTHOR*

For the past forty years, **Tom Ramos** has been a physicist at the Lawrence Livermore National Laboratory, where he was a member of the nuclear team that developed the X-ray Laser for President Reagan's Strategic Defense Initiative. He later supported U.S./USSR arms control negotiations. Ramos, who graduated from West Point, commanded combat engineers before entering MIT to earn a degree in high energy physics.

**The Naval Institute Press** is the book-publishing arm of the U.S. Naval Institute, a private, nonprofit, membership society for sea service professionals and others who share an interest in naval and maritime affairs. Established in 1873 at the U.S. Naval Academy in Annapolis, Maryland, where its offices remain today, the Naval Institute has members worldwide.

Members of the Naval Institute support the education programs of the society and receive the influential monthly magazine *Proceedings* or the colorful bimonthly magazine *Naval History* and discounts on fine nautical prints and on ship and aircraft photos. They also have access to the transcripts of the Institute's Oral History Program and get discounted admission to any of the Institute-sponsored seminars offered around the country.

The Naval Institute's book-publishing program, begun in 1898 with basic guides to naval practices, has broadened its scope to include books of more general interest. Now the Naval Institute Press publishes about seventy titles each year, ranging from how-to books on boating and navigation to battle histories, biographies, ship and aircraft guides, and novels. Institute members receive significant discounts on the Press' more than eight hundred books in print.

Full-time students are eligible for special half-price membership rates. Life memberships are also available.

For a free catalog describing Naval Institute Press books currently available, and for further information about joining the U.S. Naval Institute, please write to:

Member Services
**U.S. Naval Institute**
291 Wood Road
Annapolis, MD 21402-5034
Telephone: (800) 233-8764
Fax: (410) 571-1703
Web address: www.usni.org